Peabody &
Stearns

COUNTRY HOUSES AND SEASIDE COTTAGES

Wyndhurst, Lenox,
Massachusetts. Courtesy
of Cranwell Resort, Spa, &
Golf Club.

Althorpe, Newport,
Rhode Island. Photograph
courtesy of Salve Regina
University.

Pinecrest gatehouse,
Elkins, West Virginia.
Photograph by Annie
Robinson.

Pinecrest, Elkins, West
Virginia. Photograph by
Annie Robinson.

Krisheim, view from
the teahouse, Chestnut
Hill, Pennsylvania.
Photograph © 2009
W. F. Milliken.

The Hennery at
Vinland, Newport,
Rhode Island.
Photograph courtesy of
Salve Regina University.

Robert Peabody
Cottage, Peach's
Point, Massachusetts.
Photograph by Annie
Robinson.

Oakley, Wissahickon
Heights, Pennsylvania.
Photograph © 2009 W. F.
Milliken.

FACING PAGE
TOP
The Stable at The Cove, Beverly, Massachusetts. Photograph by Annie Robinson.

BOTTOM
Mary Stevens Cottage, North Newport, New Hampshire. Photograph by Annie Robinson.

THIS PAGE
ABOVE
Vinland, Newport, Rhode Island. Photograph courtesy of Salve Regina University.

ABOVE RIGHT
Westview entry, Bryn Mawr, Pennsylvania. Photograph by Annie Robinson.

RIGHT
Wootton details, Bryn Mawr, Pennsylvania. Photograph by Annie Robinson.

Cochran Cottage,
Manchester-by-the-Sea,
Massachusetts. Photograph
by Lincoln Russell.

Peabody & Stearns

COUNTRY HOUSES AND SEASIDE COTTAGES

Annie Robinson

W. W. NORTON & COMPANY

New York • London

For information about permission to reproduce selections
from this book, write to Permissions, W. W. Norton &
Company, Inc., 500 Fifth Avenue, New York, NY 10110

For information about special discounts for bulk purchases,
please contact W. W. Norton Special Sales at specialsales@
wwnorton.com or 800-233-4830.

Book design by Abigail Sturges
Manufacturing by Friesens
Production Manager: Leeann Graham

Library of Congress Cataloging-in-Publication Data

Robinson, Annie (Ann E.)
Peabody & Stearns : country houses and seaside cottages /
Annie Robinson. – 1st ed.
        p. cm.
Based on the author's thesis (M.A., Tufts University, 1999).
Includes bibliographical references and index.
ISBN 978-0-393-73218-4 (hardcover)
1. Peabody & Stearns (Boston, Mass.) 2. Country homes–
United States. 3. Seaside architecture–United States. I. Title.
II. Title: Peabody and Stearns.

NA737.P36R63 2010
728.0973–dc22

                                2009018466

ISBN 978-0-393-73218-4

W. W. Norton & Company, Inc.,
500 Fifth Avenue, New York, N.Y. 10110
www.wwnorton.com

W. W. Norton & Company Ltd.,
Castle House, 75/76 Wells St., London W1T 3QT

0 9 8 7 6 5 4 3 2 1

For Skip

 you are the wind beneath my wings . . .

Contents

Acknowledgments

This book has been a grand journey, one that has been facilitated every step of the way by friends, colleagues, and strangers. My research began at the suggestion of Margaret Henderson Floyd at Tufts University. In the 1960s, she and Wheaton Holden laid the groundwork for the study of Peabody & Stearns's architectural commissions; this project would have been nearly impossible without their early research.

Peabody & Stearns: Country Houses and Seaside Cottages grew into a larger undertaking than I originally contemplated. With the help of many people, I have attempted to catalog most if not all of the firm's so-called resort architecture. If there are errors, I hope that my readers will forgive me, and contact me to correct the information. A list of all those who helped with information, photographs, or encouragement would be nearly as long as this book, so I will list a few of you and hope that the rest know how much I appreciate your assistance.

Professors and mentors who guided my journey include Eric Rosenberg, Maureen Meister, Daniel Abramson, and Keith Morgan. Richard Hunnewell and Naomi Kline were early supporters. Richard Guy Wilson has been teacher, guide, and friend, and deserves special mention. To each of you, I say "thank you," meaning much more than that.

A book topic is only as good as the librarians and curators who help the author along the way. Among those who have been generous with time, patience, and information are Janice Chadbourne and the Fine Arts Librarians at the Boston Public College; Susan Lewis at the Boston Architectural College and her colleague, Sheri Rosenzweig; Lorna Condon at Historic New England; Earle Shettleworth at the Maine Historic Preservation Commission; the librarians at Harvard University and MIT; and the curators at countless historical societies. In Newport, Rhode Island, I have had so much help from friends at the Preservation Society of Newport Country and the Newport Historical Soci-ety (NHS); Joan Youngken's early help and friendship at NHS and in the years since have meant so much. I also appreciate the help of Michael Semenza and many others at Salve Regina University. Again, a "thank you" to all seems inadequate, but must do.

Architect Robert A. M. Stern deserves special thanks for his interest and help.

How many times in my journey did I think I had discovered a new Peabody & Stearns commission, only to learn that Weston Milliken had been there ten years before me! Weston has been generous with his time and advice, and with his collection of slides that has been at my house far too long. Several of his photographs are included in the book; I hope that it pleases him to see his work in print.

I have been fortunate to visit nearly every extant house included in this book; consequently, I have a long list of homeowners and descendants of original owners to whom I owe debts of gratitude. Thank you all for opening your homes and photo albums to me.

People who have become special friends beyond the world of this book include Paul and Elaine Rocheleau and Loring and Susie Catlin. And to Jim Buttrick, who is always there to take a road trip or listen to a problem—a very special thanks.

Finally, I am especially grateful to my editor, Nancy Green, and her colleagues at W. W. Norton & Company, for their confidence and patience, and for making this book possible.

15

Providence Railroad
Station, Park Square,
Boston. Courtesy of
Memorial Library, Boston
Architectural College.

Brunswick
Hotel, Boston.
Architectural Sketchbook,
December 1875, vol. 3, no. 6,
pl. 24. Courtesy of the Boston
Public Library Fine Arts
Department.

Preface

We used to go shopping in Newport. There among the many mansions
and beautiful gardens we found the prettiest houses had been designed by
Peabody and Stearns of Boston. We decided they were the only architects for
us, and they were, after a good many years of planning and waiting. We have
never regretted our choice.

— GEORGE STANLEY WOODWARD, *Memoirs of a Mediocre Man* [1]

George and Gertrude Woodward discovered
Peabody & Stearns's work in 1895. Peabody
& Stearns was in its prime, having already
completed at least a dozen cottage commissions for
Newport's summer colony alone. Elsewhere it had
completed the Providence Railroad Station and the
Brunswick Hotel in Boston (left), the Colorado College
Building (fig. 4.1) and the Antlers Hotel in Colorado
Springs (fig. 4.7) and the James J. Hill mansion in St.
Paul, Minnesota (below), among many other residential and commercial commissions. The George Stanley Woodwards did not purchase their Chestnut Hill
property in far northwest Philadelphia until 1901, but
they remained steadfast in their devotion to the Boston
architectural firm: when the house was constructed
ten years later, it had been designed by Peabody &
Stearns. At 27,000 square feet, Krisheim was one of the
largest country houses the firm ever designed, but it
exhibited the domestic scale and attention to detail
that characterized almost all of the cottages that the
firm created (fig. 2.29).

This is the story of an architectural firm that was
well known in its own time but has received little of
the public fanfare of its contemporaries: H. H. Richardson; McKim, Mead & White; Bruce Price; and John
Calvin Stevens, to name a few. It is the story of only
one segment of that firm's output—the seaside cottage
and country house commissions—but hopefully readers who become intrigued by the architectural "surf
and turf" catalogued in the pages that follow will continue their pursuit of Peabody & Stearns, and through
their interest bring to the firm the twenty-first-century
appreciation and recognition it deserves.

A few ancillary leisure-time buildings designed
by Peabody & Stearns are also included in this book,
among them boathouses at Harvard and Yale universities, several yacht-club clubhouses, a casino at Elberon,
New Jersey, and a hotel in Colorado Springs. Nonre-
sort buildings in resort towns—B. F. Stevens's business
block in Spirit Lake, Iowa, comes to mind—have been
mentioned in the introductory remarks for the region

in question, or in the write-up for the client's own cottage, when there is one. Likewise, mention is made of
commissions that have not been located or for which
information could not be secured. Further information
from readers would be greatly appreciated.

The cottages that make up this book were generally "second" homes, and fall loosely into the broad cat-
egory of resort architecture. Thus, we could begin this
story in the early nineteenth century, with the growth
of the resort movement in the United States. Or we
could begin with the developments in the national
economy that produced a clientele for resort and recreational architecture—an architecture of leisure, of
public and private commissions: casinos, boathouses,
stables, and gentlemen's farms, in addition to the so-
called cottages of our subtitle. But each of these topics
could have (and, in fact, do have) whole books devoted
to it. Instead, we will begin with the story of the men
themselves—Robert Peabody and John Stearns—and
fill in the other histories along the way.

James J. Hill Mansion,
St. Paul, Minnesota, 1905.
Courtesy of the Minnesota
Historical Society (neg. 5060).

Introduction

Narrative of a Practice

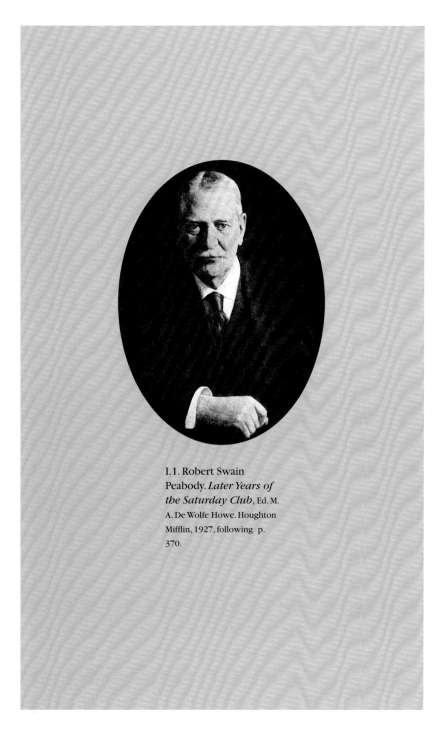

I.1. Robert Swain
Peabody. *Later Years of
the Saturday Club*, Ed. M.
A. De Wolfe Howe. Houghton
Mifflin, 1927, following p.
370.

The architectural office of Peabody & Stearns opened at 14 Devonshire Street, Boston, in the spring of 1870. The two founders, Robert Swain Peabody (1845–1917) and John Goddard Stearns, Jr. (1843–1917) (figs. I.1 and I.2), remained partners for an almost unprecedented forty-five years, during which time they secured over one thousand commissions and established themselves as one of the most important architectural firms in Boston and the Northeast. Designs for buildings of every type—warehouses and town houses, retail stores and banks, schools, railroad stations and libraries, playhouses and country houses—passed over their drafting tables. Some were famous—the original Breakers in Newport (see fig. 1.19) and Boston's Custom House Tower—others were and are virtually unknown: a log cabin in Iowa (see fig. 4.8); a 900-square-foot cottage in Jamestown, Rhode Island (see fig 1.50); a dairy building in Highland Falls, New York (see fig 2.11).

The firm became a training ground for aspiring draftsmen and designers, and many well-known New England architects received their start under the supervision of Peabody and/or Stearns: Clarence Blackall, Henry Ives Cobb, Arthur Little, and Edmund Wheelwright among them. Julius Schweinfurth and Robert D. Andrews both wrote reminiscences of their experiences at the firm—from these we get a sense of the office operation.[1] Robert Peabody was, by all accounts, the design member of the partnership. He met with clients, created thumbnail design sketches for almost all of the firm's commissions, and supervised the up to twenty-five employees of the firm.

Peabody's partner, John Goddard Stearns, Jr., was the perfect complement to Peabody's artistic personality. Stearns came to the partnership from the position of head draftsman at the prestigious Boston architectural firm of Ware & Van Brunt. Born on May 18, 1843, in New York City, he was the son of John Goddard Stearns, Sr., a manufacturer, and Elizabeth (Stearns) Stearns. His family moved back to Brookline, Massachusetts in 1861, and Stearns lived there for the rest of his life.

Stearns graduated from the Lawrence Scientific School at Harvard, a member of the Class of 1863. He and his wife, Ellen Elizabeth Abbott, had one daughter and one son, who became an architect in his father's firm. (Frank A. Stearns continued the business with Cornell Appleton as Appleton & Stearns following the death of the two original partners in 1917. This firm closed in 1965.) Stearns was well regarded in the architectural profession and was elected as a Fellow of the AIA in 1894. He was not as active in local and city affairs as his friend and partner Robert Peabody, but in 1904 he accepted an appointment from Governor John Bates of Massachusetts to serve on a special commission created to revise the building laws of the state.

Although Stearns had worked as a draftsman in the office of Ware & Van Brunt, his role in the new partnership was far more extensive. He assumed the difficult role of superintendence of the many projects that the firm undertook and ensured that the jobs were completed in the appropriate manner. He insisted upon quality and thoroughness, and required that the specification and drawing documents for each job were complete. Stearns was responsible for the on-time and on-budget execution of Peabody's designs, and the relationships with local Boston contractors that he had formed while at Ware & Van Brunt were valuable to the new firm. In these respects Stearns was equally as important as Peabody to the continuing financial success and professional esteem the partnership enjoyed. It was Peabody, however, whose design aesthetic predominated in the firm's architectural production and as such will be the primary focus of this introduction. His educational and professional training, and the architectural designs to which he was exposed as a young man, clearly influenced the work he produced during his long and successful career. The resort cottages he designed during the late decades of the nineteenth century and the early twentieth century represent a conflation of these early influences with the popularized styles of the day.

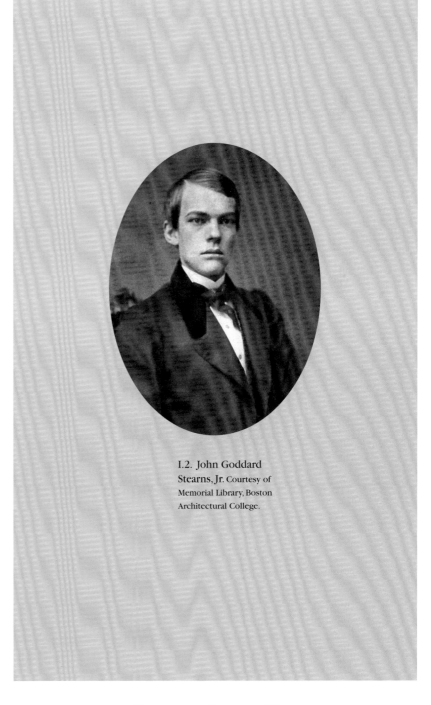

I.2. John Goddard Stearns, Jr. Courtesy of Memorial Library, Boston Architectural College.

Early Years of Robert Swain Peabody

Robert Swain Peabody was born on February 22, 1845, in New Bedford, a shipbuilding and seafaring city in southeastern Massachusetts. He was the son of Ephraim (1807-56) and Mary Jane (Derby) Peabody (1807-92)—his father was a graduate of Bowdoin College and the Harvard Divinity School, while his mother came from Salem, Massachusetts, the granddaughter of Elias Haskett Derby, an American "merchant prince" (and quite possibly the first millionaire in New England). Ephraim served as pastor at King's Chapel in Boston for nine years; its affluent parish presumably provided a good client base for Peabody's architectural firm. Prior to serving at King's Chapel, Ephraim Peabody had preached at the New Bedford First Congregational Society Church, where many in the congregation were Quakers who held "strong convictions

on the burning issue of slavery." Ephraim and Mary Jane Peabody shared their dedication to the cause, and continued their contributions to the abolitionist movement after the transfer to Boston. It is interesting to note that Charles Follen McKim, partner in the New York architectural firm McKim, Mead & White and long-time friend of Robert Peabody, was of a devout Quaker family in Pennsylvania and that his parents were also extremely active in the abolitionist cause. One cannot help but wonder if this common background provided in part the basis upon which Peabody and McKim formed their lifelong friendship.

The histories of Ephraim and Mary Jane Derby Peabody are told in a slim volume, *A New England Romance: The Story of Ephraim and Mary Jane Peabody [1807-1892] Told by Their Sons,* published in 1920 (fig. I.4). It was written, we are told, by Robert Peabody during his last illness in 1916-17. Confined

I.3. Fiske Building, Boston, Massachusetts. Courtesy of the Frances Loeb Library, Graduate School of Design, Harvard University.

to bed, he gathered all of the family papers about him and "what seemed an arduous task gave him much happiness; . . . his enthusiasm in the details was indefatigable and contagious."[2] After Robert Peabody died, his brother took on the task of editing the voluminous materials that had been assembled and had the book published. Robert Peabody also wrote *Hospital Sketches* (1916) (fig. I.5), a collection of fanciful architectural sketches and stories crafted while he was a patient at Johns Hopkins Medical Center. These books provide brief opportunities to view the man behind the architect. He admired the strong moral values of his parents and their participation in national political issues. He also admired his mother's artistic abilities as a painter, and we surmise that he inherited her artistic talents.

Robert Peabody's brother Francis Greenwood Peabody (1847–1936) grew up to be a noted Cambridge theologian, who in addition to his extensive speaking and writing career was also instrumental in the development of the School of Social Work at Harvard University. His Peabody & Stearns–designed cottage in Northeast Harbor, Maine, still stands (see fig. 1.190). Their older sister Ellen (1836–1869) married Charles William Eliot (later to be president of Harvard University) in 1858; both Robert and his brother Francis became good friends with Eliot. The younger Peabody daughter, Anna Huidekoper (b. 1838), married the Reverend Dr. H. W. Bellows and later moved to New York. This is a good time to point out the hugely intertwined family trees of the architectural clientele who were responsible for a large number of commissions in this book. At times, the relationships are positively confounding with given names repeated in successive generations and the marriage of first cousins not an infrequent occurrence. Commissions for the architectural firm were augmented by friend and family referrals for private as well as civic projects—these circumstances, when known, will be noted throughout the catalogue texts.

As a boy, Peabody attended the private school of former Boston Latin School headmaster Epes Sargent Dixwell, along with the sons of many of his prominent Boston neighbors. From there he went on to Boston Latin and was admitted to Harvard College in the fall of 1862. Peabody was well suited to life and studies at Harvard; his classmate Moorfield Storey, later a well-known Boston attorney, civil rights advocate, and the first president of the NAACP, recalled that "at college he was one of the exceptional men who excel in everything. A member of the Harvard crew, a good scholar and the chief marshal of his class, he won distinction in every walk of college life."[3] The importance of the friendships made during these school years cannot be underestimated. Sociologist E. Digby Baltzell has observed that during the mid- to late 1800s, "for the first time, upper class associations other than the family played an important role in socializing the young. The New

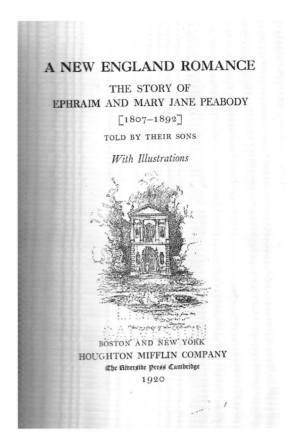

I.4. Title page to *A New England Romance: The Story of Ephraim and Mary Jane Peabody, Told by Their Sons.* Houghton Mifflin, 1920. Collection of the author.

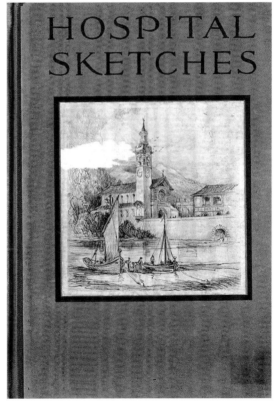

I.5. Cover to *Hospital Sketches,* by Robert Swain Peabody. Houghton Mifflin, 1916. Collection of the author.

I.6. School House,
Groton School, Groton,
Massachusetts. Postcard,
collection of the author.

England boarding school and the fashionable Eastern University became upper class surrogate families on almost a national scale."[4]

Robert Peabody, as well as many of the clients for whom Peabody & Stearns worked, attended these well-known eastern schools, and the network of influence was thus established. St. Paul's School in Concord, New Hampshire, and St. Mark's in Southborough, Massachusetts, founded in 1856 and 1865, respectively, were popular choices, along with Phillips Academy in Andover, Massachusetts, and Phillips Exeter Academy in Exeter, New Hampshire. Men such as J. P. Morgan "joined his contemporaries as trustees and benefactors of these exclusive educational associations, where they all, in turn, sent their sons to be educated together."[5] When the Groton School in Groton, Massachusetts, was founded by the Reverend Endicott Peabody in 1884, the land for the school was donated by James and Prescott Lawrence, and J. P. Morgan was a financial contributor. Peabody & Stearns was chosen to design the major buildings for the school in conjunction with Frederick Law Olmsted's landscape plan (fig. I.6). This was not their first collaboration, nor would it be their last; they worked together in apparent harmony on many other commissions, residential as well as institutional. Two years after the Groton commission, Peabody & Stearns was hired to work on financier Morgan's Highland Falls, New York, summer house, Cragston (see fig 2.9).; a dozen years later, the firm designed James Lawrence's cottage on Islesboro Island in Maine (see fig 1.190). The school "family" was an important factor in the spheres of influence that produced the residential and leisure architecture of the period.

Young Robert Peabody's architectural ambitions developed while he was at Harvard. His travel diary from a trip to Cuba in January of his junior year is full of descriptions of the buildings of Havana and includes a sketched plan of a coffee plantation. When he graduated the next year, the Class Notes of the Class of 1866 listed his intended occupation as architect. Later in life, Peabody would recall: "It must have been a relief to [my family] to hear of a new profession in which imagination was kept from harmful flights by loads of bricks and mortar and timber and plaster and other substantial things. I too, was pleased as these things had then to be studied abroad, and so,

without knowing much about what architecture was, I found myself bonded for life as its servant soon after I left college."[6]

Following graduation, Peabody worked in the architectural offices of Gridley J. F. Bryant (Bryant & Gilman, active 1859-66) and later with Henry Van Brunt (Ware & Van Brunt, active 1863-81). In Van Brunt's office he met George Tilden and Francis W. Chandler, as well as his future partner, John Stearns; during this period of time he also became acquainted with Charles McKim. Although brief, these work experiences were important to the respect with which he viewed the architectural profession. The relationships formed during this period would last throughout his career.

That Peabody was the only member of his Harvard College Class of 1866 who expressed the intention of becoming an architect at graduation is not remarkable: the architectural profession was in a state of flux at the time, teetering between the work of the craftsman-builder and the professionally educated architect. This builder/architect distinction was clearly of concern to young Peabody, who carried on a correspondence regarding becoming an "Artist-Architect" with Edward D. Lindsey, an architect in New York City. Lindsey wrote in December of 1866 in response to Peabody's queries: "I know you want to study Architecture as an Art and become not a builder but an Architect—there are so few of those in this country according to the lowest artistic standards of Europe."[7] He advised Peabody to leave employment in Boston to study in France. Years later, Peabody wrote in "Architecture as a Profession for College Graduates":

> The satisfactory architect must always in some measure unite the artist and the man of affairs . . . the practical man cannot ignore the artistic side of the art and must recognize the difference between building and architecture. . . . Rhyme is not poetry nor noise music; nor is building architecture unless it has higher qualities like dignity, simplicity, breadth, harmony, or that nameless something which makes all men recognize genius in the artist.[8]

In this assertion he perhaps knowingly echoed the words of John Ruskin in *The Seven Lamps of Architecture* (1849): "Architecture is the art which so disposes and adorns the edifices raised by man, for whatsoever uses, that the sight of them may contribute to his mental health, power, and pleasure. It is very necessary, in the outset of all inquiry, to distinguish carefully between Architecture and Building."[9]

Throughout his career, Peabody also commented on the importance of balancing the artistic manipulation of details in the creation of architecture while maintaining fiscal responsibility. His partner Stearns shared these concerns, commenting in a letter of October 1869, " . . . all these men of money think you must be a great Architect if all their accounts are kept in good order and you are still a greater Architect if you can build for them within the estimates given them at start."[10] Some measure of the continued success of Peabody & Stearns must have been in the firm's ability to respond artistically to the design challenges of each commission as well as to satisfy the client's practical need for quality work and accurate bookkeeping.

Peabody at the École des Beaux-Arts

Peabody began his formal study of architecture in 1866–67, taking a course of study at the Massachusetts Institute of Technology in Boston, where the first American academic architectural program had been created under the direction of William Robert Ware that year. Prior to this program, aspiring architects in the United States had had little choice but to apprentice with a practicing architect, or to study abroad—generally in France or perhaps in Germany, but this was expensive, time-consuming, and generally involved a difficult admission process and was therefore much less common. Peabody soon opted to take architect Edward Lindsey's earlier advice, however, and chose to attend the École des Beaux-Arts in Paris from 1867 until the spring of 1869. This decision was an important one, as it aligned Peabody with an elite group of American architects, including Richard Morris Hunt (the first American to attend, admitted in 1846) and Henry Hobson Richardson (entered in 1860). Mere attendance at the École conferred a cachet on young architects that the "home-grown" architects did not have. A listing of students admitted

into the famed school published by William Robert Ware in *The American Architect and Building News* in September 1887 documents that Robert S. Peabody, Charles F. McKim, and Sidney V. Stratton were admitted in 1868, having been preceded by Edward D. Lindsey in 1863 and Alfred H. Thorp in 1864.

And so, Peabody left Boston in May 1867 to prepare for admission examinations for the École des Beaux-Arts, traveling first to England and then to the continent. By September 12 he was in Paris, working hard toward admission. He wrote to his mother that he was "pretty sick of studying particularly as I have really given up hopes of getting in this autumn"; three days later he wrote to his family that Francis Chandler was arriving in Paris to study with him. They were joined shortly after by Charles McKim.[11]

The venerable École des Beaux-Arts is the direct descendant of the original French school of fine arts, the Académie des Beaux Arts, founded in Paris in 1648 by Cardinal Mazarin. Two programs of study allowed students to concentrate on either the fine arts or architecture. A large part of the École experience was the student's participation in an *atelier*, or studio, where a substantial amount of the actual learning about architecture took place. A student spent much of his time in the atelier and received most of his hands-on work and instruction from the *patron* and from the other students. Peabody was accepted into the atelier of Honoré Daumet along with Charles McKim, Alfred Thorp, and Sydney Stratton. Francis Chandler also attended the Daumet atelier, although he was not accepted into the École. Peabody later commented

I.7. Chateau de Mesnières (Normandy), July 13. From Robert Swain Peabody's *An Architect's Sketchbook*, Houghton Mifflin Company, 1912, p. 78. Collection of the author.

CHATEAU DE MESNIERES
JULY 13

on the system: "To me the wonderful thing about the Beaux Arts school was the way in which one learned more through the spirit of the atelier and because all lived together with a common aim rather than because of any direct instruction."[12] At the École, students like Peabody and McKim were trained in the classical manner, working with motifs from the Greek and Roman traditions in balanced and symmetrical compositions. The Beaux-Arts style came to connote an eclectic Neoclassical architecture, often associated with large masonry structures designed on an organizational axis, embellished with columns and balustrades, and ornamented with carved detail. This was in contrast to the then-popular English picturesque architectural trend that featured more loosely structured floor plans and smaller, more eclectic decorative programs. Peabody later recalled in the unpublished *Early Reminiscences:*

> Although we rendered the French projects, the thought of England and the picturesque was ever present with us. . . . When we began Victorian Gothic was at its best. You were expected to declare that you belonged to the English Gothic School or to the Classical School, and it was exactly like saying whether you were a Baptist or a heathen. We were torn with indecision as to whether we were to espouse one cause or the other, and we wished we had been born to one or the other as most men are to their theology.[13]

Peabody's body of work reveals the resulting tension between the two "schools" of design.

In December of 1867, Peabody wrote to his mother that "McKim and I both passed our first examinations. . . ."[14] They received permission to take the entrance examinations on February 13, 1868, and on April 30, 1868, were admitted to the École. Peabody placed nineteenth of the fifty-seven applicants who took the examination on that date, and McKim placed forty-first.[15] Immediately following the examination, Peabody left for a trip with Alfred Greenough and Frank Chandler to tour and sketch in Normandy: they visited Rouen, Lisieux, Caen, Bayeux, and Mont-St.-Michel. Peabody enjoyed sketching and recognized its importance in the process of architectural design. He sketched, it seems, everywhere he went (fig. I.7). Even at this time, he planned to publish his work, telling his mother not to show anyone the sketches from the École that he was sending home: " . . . they will be a book."[16] And, indeed, in addition to many commission sketches published in the architectural journals of the period, his *Notebook Sketches* and *An Architect's Sketchbook* were published, in 1873 and 1912, respectively.

Peabody was well aware of both the positive and the negative impacts the École experience would have in his architectural education. He recognized the importance of the atelier experience, and he understood that, in addition to the theoretical training, the cachet of simply having attended the École was of great importance. However, he also realized that the great French school did not address one of the issues about which he was most concerned: his lack of "practical" experience in the architectural profession. Peabody had a plan, however, to remedy this gap in his preparations: he would work a brief apprenticeship in England before returning to the United States. He wrote in a letter of June 1869: "It is just what I need to make up the very manifest deficiencies of the École—that in the way of practical matters as much as anything—."[17] It is not unreasonable to conclude that Peabody may well have been influenced or encouraged in his plan to work in London by his friend Charles McKim, whose father had commented in a letter that professionals such as Frederick Law Olmsted and Calvert Vaux considered that "a familiar acquaintance with English architecture" was important to success in the profession in the United States.[18]

In the Office of Alfred Waterhouse, London

In May 1869, Peabody left Paris to enter the second significant episode in his professional preparation. Carrying a letter of recommendation from his former employer, William Robert Ware, Peabody applied to work in the office of Alfred Waterhouse (1830–1905) in London. Peabody wrote to his mother from Wells, Somerset, England, on May 16, 1869, to let her know that he had safely crossed the English Channel. He and his traveling companions traveled from Newhaven to Arundel and Chichester, then on to Salisbury, mainly to see the cathedral. A week later Peabody was settled in rooms at No. 11 Bedford Square, London. He was dismayed at the dirt and overall ugliness of that city but hopeful of a positive experience there. He wrote: "I never have seen so black, dirty, nasty, muddy, ugly, unarchitectural, pious & drunken a city as this—Now I remember distinctly that before I got fairly settled at Paris I saw its faults as much as its beauties and so I have not the slightest doubt no end of instruction and interest will come out of this most dismal place."[19] Waterhouse was away from the office when Peabody presented himself "armed with Mr. Ware's letter," but the young American settled in to await his return and occupied himself with exploring the city with British architects Richard Phene Spiers (1838–1916) and Henry Louis Florence (1841–1916) as well as his American companions, McKim and Chandler. They visited the British Museum, the South Kensington Museum ("most interesting of places"), and the Houses of Parliament, while their British associates provided them with entry to exhibitions and lectures at the Royal Academy. At last, on June 4, Peabody met Waterhouse:

> After most provoking delays I got hold of him at last on Thursday, gave him my letter, showed him my project & the photos of the others, told him I had waited two days for him & that I w'd be pleased to serve him for two or three months. He eyed me & my drawings & at last said he thought he could give me a place in his

office but that he had just dismissed one man as not needing him and w'd have to patch things up before taking another to step into his place but he w'd tell me more decidedly Monday afternoon. . . . I told him I do not expect a salary (knowing he would not give me one) and he said I could leave him when I found I was not learning. He looked like a mighty good man and will you please thank Mr. Ware when you see him for his letter to him—It was just what I needed & all I needed as far as I see.[20]

The next week when Peabody wrote to his mother, he had even better news:

Last Monday I went to see Mr. Waterhouse and instead of talking further he took me into his back office and set me to work at once—So I have been at it all the week from 9 until 5 with 1/2 an hour for lunch until 5:30 if I take an hour. It is quite humiliating to see how green I am about what is A.B.C. in an English office but I feel it is an inestimably good thing to see something of it. It has an additionally great advantage that while I am learning something of England, English works + books, + English ways of thinking I am getting some of that practical insight into things that I must get somehow before undertaking anything on my own account.[21]

Peabody spent the summer working in the Waterhouse office. Entries from the office journals indicate that he spent nine days working on drawings for the Manchester Town Hall. More important was the time he spent on three country houses that were in the planning stages: thirty-seven days on "Blackmoor House" (fig I.8) and two days on "Coldhayes," both located in Hampshire, and three days on "Mossley Park" in Liverpool.[22] The work on the country houses was corrobo-

rated in Peabody's letter to his mother, dated June 20, 1869: "Since I have been with him he has put me on the country houses and he has three or four great big fellows going on at once—I have worked on three plans and their elevations and shortly I am going to work over their details throughout. You see then how exactly that is what I want—."[23]

This *was* exactly what Peabody had wanted—on May 16 he had written that what he should study in England was "modern work and picturesque Elizabethan and the like," and that the country houses in England were "such as the French in their dreary chateaus or country play houses never dream of." Peabody was getting practical office experience and hands-on experience in the design of large country houses—experience that would stand him in good stead when he returned to the United States and, in particular, in his extensive work in similar houses in the burgeoning seaside resorts on the East Coast. Peabody continued in his letter of June 20: "Waterhouse's is proving a perfect success. . . . I wish the office were in America and that I could stay there a few months after getting home—as it is now I don't know what I can do. . . . But there are specifications, contracts and that sort of thing to be done in American fashion that one must find out about somehow."

English country houses such as the ones on which young Peabody was working were recognized as important models for the American country and resort houses that would be built beginning in the late 1870s and 1880s in the United States. Peabody was one of the first to articulate our national interest in English houses as early as 1877 in several articles in the *Amer-*

ican Architect and Building News that promoted the nascent Colonial Revival. Signing himself "Georgian," he wrote, "Whatever the attractions of other sources, from no field can suggestions be drawn by an artist more charming and more fitted to our usages, than from the Georgian mansions of New England."[24] Later, in 1905, he wrote "On the Design of Houses" (published in *An Architect's Sketchbook,* 1912). What happens, he asked, "when a rich American who has no traditional ties wishes to build a mansion . . . ?" How does the client negotiate the many stylistic trends available in the marketplace? The influences of historical art were unavoidable for Peabody: "We cannot ignore the work of the past . . . all details of house have some degree of affiliation with some bygone art."[25] In this article he considered the historical influences of Roman and Greek architecture on later European styles, and how the associations of bygone art and architecture cannot be erased from the building elements common to all structures. While the Romans had sophisticated tastes for their resort houses—"Colonnades, courts and cloisters, great sunny baths from which the bathers have a view of the sea, tennis courts, riding-grounds and amphitheatres, marble seats and basins, flat lawns surrounded by plane trees that are linked by festoons of ivy and banked by masses of box and laurel"—Peabody preferred the English work, especially that done during the periods of Elizabeth and James I. He found the houses to be "full of quite reasonable beauty due to the well-considered use of materials and the absence of desire to surprise by learning or technical dexterity. It is difficult to name the age of such buildings . . . they are simple, wholesome and direct architecture."[26]

In "An Architect's Vacation" Peabody admired the timeless beauty of "the great mansions . . . some of brick and some of 'post and pan,' as the black oak and white plaster work is called." He liked the "long and low" elements of English building design.[27] Both of these elements were incorporated into many of his designs. But more important than style for Peabody was the scale of English residential architecture:

> . . . all English architecture starts with the home as the unit, and as the grandeur of the house increases, it is still an enlarged home. So we find scarcely a palace in England. . . . The world has never known houses more homelike than these, for in them domestic charms take the place of splendor, and that homely aspect is retained which characterizes cottage, manor house, mansion, church and cathedral throughout the length and breadth of England.[28]

This was an important characterization on Peabody's part, and it is the key to appreciating his designs for residential architecture. No matter how large the cottage, be it 2,000 or 20,000 square feet, five rooms or ninety-five, Peabody's designs have human scale, the domestic scale that gives them timeless livability and a consistent charm and grace.

In London, Peabody worked on the Blackmoor House drawings for the equivalent of seven weeks and in the course of that time would have become very familiar with Waterhouse's methodology. Because of the nature of the commission—the project had begun with the renovation of the existing farmhouse and then expanded to include the new residence attached and integrated with the old—it provided Peabody with valuable experience in both of these phases of design. Waterhouse's biographer describes an office that by its organization was able to produce a large number of commissions.[29] Waterhouse's three major works—Manchester Town Hall, Eaton Hall in Cheshire, and the Natural History Museum in London—had all been awarded at nearly the same time, during the period 1869 to 1873, a fact to which Waterhouse himself alluded with some regret. The upshot of this abundance of work was that Waterhouse was not able to supervise personally every aspect of every project. Fortunately, his men were carefully trained, so that he could depend on them in his absence to "produce Waterhouse work." In his residential work Waterhouse utilized a limited number of floor plans, enabling his staff to anticipate with some degree of success Waterhouse's intentions for a project.

This mode of working undoubtedly served as a model for Peabody's own office. Peabody also often produced only a rough perspective sketch for commissions, which he subsequently gave to the head draftsman at Peabody & Stearns for expansion and clarification. The simple perspective sketch would then be translated into plans and elevations. Peabody was able to work in this manner because he too utilized a series of plan types that were recognizable from the massing of the building in his original drawing.[30] Additionally, Waterhouse had built up relationships with a small group of subcontractors and suppliers whom he considered reliable. This kind of downline organization ensured consistency in the work produced by the firm, as craftsmen and vendors were fully aware of the style and quality demanded of typical Waterhouse work. Similarly, Peabody & Stearns employed a small number of craftsmen on whom they could rely; Stearns wrote to Peabody: ". . . for the quality of the work depends upon the honesty of the mechanic as it is impossible to superintend every stone that is put upon another."[31]

Waterhouse was as successful a businessman as he was an architect, fully aware of the importance of cost control. While his personality and charm were important assets, his attention to the details of business were of primary importance to the success of his practice. These elements of Waterhouse's success could not have been lost on young Robert Peabody—he was, after all, anxious to learn the business of architecture. Certainly, he learned much about the importance of good business practices in Waterhouse's employ. He must also have observed Waterhouse's design aesthetic—how utility of plan and soundness of structure were of primary importance and that decoration might come after. Like Waterhouse, Peabody would be comfortable designing buildings in a variety of styles—Gothic, Queen Anne, Italian Renaissance, and Colonial Revival in Peabody's case—viewing individual style as secondary to function and artistic composition.

By the Fourth of July, 1869, Peabody was tired of London's dismal atmosphere and pined for "green woods and country life." His work in Waterhouse's office was still "very instructive," however, and Peabody chose to remain another five weeks. By August 11, he was ready to move on: "The gov'nor as Mr. Waterhouse is called in the office has just gone off on a long holiday. I said goodbye to him before he went and can leave now when I choose—I think I shall let this be my last week. Next week I think can be spent profitably at Canterbury."[32] The Waterhouse experience had provided just what Peabody had hoped it would. Bolstered by his education at the École and by his practical experiences in England, Peabody was prepared to enter the last phase of his preparatory study: he traveled throughout Europe for the next six months.

Peabody & Stearns, Architects

While Peabody was still in Europe, he and John Goddard Stearns, Jr., decided to form their architectural partnership in Boston. Both felt that it would be a good fit—Stearns would benefit from Peabody's European education and travel experience, and Peabody could rely on Stearns's practical knowledge, acquired in seven years of experience at Ware & Van Brunt. In September 1869, Peabody wrote to his mother, "[The partnership will be] a mighty good thing for me if only it can be arranged."[33] By October 6 the deal had been made, and the two men were making plans for Peabody's return.

According to the Harvard University *Class of 1866 Class Report, June 1869-June 1872*, Robert Peabody had "remained in Europe, studying architecture, until May, 1870." He returned to Boston in time for "Peabody and Stearns, Architects, 14 Devonshire Street" to appear in the 1870 Boston City Directory.

Robert Peabody and John Stearns's timing in 1870 couldn't have been better. Several social and economic factors converged at about this time, and American resorts were blossoming. Industry and financial markets created great wealth, part of which found its way into the developing leisure market. The expanding railroad networks opened new territories for settlement, and railroad entrepreneurs designed destination resorts to encourage railroad travel. A growing middle class found the money and leisure time to pursue the activities once reserved for only the very wealthy. There were dips along the way, to be sure—the financial panics of 1873 and 1893, for example. But overall the resort market continued to expand, and architects found great opportunities to design and build all manner of projects.

The literature of the period fed into the popularity of resort life and the concept of the cottage or country house. Andrew Jackson Downing articulated the architectural genre with publication of *The Architecture of Country Houses* in 1850, but it was not until after 1865 that the resort explosion really took hold. Guidebooks and travelogues abounded, as did publications that celebrated both specific destinations and the architectural developments that seemed to characterize the age. Charles H. Sweetser published the *Book of Summer Resorts* in 1868. In Newport, Rhode Island, cottage construction was strong in the 1850s, flagged during the war years, and then picked up with

I.9. Peabody & Stearn's design for a summer hotel, c. 1880. *American Architect and Building News*, January 31, 1880. Courtesy of the Frances Loeb Library, Graduate School of Design, Harvard University.

SKETCH · FOR · SUMMER · HOTEL :::

I.10. Gazebo on the waterfront of The Breakers, Newport, Rhode Island. Courtesy of Redwood Library and Athenaeum, Newport, Rhode Island. Gift of Gladys Moore Vanderbilt Szechenyi.

renewed gusto in the 1870s; George Champlin Mason responded with *Newport and Its Cottages,* published in 1875. Mrs. John King Van Rensselaer published *Newport, Our Social Capital* in 1905 and included remarks on several Peabody & Stearns clients and their cottages in her text. By 1904 the North Shore of Massachusetts was so popular that a special publication was warranted: *The North Shore Breeze: A Weekly Journal Devoted to the Best Interests of the North Shore.* Its introductory remarks contained a prediction for the future of summer and resort life:

> The Breeze and its Purpose: The population of the North Shore as a resort is growing from year to year. It now attracts hundreds of wealthy people the country over who spend the greater part of the year here. In fact, if present indications are any criterion, we have reason to believe that the "summer season" is fast outgrowing itself, and ere long these picturesque shores and wooded hills will have equal attraction for wealth in winter as in summer.[34]

The mid-1880s witnessed the publication of Mrs. Mariana Griswold Van Rensselaer's series "American Country Houses" in the *Century Magazine* as well as George William Sheldon's classic *Artistic Country-Seats.* *Scribner's Magazine* highlighted resort communities in the feature articles of four editions of the magazine in 1894: July—the North Shore (Massachusetts); August—Newport, Rhode Island; September—Bar Harbor, Maine; and October—Lenox, Massachusetts. Social columns in the newspapers of major cities carried the lists of summer residents who were arriving in Newport or traveling to Bar Harbor, and Social Blue Books frequently indicated which of their elite members were year-round and/or summer residents.

The development of any number of resort communities followed what seemed to be a proscribed route. A location became locally and regionally known for healthful surroundings or a beautiful landscape. As its popularity increased, more socially progressive activities were demanded, and tourist accommodations expanded from boardinghouses to inns and hotels, and later, "grand" hotels and finally, to cottages. Architect Bruce Price commented on this transition in an article in *Scribner's Magazine* in 1890: "The fashion, almost universal at this time with city people, was to spend a few days, or weeks at most, during the heated term, at the great hotels of "the springs," "the summer resort," or the seashore.... But from the whirl and heat of the city, the summer hotel, with its artificial life and huddling quarters, was a poor resource, and early in the seventies the country cottage . . . began to appear."[35] Although Peabody & Stearns was commissioned to design several resort hotels—the design that appeared in the *American Architect and Building News* in 1880 (fig. I.9) was apparently never built, but their Antlers Hotel in Colorado Springs (1883) received rave reviews—the national trend was toward the individual retreats that form the basis of this book.

A key element in the burgeoning American resort movement was an American interest in the landscape—due in part to the closing of the West and the romanticizing of a vanishing landscape, to the perceived contrasts in the nineteenth century between the city and the country, and to the idealization of country life. All of these contributed to an aura of myth and fantasy around the resort locale. The natural surroundings became an integral part of the resort cottage, bringing with them suggestions of nostalgia, boundless potential, and images of the sublime. In coastal and mountain communities the potential of the landscape view was carefully considered. Implicit in the siting of the house was its potential to control the landscape, and hence, the viewer's experience of it. Two distinct approaches could be adopted: the subordination of architecture to an Arcadian landscape or the conscious manipulation of view and natural landscape. Homes built next to towering rock formations or deeply carved fjords, such as Peabody & Stearns's Glen Eyrie in Colorado Springs (see fig. 4.4) or Ravenscleft in Seal Harbor (see fig. 1.195), reflected the associative power in landscapes where the natural elements nearly dwarfed the man-made structures. Alternatively, Pierre Lorillard's Breakers dominated the carefully managed lawns and gardens, just as his gazebo and yacht, the Rhoda, dominated the nearby oceanscape (see fig. I.10). Thus, the choices made by architect and client in the siting of a resort cottage were critical to the experience created by the building. Peabody & Stearns worked with landscape architect Ernest Bowditch on several of the Newport projects and paired with Frederick Law Olmsted's landscape design firm for numerous other residential and commercial projects. Surviving letters indicate that there was a necessity for give-and-take not only between the client and the design firms, but between the two designers as well.

Peabody & Stearns's fledgling firm was busy, apparently, from the very beginning. The first year and a half seem to have been occupied with alterations to existing buildings, primarily in the Boston area. According to office records, there were approximately twenty of these alteration commissions in the first eighteen months. The Bussey Institute Building in Jamaica Plain, built for Harvard University in 1870–71, may have been the firm's first executed work (fig. I.11). Other early commissions included two buildings for Nathan Matthews: a dormitory, Matthews Hall, at Harvard University (fig. I.12); his summer home, Manshurd Hall, in Newport, Rhode Island (see fig. 1.13); and two blocks of townhouses in Boston's Back Bay. Peabody & Stearns was aggressive early in its career: it was one of the fourteen architectural firms that entered the competition for the new Boston Museum of Fine Arts building in Copley Square on October 1, 1870. The fact that the young firm placed among the top six contestants in this competition must have influenced the Building Committee at nearby Trinity Church to invite Peabody & Stearns to participate in that competition in 1872, along with W. A. Potter, H. H. Richardson, John H. Sturgis, Ware & Van Brunt, and Richard Morris Hunt. While Peabody's design did not win the committee's final approval, Peabody & Stearns was competing at the highest level, and the two young men were obviously held in high regard, both at home and abroad.

While Boston was always home base for Peabody & Stearns, the firm moved within the city: from 14 Devonshire Street to 60 Devonshire Street in 1874, and to 53 State Street in 1891. The firm expanded its geo-graphical boundaries twice—once to open an office in New York City for a brief time (1881–82) and the other to operate the office of Peabody, Stearns & Furber in St. Louis during the 1890s. Pierce P. Furber had been an employee of the Boston firm and later became a partner in his hometown of St. Louis. We do not know at this time how much of the design work in St. Louis he was responsible for, but he was certainly the "architect on the site" in most of the firm's western work—for example, the Antlers Hotel and the Signal Station in Colorado Springs, the Union Depot in Duluth, and the Hill House in St. Paul.

While Peabody & Stearns received commissions for country houses and seaside and resort cottages almost from the start, their busiest period of residential and resort building appears to have been during the decades of the 1880s and 1890s, when the firm produced approximately sixty-four significant resort commissions. The period 1900 to 1909 was productive as well, with at least twenty-one summer houses and related buildings designed, including the majority of the work in Northeast Harbor, Maine—all of this in addition to commercial, educational, and ecclesiastical commissions. During these years, Peabody returned to England and the Continent several times, including a trip in 1876 with his wife, Annie Putnam Peabody, and one in 1882 with Francis Chandler. The influences of the architecture there, combined with the vernacular architecture of the American Colonial Revival, as well as the residential work of other American architects such as McKim, Mead & White, William Ralph Emerson, Bruce Price, and Richard Morris Hunt would help to produce a body of Peabody & Stearns'–designed resort cottages that were both stylish and highly esteemed in their market.

I.11. Bussey Institution, Jamaica Plain, Massachusetts, c. 1870–71. Collection of the author.

I.12. Matthews Hall,
Harvard University,
c. 1871. Courtesy of
the Frances Loeb Library,
Graduate School of Design,
Harvard University.

In 1893, Peabody & Stearns created the Machinery Hall and Colonnade at the World's Columbian Exposition in Chicago (fig. I.13), as well as the iconic Massachusetts State Building, based on the historic John Hancock house (figs. I.14 and I.15). Eight years later, Peabody designed the Horticulture, Mining, and Graphic Arts Building, as well as the pavilion for chocolate maker Walter Baker & Company at the Pan-American Exposition in Buffalo, New York (1901–2), and the

American Telephone & Telegraph Building at the Louisiana Purchase Exposition held in St. Louis in 1903–4. While still involved with the design work of the firm, Robert Peabody became increasingly involved in service and civic organizations. He served a term as president of the American Institute of Architects, was a member of the jury on architecture for the Paris Exposition in 1900, was chairman of the Parks Department of Boston from 1909 through 1914, and again

I.13. Machinery Hall,
World's Columbian
Exposition, 1893. From
*The Columbian World's Fair
Atlas*, Colchester, Illinois.

I.14. Massachusetts State Building, World's Columbian Exposition, 1893. Courtesy of Memorial Library, Boston Architectural College.

from 1916 until his death in 1917. He was called upon to be a member of the Committee on Public Improvements and the Committee on Metropolitan Improvement for the City of Boston, and in 1908 authored *A Holiday Study of Cities and Ports* as part of his study of the potential development of the port of Boston. He was an overseer at Harvard University in 1898 and 1899 and from 1907 to 1912, and was a member of the Massachusetts Institute of Technology Corporation for many years. In this way Peabody's education and

expertise extended beyond the design of individual buildings to benefit his profession and the community at large.

Robert Swain Peabody died at his cottage on Peach's Point in Marblehead, Massachusetts, on September 23, 1917, after a long illness. In an unusual twist of fate, his partner, John Goddard Stearns, had died the previous Sunday, September 16, at his own summer home in Duxbury, Massachusetts.

I.15. John Hancock House, Boston, Massachusetts. From Moses King's *King's Handbook of Boston,* Cambridge, Massachusetts, 1885.

Chapter 1

New England

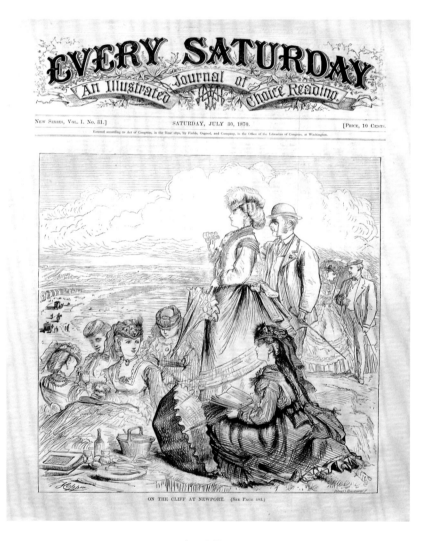

1.1. On the Cliff at Newport.
From *Every Saturday: An Illustrated Journal of Choice Reading*, vol. 1, no. 31, Saturday, July 30, 1870. Collection of the author.

I t is no surprise that a large percentage of Peabody & Stearns's summer house commissions were located in New England, whose cool temperatures and refreshing landscapes attracted visitors from all over the country—Peabody & Stearns did not have to go far afield for clients or commissions.

Newport, Rhode Island, is arguably the best-known resort town on the eastern seaboard of the United States, with a long-standing history as a favorable location, as an important eighteenth-century mercantile center, and as a healthful summer destination (fig. 1.1). By the late nineteenth century, it had become a "super" resort, principally because of its wealthy residents and their cottages. Indeed, Newport's success, and subsequent interest, can be attributed in large part to its cottages. Of particular interest to our study is the fact that Newport boasted the largest concentration of Peabody & Stearns–designed buildings outside Boston. The fact that the firm was engaged at Newport throughout much of its forty-seven-year existence, as well as the range of designs created there, makes it a primary site for the serious contemplation of Peabody & Stearns's residential resort architecture.

Newport was the site of one of Peabody & Stearns's first commissions for an important client. Manshurd Hall (figs. 1.13–1.15)) was designed in 1871 in the prevailing Stick Style, as were the firm's next two cottage commissions. Shortly after, by 1874-75, Henry Hobson Richardson completed the William Watts Sherman House on nearby Shepard Avenue, and the shift to the Shingle Style became apparent. This proved to be a successful design vocabulary for Peabody, whose repertoire of English cottages, Queen Anne massing, and Colonial American building forms sheathed in cedar shingles became a signature architectural formula, in Newport and beyond.

The conditions that made Newport popular extended to the surrounding area, and towns such as Narragansett and Jamestown attracted development, although to an understandably lesser degree. The Peabody & Stearns designs in these two smaller locations are a contrast to most of their work in Newport and belong to a lesser-known body of their work.

While the Commonwealth of Massachusetts is only the fourth-largest of the New England states physically, it is the most diverse in terms of its historic resort communities. The state's eastern boundary is the Atlantic Ocean, and a variety of seaside communities constitute the distinct summer resorts of the North Shore and the South Shore with Cape Cod. In the far west of the state, the Berkshire Hills and Berkshire Valley provide the setting for the Lenox-Stockbridge resort area.

The North Shore comprises the northernmost coastline of Massachusetts Bay, from Nahant and Swampscott on the south to Gloucester and Cape Ann on the northeast (figs. 1.2 and 1.3). Nahant was a popular Bostonian watering hole for several generations before other towns on the North Shore became popular; although smaller and with fewer social amenities, it was accessible from Boston by daytrip steamboat ride for a number of years, while travelers to other North Shore communities still had to make a railroad excursion. Soon, however, all of the North Shore was discovered and developed, prompting the observation that

> unlike Newport, Lenox, and Bar Harbor, the North Shore is first of all a dormitory. The busy men of affairs, who spend the summer at Beverly Farms or Manchester, go to Boston every day and return home in the early afternoon....[1]

While the North Shore was popular primarily for its ocean frontage, inland areas also had their appeal, and the Myopia Hunt Club was established in Wenham for horsemen in the surrounding towns of Hamilton and Beverly. Peabody & Stearns designed elegant farm buildings in Topsfield for Dr. Henry Sears, a client who commissioned a shorefront cottage in Beverly as well as a town home for his sister in Boston. Robert Peabody's own family purchased a cottage on Peach's Point in Marblehead, which the architect took delight in expanding over the years.

To the south of Boston, the South Shore, Cape Cod and the islands, and the so-called South Coast are quite different in terrain. Peabody & Stearns had cottage commissions in Duxbury and Hull, and worked on the historic First Parish Church in Hingham—all part of the

1.2. President Taft's summer home, Beverly, Massachusetts. Postcard, collection of the author.

1.3. Swallows' Cave, Nahant, Massachusetts. From *Picturesque America*, New York, New York, D. Appleton & Company, 1872. Wood engraving. Collection of the author.

South Shore of Boston. Cape Cod, the arm-shaped peninsula that stretches out from the southeasternmost point of the state, became one of Massachusetts's most popular shore resorts (figs. 1.4 and 1.5). "The Cape" was once attached to the mainland, but in 1909 August Belmont, Jr. created the Boston, Cape Cod & New York Canal Company and began the excavation of what would become the Cape Cod Canal. Belmont's canal opened with limited success in 1914; the U.S. Army Corps of Engineers revisited the project in 1935–40 and created the canal that exists today, spanned by two traffic bridges and one railroad bridge. Most of Cape Cod is located on the far side of the canal, although parts of Bourne and the town of Buzzards Bay were left on the mainland side.

Of the fifteen Cape towns, Peabody & Stearns received commissions in Falmouth and Woods Hole, as well as in Bourne, Cataumet, and Naushon Island—all areas located in the upper Cape region. Only their commission for Nathan Matthews for additions and alterations to the Yarmouth Library took the firm to the mid-Cape region. Nantucket Island provided an alternative island site, and the Cliff Beach Bathhouses pro-

vide a look at the public recreational architecture of the period. The area of Massachusetts now called the South Coast includes the southeastern shore region of the state approaching Rhode Island. At the turn of the twentieth century it was still close enough to Boston to be an attractive summer destination for wealthy city residents, and near enough to New Bedford to make use of its facilities for water transportation. Peabody & Stearns received many residential and commercial commissions in New Bedford, Peabody's birthplace, as well as commissions for summer cottages in Dartmouth and nearby Wareham.

During the same period, the towns of Lenox and Stockbridge in the Berkshire Hills of western Massachusetts were developing as communities favored first for simple, country life and later for more lavish country homes and estates. On par with Newport, Rhode Island, and Bar Harbor, Maine, Lenox was even referred to by a writer at the *Newport Mercury* as "this inland Newport," with the observation that "Everybody who is anybody is now at [Lenox].[2] Unlike Newport and Bar Harbor, the "season" in Lenox was autumn. In a letter dated August 24, 1886, English author Matthew Arnold wrote: "This place [Stockbridge] has become very enjoyable. I see at last what an American autumn which they so praise is, and it deserves the praise given it."[3] Like its oceanfront counterparts, Lenox was featured in an October 1894 article in *Scribner's Magazine* and in an August 1897 article in *Munsey's*. The history and country charm of the Berkshire Hills pleased Robert Peabody during a visit in 1877, resulting in his well-published sketch of the early Lenox house, Yokun (later remodeled by Charles McKim in the 1880s). Peabody captured the house, however, in his "Georgian" days, and the sketch appeared in the *American Architect and Building News* (fig. 1.6). A few years later, Peabody & Stearns began to receive commissions for country houses in Lenox, totaling seven during the period 1882–93.

In 1908, Frank Crowninshield, editor of *Vanity Fair* magazine, compiled a list of the country's great eastern resorts: Palm Beach; Hot Springs, Virginia; Narragansett Pier, Rhode Island; the Berkshires; Tuxedo Park, New York; Long Island; and Newport.[4] The resorts along the coast of Maine, including Bar Harbor and Northeast Harbor on Mount Desert Island, and Dark Harbor on Islesboro, are conspicuous for their absence. (A puzzling omission, since four years later, the 1909 *Baedecker's United States* guidebook considered Bar Harbor to be the only resort at the time "vying in importance" with Newport.) However, if we read further in Crowninshield's remarks, we learn that his purported purpose in providing the rating list was "for the benefit of millionaires from the West whose wives are bent upon breaking into Society." Evidently, the folks who vacationed in Maine had either already broken into society, or just didn't care. And it turns out that the truth was a little bit of both.

1.4. Highway alongside Cape Cod Canal, near Wareham, Massachusetts. Postcard, collection of the author.

1.5. An old Cape Cod House. Postcard, collection of the author.

Peabody & Stearns received commissions for nearly a dozen projects in Maine. The firm's Bangor Public Library (1912) (fig. 1.7) is still well regarded in that northern city; in 1998 the library received an acclaimed Robert A. M. Stern–designed addition, making it the second-largest library in the state. This solid Italian Renaissance structure constructed of yellow brick and trimmed out in granite, marble, and terra cotta stands next door to the complementary Peabody & Stearns–designed Bangor High School, also completed in 1912. Both structures inspired newspaper articles extolling their many virtues and state-of-the-art features. In the seafaring city of Bath, the William D. Sewall house, York Hall (fig. 1.8), is an excellent example of a Georgian Revival residence in a city neighborhood setting. Built in 1896 at a cost of $22,700, it still stands as an elegant monument to the seafaring family that built it and to the architects who designed it. The City of Portland consulted the firm for advice regarding a new City Hall in 1908 and, a few years later, for advice regarding the Portland Bridge. But it was in the two island communities of Northeast Harbor on Mount Desert Island and Dark Harbor on Islesboro that the architectural firm made its mark in Maine. Peabody & Stearns designed nine cottages as well as a church; six of the cottages are still serving their original purpose.

Mount Desert Island's reputation as a summer resort began during the 1840s and, like Newport, it was "discovered" by artists and intellectuals. Unlike Newport, however, this artistic and academic population did not abandon the area when New York society invaded; instead, several different resort communities, catering to different clientele, developed simultaneously. Bar Harbor became home to the likes of the Vanderbilts, the J. P. Morgans, and the Astors, while Northeast Harbor and Seal Harbor attracted members of the clergy, such as Bishop Doane of Albany, scientists like Louis Agassiz, and university presidents and professors, such as Charles William Eliot of Harvard University and Seth Low of Columbia. The distinct difference between these villages caused maritime historian Samuel Eliot Morison, a longtime resident, to remark that "it used to be said that to be a summer resident at Bar Harbor you needed money but no brains; at Northeast Harbor you wanted brains but no money; but at Southwest Harbor, neither brains nor money!"[5]

While Mount Desert Island was becoming a destination resort for people from New York, Boston, and Philadelphia, the island community of Islesboro (south of Mount Desert Island, three miles out to sea in Penobscot Bay) began drawing clientele from nearby Bangor, Maine. Small summer communities soon developed at Ryder's Cove, Hewes Ledge, and North Haven. In 1888, James D. Winsor, a wealthy Philadelphia steamship owner, devised the Islesboro Land & Improvement Company, eventually acquiring about 1,500 acres of land—nearly 25 percent of the total community acreage. He marketed lots primarily to Philadelphia businessmen, with the result that the community at Dark Harbor provided

New Public Library, Bangor, Maine.

1.6. Robert Peabody's sketch of Yokun, Lenox, Massachusetts. *American Architect and Building News*, October 20, 1877, vol. II, no. 95, p. 95.

1.7. New Public Library, Bangor, Maine, 1911. Postcard, collection of the author.

1.8. House for W. D. Sewall, Esq., Bath, Maine. South Elevation. Peabody and Stearns Collection, courtesy of the Boston Public Library Fine Arts Department.

1.9. Postcard showing cottages of Dr. White, William Pratt, and Henry Howe in Dark Harbor, Maine. Courtesy of the Maine Historical Preservation Commission.

commissions for larger cottages and a more national clientele than did Northeast Harbor (fig. 1.9).

In addition to the cottages included in this catalogue, the Peabody & Stearns project record cards indicate that commissions were received from James Garland for a cottage in Bar Harbor in 1891 (not built) and for two cottages for W. W. Vaughan in Northeast Harbor—one in 1893 (destroyed) and another in 1902 (fig. 1.10). It has been suggested that these commissions were handled in conjunction with local architect Fred Savage, who had received his early architectural training in the Peabody & Stearns office in Boston during the period 1882-84. Alterations for the Carroll S. Tyson cottage in Northeast Harbor and an addition to the Northeast Harbor Library, both in 1915, were perhaps similarly managed.

Peabody & Stearns produced a surprisingly small number of commissions in the three remaining New England states—for either resort or other residential or commercial clients. In Connecticut, Peabody & Stearns's principal cottage commission was for Henry O. Havemeyer in Greenwich. Located on Long Island Sound, Greenwich was certainly well located for a summer retreat, with all of the amenities—yachting,

waterfront and waterview house sites, carriage roads, and healthful surroundings (fig. 1.12). Not surprisingly, the town was identified in the *Encyclopaedia Britannica* of 1910 as "a summer resort, principally for New Yorkers."[6] The establishment of rail service to the area provided the stimulus for development both for year-round residents who could commute to the city and for seasonal cottagers. Elsewhere in the state the firm may have designed or worked on a cottage in Farmington for George Goodwin Williams in 1908, as well as houses in New Haven for L. E. Stoddard, Hayes Quincy Trowbridge, and Victor Morris Tyler; a house in Noank for Arthur Anderson; a house in Waterbury for Charles Benedict; and a house in Wauregan for J. A. Atwood. Commercial commissions in Hartford included the Hartford National Bank, which was well published; the Scottish Union and National Insurance Building; and the Society for Savings Bank. Additions and alterations to the John Rogers Studio in New Canaan in 1878 may have been designed by Peabody as well. The Adee Memorial Boathouse for Yale University in New Haven was an opportunity for Peabody & Stearns to work on one of the ancillary kinds of structures that were developing during the later nineteenth century as physical education, fitness, and sport became part of the experience of an ever-increasing swath of the American population, and is included for that reason (see fig. 1.231).

Peabody & Stearns had very few commissions in Vermont. What little work it did was located in the larger towns or cities in the state—tentatively, alterations for the Brattleboro Hospital Asylum in 1887, and the Burlington Bank Building in 1903. Plans in the Boston Public Library indicate commissions for house designs in Burlington for D. W. Robinson (1886) and for F. W. Ward.

Alternatively, Peabody & Stearns's notable work in the state of New Hampshire was primarily concentrated in the hill farm country of the mid and western

1.10. Alteration of and addition to house no. 2 at North East Harbor for W. W. Vaughan, Esq. Peabody and Stearns Collection, courtesy of the Boston Public Library Fine Arts Department.

1.11. South Main Street, looking north, Newport, New Hampshire. Postcard, collection of the author.

parts of the state. The state's proximity to the Peabody & Stearns client base might lead to the expectation of more New Hampshire cottages and country houses, but the firm's resort commissions were limited to Chocorua, Dublin, and Newport.

Beginning as early as the 1820s and 1830s, New Hampshire began to benefit from its reputation as a summer retreat for artists, academics, and businesspeople from Boston, as well as from more distant locales such as St. Louis, Philadelphia, and Chicago. Grand hotels were constructed in the coastal areas and in the White Mountains, following the paths of the railroads that were constructed to haul lumber and produce to the urban centers of Portland and Boston. People eventually began buying up old hill farms for use as summer homes. So common was this activity that Nahum Bachelder, secretary of the State Board of Agriculture and briefly state governor, published an annual "New Hampshire Farms for Summer Homes" from 1901 through 1913. Two of the towns that contain Peabody & Stearns cottage designs were remarkably similar (although the same cannot be said for the cottages). Both Chocorua and Dublin were renowned for their namesake lakes as

well as for the breathtaking views of a signature local mountain. Both were agricultural communities that gradually accommodated (and in some senses were appropriated by) a growing number of tourists and summer residents. Newport, New Hampshire, seems a less likely location for a Peabody & Stearns cottage (fig. 1.11). Although it is the county seat of Sullivan County, it is a small town with few if any resort amenities. Perhaps its greatest claim to fame is the fact that Sarah Buell Hale, the author of "Mary Had a Little Lamb," was once a resident of the town. The cottage in Newport designed for Miss Mary Stevens is a classic small cottage—as unlike its contemporaries in Newport, Rhode Island, as Miss Stevens, a schoolteacher from Framingham, Massachusetts, was from the clientele who built in the larger "watering holes" of New England. In other areas of the state, the firm designed the Baptist church on Front Street in Exeter in 1875-76 and worked on a building for the Philips Exeter Academy in the early 1870s. In Concord the firm produced designs for the Conway National Bank, for the 1909-10 addition to the New Hampshire State House, and for additions and alterations at St. Paul's School in 1911.

1.12. The sea wall, Seaside Park, Bridgeport, Connecticut. Postcard, collection of the author.

Rhode Island

Newport and Surrounds

This Island . . . is deservedly esteemed the Paradise of New England for the . . . temperateness of the climate; that though it be not above sixty-five miles south of Boston, it is a coat warmer in winter, and being surrounded by the ocean is not so much affected in summer with hot land breezes, as the towns on the continent.
— DANIEL NEAL, *Evening Post,* July 23, 1739

Newport is damp and cold and windy and excessively disagreeable, but it is very select.
— MARK TWAIN, *The Gilded Age*, 1873

Manshurd Hall

Newport, Rhode Island, 1871–72

Nathan Matthews, 1814–1904

. . . . one of the most picturesque in Newport.
— George Champlin Mason,
Newport and Its Cottages [7]

Nathan Matthews built his Stick Style cottage, Manshurd Hall, on a waterview site on the east side of Bellevue Avenue at Shepherd Avenue. Matthews, a Boston businessman with many financial successes as well as failures, was an important investor in real estate: as president of the Boston Water Power Company he was a prime mover in the development of the Back Bay. His obituary stated: "To-day the people who walk along Beacon Street, Marlborough Street, Commonwealth Avenue and all the thoroughfares above Arlington Street that run into these great avenues, can see the property that existed very clearly forty years ago in the mind's eye of Nathan Matthews.[8] In 1870 he was reported to be the largest individual real estate taxpayer in Boston.

Three of Nathan and Albertine Bunker Matthews's seven children attended Harvard University. Matthews was interested in Harvard as both an educational and a cultural institution, and it seems logical to speculate that he and Robert Peabody were introduced by mutual friends when his oldest son, Nathan, Jr., enrolled there in 1870. The senior Matthews became an important client for the young firm of Peabody & Stearns: in 1871 he commissioned Matthews Hall, a dormitory at Harvard University (fig. I.12); additions

and alterations to his hometown library in Yarmouth Port, Massachusetts; and his new summer home in Newport.

According to the *Newport Mercury*, Matthews's cottage was completed during the winter of 1871–72 at a cost of about $75,000. The main house measured 60 by 65 feet, with a 45-by-46-foot addition. The first story was of face brick with brownstone trimmings, "inlaid here and there with wall tiles," as well as black bricks and soapstone for decoration. The second and third stories were of wood, in the style, as Mason put it, of "the old timber houses of a former age, which are so justly noted for their pleasing effect."[9] Bargeboarded and jerkinhead gables added to the effect of an old English house. From the perspective of a later age and aesthetic, Henry-Russell Hitchcock criticized it as having "all the vices of the American Victorian Gothic domestic vernacular: confused massing, a conglomeration of different materials, and quantities of the crudest sort of gingerbread."[10] The residence was oriented to its view of the ocean to the east with numerous piazzas, a covered verandah in front of the first-floor billiards room, along with multiple balcony areas and bargeboarded gables. These transitional spaces linked the interior of the house to the manicured lawns and cooling ocean breezes outside.

Inside, Manshurd Hall was based on a central-hall plan. The grand staircase in the hall was separated from a passage to the billiards room by an openwork screen of ash, the wood finish throughout the house. Stained-glass windows designed and manufactured by the McPherson Stained Glass company adorned the hall door and windows.[11] A morning room and formal parlor were situated to one side of the large entry hall; the study and billiards rooms were on the opposite

1.13. House on Bellevue Avenue, Manshurd Hall, front façade. *Architectural Sketchbook*, October 1873, vol. 1, no. 4, pl 14. Courtesy of the Boston Public Library Fine Arts Department.

1.14. House on Bellevue Avenue, Manshurd Hall, rear façade. *Architectural Sketchbook,* October 1873, vol. 1, no. 4, pl. 14. Collection of the author.

1.15. Manshurd Hall, detail, first floor plan. *Architectural Sketchbook,* October 1873, vol. 1, no. 4, pl. 14. Courtesy of the Boston Public Library Fine Arts Department

side. There is a suggestion in Peabody's *Architectural Sketchbook* that the furniture was designed by the architects, "in keeping with the house."[12]

In February of 1873, Matthews purchased two and a half acres of land on nearby Coggeshall Avenue and erected a stable and a small cottage with mansard roof for his gardener. However, by 1877 he may have been experiencing adverse economic conditions, as Pierre Lorillard rented the "Matthews villa" for that season. The next April it was reported that "the estate containing 128,520 square feet of land, with house, stable and porter's lodge" had been sold at a mortgagee's sale.[13] While that 1878 bankruptcy report was premature (and later retracted by the newspaper), the estate *was* sold in 1879 to James R. Keene, a California and New York stock speculator.

The original Matthews house burned in December of 1881. Peabody & Stearns was reported to be drawing plans for the new villa, but then the *Newport Mercury* reported that Clarence S. Luce had won the bid for a Queen Anne design of two stories and "a handsomely gabled and ornamented attic. The interior finish will be exceedingly rich and the house will be one of the most attractive on the Avenue."[14]

The exterior features of the original Matthews house—the heavy Gothic ornamentation and Stick Style trim—soon passed from fashion and were replaced by Queen Anne and Shingle Style cottages. Before that change, however, Peabody & Stearns designed several other Stick Style houses in Newport, including the D'Hauteville Villa, which was, like Manshurd Hall, featured by George Mason in *Newport and Its Cottages*.

Following the loss of Manshurd Hall, Nathan Matthews began summering in Bar Harbor, where he purchased a cottage, and where he died in August of 1904.

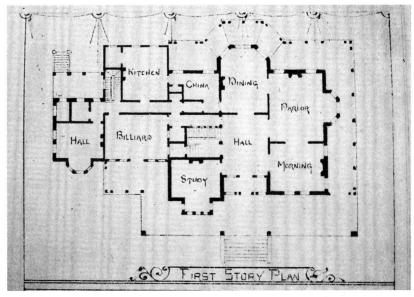

D'Hauteville Villa

Newport, Rhode Island, 1871-72

Frederick Grand D'Hauteville, 1838-1918

The principal rooms. . . . have eastern and southern exposure, giving a commanding view of the avenue in the east, and a long stretch of water on the south and west, particularly from the upper windows. . . .
— George Champlin Mason, *Newport and Its Cottages* [1]

The D'Hauteville villa was built in 1871 for Frederick Sears Grand D'Hauteville of Boston, the son of Ellen Sears of Boston and Paul Daniel Gonsalve Grand D'Hauteville of Switzerland. It was a three-storied structure bucolically sited on the west side of Bellevue Avenue, with views of Coggeshall Pond and the partially wooded hillsides of Rocky Farm to the west. According to Mrs. Van Rennselaer, the villa was occupied only in alternate seasons; family estates in Switzerland claimed D'Hauteville at other times.

D'Hauteville purchased the 30,900-square-foot lot for $10,000 in October 1871. The *Newport Mercury* later reported that the house was planned to measure 37 feet by 64 feet, in a "style of architecture similar to Mr. Matthews," but with a projected cost of $25,000.[16] In addition to the villa, Peabody & Stearns designed a stable and performed alterations to the main house in 1899, according to the *Newport Journal* (January 21, 1899). The Boston Public Library collection contains two small portfolios of Peabody & Stearns's estimates and bills for this house, but no plans or elevations.

Like the Matthews house, the predominant style of the D'Hauteville villa was the Stick Style, with Gothic ornamentation. A formal porte-cochere was located on the north entrance to the house, with porches on the east and west and a room built above. Mason commented on the graceful proportions of a tower. On the interior, all of the principal rooms again opened from a wide entry hall, with the porches allowing an interaction between interior and exterior space.

Frederick D'Hauteville was educated at Harvard, a member of the Class of 1859. He served in the Civil War, first as an aide-de-camp on the staff of General Nathaniel Banks and later as a captain and assistant adjutant general. After the war he was active socially in the leading clubs of Newport and New York, including the Knickerbocker, Union, Metropolitan, and New York Yacht clubs and the Newport Reading Room and Casino. He was married twice and, at his death in Newport, was survived by his widow, Susan Macomb, a daughter, and two sons.

D'Hauteville's mother, Ellen Sears, was the daughter of David Sears of Boston, a gentleman of great wealth and position in that city. According to the *Sears Genealogical Catalogue*, David Sears had been one of the first to own and occupy a summer residence at Nahant, but "finding it too bleak for his own taste," he relocated to Newport, where in 1845 he built the villa which he named Red Cross.[17] D'Hauteville's aunt, Grace Winthrop Sears, was the wife of William Cabell Rives, Jr., for whom Peabody & Stearns designed Rosevale, located on Red Cross Avenue in Newport.

In retrospect, the D'Hauteville villa, like the Matthews house, was unremarkable in the resort movement for its size or layout; these early houses merely provided a preparation for the cottages to come. According to the Preservation Society of Newport County, this cottage was acquired in 1929 by Francis Drury of London and his wife, Mabel Gerry, of Newport, and renamed Drury Lodge. A fire in the 1950s destroyed much of the original fabric of the house, although fragments of the structure were incorporated into a later residence.[18] The property is privately owned.

1.16. D'Hauteville Cottage, front façade.
From *Newport and Its Cottages*, Boston, Massachusetts, James R. Osgood & Company, 1875. Courtesy of Newport Historical Society.

Rosevale

Newport, Rhode Island, 1876

William Cabell Rives, Jr., 1825–1889

The house is of brick, a material that can only be, or should
only be, used in summer, that the walls may harden before
cold weather sets in. . . .
— *Newport Journal*, January 24, 1877

Family connections intertwine all of Newport's
comings and goings. The Rives built a Peabody
& Stearns' designed cottage on land that had
been part of the original estate of the Sears family mentioned in the previous section.

William Cabell Rives, Jr., was born at the family's
country estate Castle Hill in Virginia, while his father
was a member of the United States House of Representatives (1823–29); Representative Rives then served
as U.S. minister to France (1829–1832). Consequently,
young Rives was educated in both France and the
United States, by private tutors and at private schools.
He attended the University of Virginia (Class of 1845)
and graduated from Harvard Law School in 1847. He
practiced law for a time, but according to the Rives
family genealogy, he abandoned his career upon his
marriage in May 1849 to the well-to-do Grace Winthrop Sears.

The Rives's twenty-room cottage, Rosevale, measured 60 by 68 feet with bay windows up two stories
and was constructed, beginning in 1876, for the sum of
$37,663.60, considerably less than its original estimate.
It is quite different from the cottages designed by Peabody & Stearns just three or four years earlier. Notably,
it was constructed of brick: the "best Eastern brick and
trimmed with olive stone."[19] Its decorative program is
also very different. One of the few Newport cottages
designed in High Victorian Gothic, the house features
pointed arches above the doors, steeply pitched dormers, and a prominent turret incorporated asymmetrically in the front façade. Even though Rosevale
originally had decorative bargeboarding at the gables,
at the time of its construction it appeared to be quite
plain in comparison to, for example, the Matthews villa
with its Stick Style trim. In fact, it was noted in a discussion of Rosevale in the *Newport Journal* in 1877 that
"there has evidently been a reluctance to allow ornamentation and this to a degree that is perhaps questionable. We are too apt to run to the other extreme, to
an excessive use of ornaments which becomes wearisome, and it is a hopeful sign that architects of late
years have seen this, and are among the most strenuous to check it."[20]

The interior finish of the 18 by 19 foot parlor
was butternut and wainscoted. The *Newport Journal*
reporter continued: "The arrangement of the interior
of the house is very good; the hall is particularly fine,
with its broad staircase and large windows on the land-

ing. The finish is in hard woods, and a liberal use has
been made of marquetry, tiles, etc." The second level
was comprised of six large chambers and the third had
three chambers and several smaller rooms.

Rosevale still stands in the Kay Street–Catherine
Street–Old Beach Road Neighborhood and is operated
as the Hambly Funeral Home.

1.17. Rosevale, front
façade, c. 2006.
Photograph by author.

1.18. Rosevale, front
façade, c. 1900. Courtesy
of Newport Historical Society.

The Breakers

Newport, Rhode Island, 1877-78

Pierre Lorillard IV, 1833-1901

The situation is one of the noblest, from an ideal seaside point of view, that this country can show, the grounds comprising many acres on the ocean-shore, which here rises abruptly ten or twelve feet above the surface of the water.... The Breakers dash incessantly below it...."
— GEORGE SHELDON, *Artistic Country-Seats*, 1886 [21]

Since 1892, "The Breakers" has evoked images of Richard Morris Hunt's massive marble palace on the Cliff Walk of Newport. However, for fifteen years before that the name and site belonged to the picturesque Queen Anne cottage created by Peabody & Stearns for Pierre Lorillard IV. It was the first significant cottage to be built in Newport's millionaires' row and without question set a standard for the resort estates that were to follow. The Breakers appeared twice in *American Architect and Building News* (1878 and 1880), was pictured in George Sheldon's *Artistic Country Seats* (as the Cornelius Vanderbilt house), and references to its great cost and lavish decor were made in Charles H. Dow's *Newport Past and Present* and the *American Builder* magazine. The *American Builder* claimed that "Pierre Lorillard's new mansion at Newport will be the largest and handsomest in New England,"[22] while Dow enthused: "Within it is spacious and elegant. The furnishings and fittings are superb and the decorations are magnificent."[23]

The Breakers represented a discernible transition in Peabody & Stearns's cottage architecture in style and especially in terms of the size. The façade documents Peabody's movement from the stick framing of the Matthews house toward the newly popularized Queen Anne style. It was designed during the same year that Peabody published two articles in the *American Architect and Building News*, in which he drew comparisons between the Queen Anne revival taking place in English architecture and the desirability and appropriateness of using English and Colonial American motifs in contemporary American architecture. The house measured 182 feet in length and covered about 10,920 square feet—equal to one-quarter of an acre. The site, an extraordinary piece of oceanfront property on Ochre Point Avenue at Victoria Avenue that purportedly cost $100,000, "commanded an uninterrupted view of the limitless expanse of the ocean."[24] It was clear that the cultivated landscape had to measure up to the spectacular natural setting—here was an opportunity for owner and architect if not to rival, at least to complement, what nature had created. Ernest Bowditch, the Boston landscape architect, visited the site with Robert Peabody on August 31, 1877. Together, they walked the property with the Lorillards, staking out the location for the house and gardens. Two years later, Peabody noted in his diary that 11,000 shrubs and 5,000 to 6,000 trees had been planted at the Lorillards'.[25] Lorillard's final coup was the construction of a pier over the reefs in front of the Breakers. Maud Howe Elliott recounted in 1944, "Pierre Lorillard did what now seems the impossible—anchored

1.20. The Breakers,
waterfront façade.
Courtesy of the Preservation
Society of Newport County.

his yacht, the *Rhoda,* off the Cliffs and landed his guests at the very door to his home . . . in a launch. This perilous undertaking was made possible by a pier built over a reef; the remains of this landing can still be seen from the Cliffs."[26]

On the exterior of The Breakers, Peabody employed a three-gabled façade. The first story was constructed of Philadelphia pressed brick, with courses of enameled brick, Hudson River bluestone, and Nova Scotia brownstone. The second and third floors and roofs were made of spruce, and the roof shingles were painted red. Photographs show an exterior rife with decorative detailing—a mélange of Classical and Colonial Revival motifs. Patterned shingling accents and tall English chimneys were accompanied by myriad Classical details, broken scrolls, wreaths, and urns. Curved pediments graced the pair of windows in each of the large gables, while shutters framed the second-story windows. On the water side, covered porches flanked the south and east walls of the house and wrapped around the shaped drawing room to the south. A porch and second-story balustraded deck to the east overlooked the ocean.

A two-story Great Hall set the tone for the interior of the cottage. Sheathed in rich dark paneling and lit by 480 gas fixtures, it had an old English air, with an oversized fireplace that dominated the north end of the room. Traffic between drawing room and dining room, dining room and billiards room, morning room to staircase, all passed through the Great Hall. Two large staircases swept up to a wide hallway on the second floor, and two galleries overlooked the Great Hall below. For the family and guests, there were five large sleeping

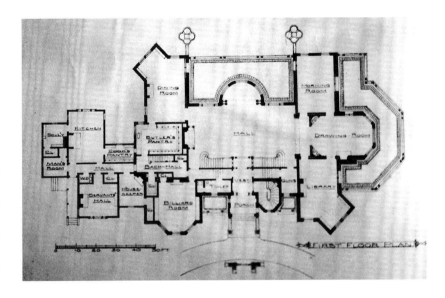

chambers with fireplaces, dressing rooms, and closets; two bathrooms, and a nursery. In addition, a large linen closet; and six servant bedrooms plus separate bath (!) in the carefully segregated servants' area assured that staff were close by to see to the needs of the household.

Previous generations of the Lorillard family were involved in a successful snuff and tobacco business. Pierre was more interested in horse breeding and real estate. Several years after he built the Breakers, he began plans for a game and fish preserve in Orange County, New York—what would become the highly desirable Tuxedo Park development. He sold the Breakers to Cornelius Vanderbilt II in October 1885 for $400,000. Peabody & Stearns was hired almost immediately to

1.21. The Breakers, first
floor plan. *American
Architect and Building News,*
July 6, 1878. Courtesy of the
Boston Public Library Fine
Arts Department.

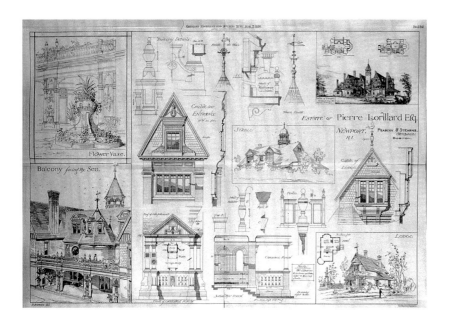

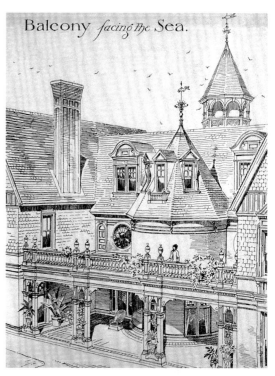

1.22. The Breakers, details from Estate of Pierre Lorillard, Newport, Rhode Island. *American Architect and Building News*, June 5, 1880. Courtesy of the Boston Public Library Fine Arts Department.

prepare the plans for a major renovation. The *Newport Mercury* reported on December 4, 1886, that "the hall, which was a noted feature of this elegantly furnished cottage, has been pulled to pieces and is to be remodeled. Other rooms have also been relieved of their elegantly carved mantels and panelings to allow of a finish more to the taste of the new owner." Vanderbilt had the kitchen cut away from the main house in order to insert a 40-by-70-foot dining room in between, thus creating the largest and most elaborate dining room in Newport. The residence now comprised a total of fifty-eight rooms exclusive of smaller dressing rooms, closets, and the basement; despite this, young Gertrude Vanderbilt would later complain that her bedroom had had to be used to store visitors' coats.[27] It was obvious that the Vanderbilts needed more room.

Ultimately, Cornelius Vanderbilt was able to do more than merely remodel Pierre Lorillard's cottage, because The Breakers burned on November 25, 1892. Vanderbilt immediately made plans to rebuild, but Peabody & Stearns was not chosen for the job. Richard Morris Hunt was working nearby on Marble House for Cornelius's brother, William K. Vanderbilt, and was hired to design the new Renaissance Revival–style palace that would also be known as The Breakers.

Very little is left of Peabody & Stearns's original designs for The Breakers—only the Children's Playhouse commissioned by Vanderbilt in 1886 still stands in its original condition on the grounds. A stable and parts of the greenhouses designed in the same year were later moved to their current location at the corner of Coggeshall and Bateman avenues. The Breakers is owned and maintained by the Preservation Society of Newport County and may be toured by the public.

1.23. The Breakers, details from Estate of Pierre Lorillard, Newport, Rhode Island. American Architect and Building News, June 5, 1880. Courtesy of the Boston Public Library Fine Arts Department.

1.24. The Breakers, details from Estate of Pierre Lorillard, Newport, Rhode Island. *American Architect and Building News*, June 5, 1880. Courtesy of the Boston Public Library Fine Arts Department.

1.25. The Breakers,
children's playhouse.
Courtesy of Memorial Library,
Boston Architectural College.

1.26. The Breakers,
loggia interior. Courtesy
of Redwood Library and
Athenaeum, Newport, Rhode
Island. Gift of Gladys Moore
Vanderbilt Szechenyi.

1.27. The Breakers, Great
Hall interior. Courtesy
of Redwood Library and
Athenaeum, Newport, Rhode
Island. Gift of Gladys Moore
Vanderbilt Szechenyi.

Lion's Head

Narragansett, Rhode Island, 1880

Reverend William Wilberforce Newton,
1843–1917

Lion's Head faces east onto Rhode Island Sound on a point just north of Gunning Rock. Built in 1880 on an undeveloped parcel of land slightly south of the Narragansett Pier for Reverend William W. Newton, it was soon surrounded by cottages designed by other architects for members of Mrs. Newton's family: Stonlea, designed by McKim, Mead & White in 1884 for Mrs. Newton's sister, Mary Beavan Cooke Cresson, was built across the street from Lion's Head. In 1887, James Welsh Cooke commissioned Boston architect William H. Dabney, Jr. (1855–1897) to create Sea Meadow west of Lion's Head, and Suwannee Villa was built on the far side of Stonlea for David Stevenson, a distant relative of Mrs. Newton.

Narragansett lies just across Rhode Island Sound from Newport. Its long and narrow peninsular form is approximately ten miles from north to south and terminates at Point Judith. Summer visitors from New York, Philadelphia, Chicago, and St. Louis began to favor Narragansett in the 1860s and 1870s, staying at hotels constructed at the pier and building small cottages with Stick Style detailing. By the 1880s and 1890s, larger Shingle Style, Queen Anne, and Colonial Revival cottages were constructed, both as owner-occupied cottages and as rental properties. Summer visitors came for extended vacations, favoring the sandy beach near the Narragansett Pier Casino, fishing, games of croquet and lawn tennis, and strolls and drives along Ocean Road. The season ran from mid-June through mid-September. Narragansett's reputation continued into the twentieth century, when the popularity of automobile travel transformed it into a day-trip destination for Rhode Island residents.

Although some of Narragansett's residents built substantial summer cottages (e.g., Robert G. Dun of Dun & Bradstreet at Dunmere, and Joseph Peace Hazard at

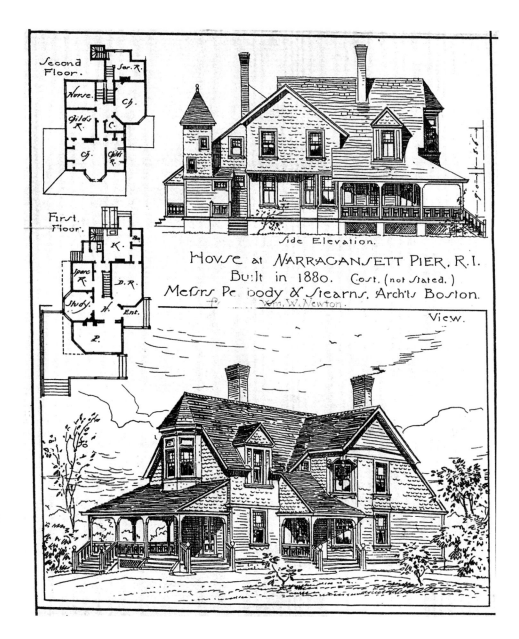

1.28. House in Narragansett Pier, Rhode Island, Lion's Head. *The American Architect and Building News*, July 3, 1880, vol. VIII, no. 236. Collection of the Frances Loeb Library, Graduate School of Design, Harvard University.

1.29. St. Stephen's
Church, Pittsfield,
Massachusetts, 1890.
Courtesy of Memorial Library,
Boston Architectural College

Hazard's Castle), the community could not compete with Newport. In a July 1906 article in *Harper's Weekly*, Brander Matthews, a New York critic wrote: "In the more thickly settled part of the village, from the Ocean Road and the Kingston Road back to the neat railroad station, ... the houses are truly cottages; but out on The Rocks . . . . the places are far more spacious . . . even if none of [the houses] are sumptuous enough to vie with the marble palaces of Newport." As appropriate for the cottage of a minister, Lion's Head was more modest than many of its Ocean Road neighbors. The Rhode Island Historical Preservation and Heritage Commission describes the cottage as a "two story shingled building . . . [with] a gable roof enlivened by dormers and pavilions. A Tuscan-columned veranda overlook[s] the ocean."[28] Lion's Head was featured in an *American Architect and Building News* article, "A Parallel of Low-Cost Country Houses," in its July 3, 1880, issue, and the Peabody & Stearns record card for the property documents a total cost of $3,550.35 for the original cottage. It was planned with a living room, dining room, study, and kitchen on the first floor, and two good-sized chambers, one with a bay window surveying the ocean view, on the second floor. A large porch wrapped around two sides of the living room and a small two-story tower decorated the rear elevation, while the low sloping roof over the kitchen referenced local Colonial farm structures. This original cottage was considerably enlarged in 1888 when Wil-

liam H. Dabney, Jr. was hired to design additions and alterations.

William Wiberforce Newton was born in Philadelphia, Pennsylvania, the son of a clergyman. He studied at the University of Pennsylvania and graduated in 1865; in 1868 he received his A.M. degree and graduated from the Divinity School of the Protestant Episcopal Church in Philadelphia. Rev. Newton was a popular speaker and a prolific writer of religious and children's books. He was the pastor at St. Paul's Episcopal Church in Brookline from 1870 to 1875; Robert Peabody was a parishioner and presumably made his acquaintance in that way. Ten years after the Lion's Head commission, the firm designed St. Stephen's Church in Pittsfield, Massachusetts, also during Newton's tenure there (fig. 1.29).

Lion's Head has remained in the current family's ownership for over fifty years. Although it has been significantly altered since it was first constructed, including the enclosure of the Tuscan-columned porch, its original Peabody & Stearns design is still recognizable and its situation overlooking a large undeveloped rocky shorefront remains as it must have appeared in 1880 when Rev. Newton first visited the site.

Lion's Head (now known as Lion Head) is listed in Rhode Island's State Register of Historic Places and the National Register of Historic Places. It is a private residence.

1.30. Hillside, street view.
Courtesy of current owners.

Hillside

Newport, Rhode Island, 1882

Arthur Brewster Emmons, 1850–1922

1.31. Hillside, street view.
Sanitary Engineer, August
26, 1886, vol. 14, no. 13, p. 299.
Courtesy of the Boston Public
Library Fine Arts Department.

...the charm of his collection of Monets was not
due to chance, but that ... it had been understood
in New York and Paris that he would not hesitate
to pay the best prices....

— *New York Times*, January 15, 1920

The *Newport Mercury* reported on November 5,
1881, that Mrs. E. W. Emmons of Boston had purchased 80,000 square feet of land at the corner
of Catherine Street and Gibbs Avenue (formerly Channing Avenue) and had engaged a Boston firm of architects to prepare the plans for her villa. The financial
records for Peabody & Stearns indicate that the client
for Hillside was Arthur B. Emmons and "E. W. Emmons"
(Elizabeth Wade, his mother), that the house was built
on Gibbs Avenue, and that a stable was constructed at
Catherine and Channing. What we see now on Gibbs
Avenue is Hillside looking very much as it did in the
early 1880s, along with a carriage house and several
other outbuildings on water-view property overlooking Easton's Pond.

The Gibbs Avenue neighborhood appears to have
been built up by a congenial group. Many of Emmons's
neighbors were faculty from Boston-area colleges and
took a great interest in the planting of the area. Richard Champlin, a Newport Botanist, stated, that "Of all
the neighborhoods in Newport this one . . . shows
the effect of long years of pride in landscaping."[29] He
also reported that Emmons's property was beautifully
landscaped with many specimen trees, including Atlas
cedar, Serbian and Alberta spruce, as well as four varieties of European beech.

Hillside was pictured and described in *Sanitary
Engineer* magazine in 1886. Like many of Peabody's
designs of the period, it is an eclectic mix of styles and
materials. One view from the street and entry court
presents a house constructed of red brick: a stepped-
gable façade with prominent chimney piece greets the

1.32. Hillside, garden view. Courtesy of current owners.

visitor at the sloped-roof porte-cochere. The rest of the cottage features a mélange of a prominent tower, gables, and dormers, all sheathed in unpainted shingles. On the garden façade, porches open off of the first-story main rooms and invite in the view and the summer breezes; a large porch on the second floor provides an outdoor living area to the bedroom level. The cottage is larger than it appears, comprising 10,000 square feet. The hall and staircase and the dining room are of oak, with unique and compelling carved detailing. Other interior rooms are "elaborately finished in hard wood." The parlor was originally designed with white-painted pine.

Arthur Emmons was born in Quincy, Massachusetts. Following his graduation from the Boston Latin School and the Massachusetts Institute of Technology, he attended the Polytechnikum in Stuttgart and the universities of Heidelberg and Leipzig. He was awarded the degree of L.L.C. from Harvard in 1877 and passed the exam for the Suffolk bar the following year. While Hillside was originally conceived as a summer residence, Emmons and his wife, Julia W. Parish, the daughter of one of Newport's early resort residents, later made it their permanent home.

Articles in the *Newport Mercury* identify Emmons as the head of the citizens group of summer residents that constructed the buildings at nearby Easton's Beach. Not coincidentally, the Easton's Beach pavilion was designed by Peabody & Stearns in 1886.

Hillside is a private residence. The Peabody & Stearns–designed carriage house is a separately owned residence.

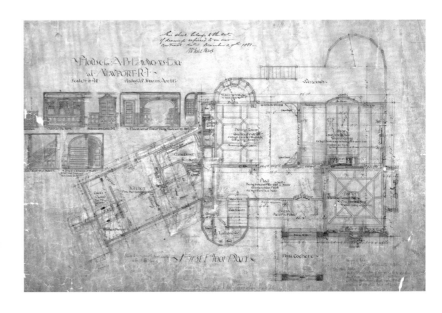

1.33. House for A. B. Emmons, first floor plan, Hillside. Peabody and Stearns Collection, courtesy of the Boston Public Library Fine Arts Department and current Hillside owners.

Vinland

Newport, Rhode Island, 1882

Catharine Lorillard Wolfe, 1828-87

... one of the most comfortable, commodious and
beautiful country seats in the world ..."
— GEORGE SHELDON, *Artistic Country-Seats*, p. 185

Vinland stands resolute at the ocean's edge, seeming to scan the horizon for the Viking adventurers who, according to local legend, settled Newport's shores in the eleventh century A.D. One of Newport's prominent monuments, the Old Stone Tower in Touro Park, was popularly thought in the Gilded Age to be an ancient Viking relic. Catharine Lorillard Wolfe's first Newport summer house looked out over the tower, and so, when she built her new cottage on Ochre Point in 1882, it was intended to be a celebration of Newport's legendary Norse heritage.

Catharine Lorillard Wolfe was the only surviving child of John David Wolfe, a wealthy hardware merchant in New York City, and Dorothea Ann Lorillard, the sister of Pierre Lorillard next door at the Breakers. Miss Wolfe was a great patroness of the arts; indeed, she left her personal art collection along with a $200,000 administration fund to the Metropolitan Museum of Art when she died, the first woman benefactor of that newly founded institution. The Wolfe collection was well known: Edith Wharton's fictional Madame Olen-

ska and Newland Archer avoided "the popular 'Wolfe collection,' whose anecdotic canvases filled one of the main galleries ..."[30]—obviously hoping for a more private meeting place.

Miss Wolfe assembled an impressive and respected team of design professionals for her cottage on the fourteen-acre parcel next to the Breakers: Peabody & Stearns, architects (McKim, Mead & White was also invited to compete; the firm's unexecuted plan was published in *The Brickbuilder*[31]); Ernest Bowditch, landscape architect; and Richard Codman, interior designer. She contacted Robert Peabody with the idea of building a villa in what was to be of "a Scandinavian character" with "steep high-pitched, brown shingled roof, and spired turrets."[32] The resulting cottage was enormous—168 feet long (over half the length of a football field) by 58 feet deep. It was constructed of red sandstone from Longmeadow, Massachusetts, with heavily ornamented friezes and window surrounds carved with fanciful Celtic human and animal faces and Anglo-Saxon interlace motifs. Outbuildings included a gatehouse, a caretaker's cottage (1907), and a potting shed built of the same stone, and these remain on the property. The Vinland estate also included shingled farm buildings—a gardener's cottage and the Hennery among them. In form and inspiration Vinland was unlike anything that was being built in Newport at the time.

Richard Codman of Boston (uncle of the well-known designer Ogden Codman) designed the interior in the modish style of the Aesthetic Movement. He commis-

1.34. Vinland, ocean elevation. Courtesy of The Newport Historical Society (P2689).

1.35. Vinland, gate lodge.
The American Architect and Building News, August 20, 1887, no. 603. Collection of the author.

Residence of H. McKay Twombly, Newport, R.I.

sioned Arts and Crafts master William Morris and his associates to provide much of the interior embellishment for Vinland. Sir Edward Burne-Jones designed seven stained-glass windows for the staircase hall that illustrated Viking gods and heroes and a Viking ship under full sail. English artist Walter Crane designed the stained-glass windows in the library as well as the cottage's decorative *pièce de résistance:* a multipaneled frieze in the dining room to illustrate Henry Wadsworth Longfellow's poem "The Skeleton in Armor," a romantic Newport tale well suited to the Aesthetic Movement mood of the interior. Miss Wolfe was reported to have personally sent a copy of Longfellow's poem, along with a picture of the Old Stone Tower, to Crane for his inspiration. The panels were wildly successful, publicly displayed in England and France as well as published in popular journals of the day before they were sent to Miss Wolfe's cottage in Newport.

Ernest Bowditch was hired to make the grounds of the new villa appear to be old and established; in order to accomplish this, two full-sized fern-leafed beech trees—one of which still stands majestically in front of the porte-cochere—were transported by ship from the Wolfe family's Westchester County estate to the docks at Newport and thence dragged by oxen to Vinland, at great expense and amid much fanfare. He incorporated many of the existing trees from the property into his landscape plan and added exotic varieties, as well as a lily pond, a palm house, and unusual antiquities that were scattered about the property. The overriding aspect of the property

must have been of old plantings, old architecture, and old money. George Sheldon paid Vinland and her creators what must have been the supreme Gilded Age compliment: "The painful air of a plebeian newness is missing. One thinks of the English manor-house, and its centuries of associations."[33] Robert Peabody had learned his lessons well when he worked for English architect Alfred Waterhouse designing ancestral country houses. Vinland was a success.

The original cottage is much changed. When Catharine Lorillard Wolfe died in 1887, her cousin Louis L. Lorillard used Vinland for several years but then sold it in 1896 to Hamilton McKown Twombly, whose wife, Florence Adele Vanderbilt Twombly, was the sister of Cornelius, William Kissam, and Frederick William Vanderbilt, whose own Newport cottages, the Breakers, Marble House, and Rough Point respectively, were all located close by. In 1907, Twombly, perhaps in competition with his expansive brothers-in-law, decided to increase the size of Vinland by cutting it in two and moving the kitchen section some 60 feet northward. Peabody determined that the resulting horizontality of the now 228-foot-long house would destroy the pleasing proportions of the façade. The solution was to raise the entire structure several feet, not at the roofline, but between the first and second floors. Newspaper accounts of this engineering feat describe how the entire house was cribbed inside and out, and how hundreds of screws were installed to enable workers to raise the blocking a fraction of an inch at a time. The men moved from one screw

1.37. The Hennery on
the grounds of Vinland,
Courtesy of Memorial Library,
Boston Architectural College.

to another, around and around the house, and the entire structure was painstakingly lifted. This extreme renovation understandably necessitated the destruction of whatever remained of Miss Wolfe's Aesthetic Movement décor; it was replaced by an interior in the French style, which was artfully chosen by Mrs. Twombly.

Vinland was reborn in 1955 when it was donated to Salve Regina University by Mrs. Florence Vanderbilt Twombly Burden. Mcauley Hall currently serves the university as classroom and office space. The Hennery, now known as Stonor and Drexel halls, received a total restoration in 2006, including the refabrication of its signature dovecote. The caretaker's cottage (Marian Hall) and the gatehouse also survive under Salve Regina's exceptional care. Vinland's vast windswept lawns and stolid visage are vivid reminders, however, of her previous cottage life.

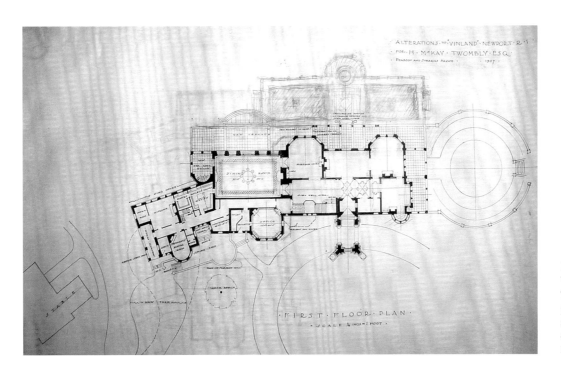

1.38. Alterations to
Vinland for H. McKay
Twombley, first floor
plan, 1907. Peabody and
Stearns Collection, Courtesy
of the Boston Public Library
Fine Arts Department.

1.39. Honeysuckle
Lodge, street view.
Courtesy of Memorial Library,
Boston Architectural College.

Honeysuckle Lodge/
Mason Lea

Newport, Rhode Island, 1885

Josiah M. Fiske, 1821-1892

...one of the most attractive places in Newport on
account of the architecture and the beautiful layout
of the grounds ...
— *Newport Journal*, December 11, 1909

Honeysuckle Lodge was originally referred
to as Mason Lea; its name was presumably
changed during the early 1900s to reflect the
large amount of Chinese and Japanese honeysuckle
planted on the property by landscape architect Frederick Law Olmsted.

Josiah M. Fiske was born in Cambridge and began his
career as a flour merchant in Boston. In 1850 he moved
to New York City to establish the firm of Josiah M. Fiske
& Company, later Smith, Fiske & Company. He retired
from active mercantile life in the early 1880s and pur-

chased this property on Ruggles Avenue, where from
then on he would spend several months each summer
in his Peabody & Stearns–designed cottage. Fiske was
a director of the American Exchange Bank, the Central
Trust Company, and the New York Guaranty & Indem-
nity Company; he was a member of the Union League
Club and the New England Society. Following his death
in 1892, Fiske's widow continued to make Mason Lea
her summer home, even after her marriage to George
W. Collard. Articles in the *New York Times* report that
she took honors at the Newport Flower Show in 1895
for her palm trees as well as her grouping of chrysan-
themums, palms, and ferns, all grown at this Ruggles
Avenue property.

Documents from the Frederick Law Olmsted
archives suggest that work began on "Mason Le" in
early 1885. Plans dated March 1885 indicate the location of buildings and roads, along with several sketches
showing one or two figures standing at the edge of
the Cliff Walk looking inland, with sight lines drawn
in. Stone walls enclosing the nearly two-acre property
were constructed during the fall of 1886, at the same
time that Caroline Ogden Jones's Peabody & Stearns–

designed cottage next door was "receiving its finishing touches."[34]

Early photographs of the property present a cottage not so different in form from the current residence. The ground story is walled with rough stone, with shingles above. A simple twin-gabled façade faces the water, with ample porches on first and second floors to catch the ocean breezes and provide the occupants with views across the water. The cottage was designed with multiple building masses and rooflines, giving an impression of a building grown over time. Russell Sturgis described the cottage in The Great American Architects Series as an example of "the effective use of the shingled roof in the simple form. . . . A really admirable design has been made of . . . . simple materials."[35] The open porches were enclosed by later owners, and the twin gables have been clapboarded over the original shingles.

Inside, a sweeping staircase curves up from the entry hall to the second floor. Living room and dining room are on the water side of the house, with the now-enclosed porch area still providing dramatic views of the Cliff Walk and the ocean beyond.

Mason Lea was purchased in 1909 by T. Suffern Tailer of New York. Tailer married Maud Lorillard, daughter of Pierre Lorillard (The Breakers) in 1892, but they divorced ten years later, and in 1909 he married Martha Brown of Baltimore. The Tailers reportedly made few changes to Mason Lea other than interior woodwork, mantels, and its name. A ballroom was added to the water side of the cottage in the 1920s. The property was later affiliated with the Newport School for Girls, which closed in the late 1960s.

Undated materials in the Peabody & Stearns collection at the Boston Public Library indicate that the firm was also commissioned to design Fiske's farm in Portsmouth, Rhode Island. The gentleman-farmer phenomenon in Portsmouth was remarked upon at length in the Newport Mercury of February 27, 1892 ("Farming as an Adjunct to Newport Summer Life"), as well as in the New York Times on June 5 of that year ("Newport's Rich Farmers"). Other Newport summer residents who purchased farmland in the surrounding area included some of the wealthiest cottagers: Cornelius Vanderbilt II, O. H. P. Belmont, Ward McAllister, Charles H. Leland.

Honeysuckle Lodge is a private residence.

Midcliff

Newport, Rhode Island, 1886

Caroline Ogden Jones, d. 1915

... the whole interior is arranged well for
every comfort and convenience ..."
— *Newport Mercury*, July 2, 1886

Next door to Mason Lea on Ruggles Avenue, Midcliff was constructed for Miss Caroline Ogden Jones of New York, her sister Miss Frances Ogden Jones, and their half-brother, Louis McCagg. Like Josiah Fiske's charming cottage, the house was designed by Peabody & Stearns, constructed by C. E. Clark of Boston, and landscaped by the firm of Frederick Law Olmsted.

Midcliff was described in the *Newport Mercury* as a "three-story Queen Anne cottage, in the form of a right angle, 68 feet on the south by 68 feet on the east, with several projecting windows, piazzas, balconies and other ornaments."[36] Although of similar scale to its neighbor, Midcliff has a very different look. The main entrance to the cottage is at the inner corner of the right angle, and while the materials used are similar—stonework on the ground level and shingles above—the primary gable on the street façade of the residence is finished in half-timbering, providing a very Old English appeal. Although the Peabody & Stearns plans for the cottage have not survived, the newspaper indicated that "hardwoods will be used in finishing the more important parts" and that the cost was estimated to be $60,000. Unlike many of the Newport cottagers, Miss Jones resided at Midcliff for the entire

1.41. Midcliff, street
view. *The American
Architect and Building News,*
September 15, 1888, no. 664.
Collection of the author.

summer, arriving early in the spring and remaining until late in the fall.

Numerous letters to Miss Jones survive in the Olmsted Brothers files, in which comparisons were made with the neighboring property. Midcliff had fences and stables less handsome and imposing than those at Mr. Fiske's, thus requiring more shrubbery and small trees to camouflage the property. Because of the Cliff Walk location, however, Olmsted recommended that the lawn should be kept "as simple as possible with nothing about it to strike the eye or hold it from the infinitely greater beauty and fascination of the sea."

The ultimate notoriety of the Misses Jones appears to be that during 1894 they withheld money left by their mother's estate to their two nephews. The difference of opinion was apparently ignited by one of the nephew's intention to marry without the approval of his aunts, and they declared that the distribution of funds (amounting to approximately $200,000) was discretionary. The judge and attorneys did not agree, and "the two spinster sisters," "those redoubtable maiden ladies," were threatened with incarceration unless they complied with the New York courts. They promptly removed themselves to their Newport cottage, Midcliff, to be out of the court's jurisdiction. Compromise was reached by the parties weeks later, and the flurry of media attention subsided. Further indication that Miss Jones was a force to be reckoned with is a note from Robert Peabody to Frederick Law Olmsted stating that Miss Jones had written him "a most disagreeable letter." Caroline Ogden Jones died in September 1915 at Midcliff, at an undisclosed age.

Midcliff is now a private multifamily residence.

1.42. Easton's Beach, Newport, Rhode Island. Postcard, collection of the author.

Easton's Beach Pavilion

Newport, Rhode Island, 1887

The ladies and their escorts assemble for bathing at 10.
Omnibuses and stages run to and from the hotels....
At noon, all is changed. The white flag [signifying that
ladies are bathing] is hauled down, and red bunting takes
its place. The ladies retire, for a few hours, and
the beach is given up to the gentlemen."

— George Champlin Mason,
Newport and Its Cottages[37]

The beaches of Newport are named, but they are numbered as well; Easton's Beach is often referred to in the literature as First Beach. It was popular with middle-class beachgoers, hotel patrons, and day-trippers, while nearby Bailey's Beach (Second Beach) was reserved for a more elite clientele. Mason described Easton's Beach as crescent-shaped, a mile in length, "seen to best advantage from the Cliffs."

Frederick Law Olmsted was contacted in 1883 to lay out the Easton's Point area for development. In November of 1886, Robert Peabody indicated in his diary that he had met with Arthur Emmons at the United States Hotel regarding the Newport Bathing House. A few days later, the *Newport Mercury* reported that the plans had been presented to the City Council for approval.

. . . They present a handsome, commodious building about 400 feet in length with some 300 bath houses. The entrance is a large hall or rotunda in the center of the building from which opens the office, a large restaurant and several hot baths for ladies and gentlemen. Along the center of the waterfront of the building is a covered piazza measuring about 130 feet in length by 20 deep. The bath houses are in the two ends of the building, those on the west of the centre being public and those on the east being private.... The work will begin on Monday and pushed forward as far as possible before the frost sets in....[38]

This announcement was apparently premature, because in March of 1887 the *Mercury* again reported that the plans had been accepted and that construction was due to begin, with the building to be ready for occupancy June 1. The grading of the grounds, landscaping, etc., was to be accomplished at the same time. In April 1887, the *Mercury* reporter marveled at the "great advancement which twenty or thirty men can accomplish in six days' labor." About half of the 400-foot extension of the seawall was completed, and the previous buildings on the site—an office building and bathhouses—had been moved across the road. He took the reader on a virtual tour of the building that was under construction.

The building had three wings, shaped nearly like a Y. The main entrance at the junction of the northeast and west wings admitted the visitor into a large

hall, 36 by 38 feet. From the hall, the visitor might go to the spa, or refreshment counter, or to the dining room vestibule. The dining room–restaurant, which took up the west wing and measured 26 by 40.5 feet, could also be entered from the piazza. The kitchen, and 48 private bathhouses (dressing rooms) finished the wing. The northeast wing was comprised of the office, a linen room, and eight hot saltwater bathrooms, along with a boiler room, drying room, and laundry. The east wing was devoted entirely to bathhouses—160 in all—reached by a 6-foot-wide covered walkway.

On the exterior, the finish was shingled and painted; two 50-foot conical towers provided the dramatic counterplay to the long, low verandahs that ran along the perimeters of the building. Located some 25 feet from this main building was yet another series of bathhouses, two hundred in number, as an "overflow"—indicating the extreme popularity of the facility.

The project did not come to completion as quickly as observers would have liked. Although it was reported on June 25 that the dining room was ready for patronage and that the private bathhouses were being engaged by patrons, an article in the July 9, 1887, *Mercury* admonished the gentlemen responsible for the project to "pray go on . . . make the Beach again become as it was of yore one of the chief attractions of Newport." Competition was evidently felt in Newport from other resort destinations—among

them the neighboring Narragansett Pier Casino (McKim, Mead & White, 1886). "In view of the desperate efforts of our neighbors of the Pier to tap our summer travel and the Bar Harbor boom we must be up and doing—*Now* is the appointed time." The push to make the area comparable to others is supported by the announcement in the September 3 *Newport Mercury* that William Ralph Emerson had been chosen as the architect for the Newport Land Trust Hotel at Easton's Beach.

The City of Newport was only partially responsible for funding the beach renovation project. The improvements were estimated to total about $34,000—$15,000 for the buildings and $19,000 for road improvements and landscaping—and Newport was providing only $6,000 toward the final bill. Approximately $5,000 came from the neighboring town of Middletown and neighbors who would benefit from the road improvements on avenues near First and Second Beach. An additional $10,000 had been pledged by "a syndicate of wealthy and public spirited summer residents, with Mr. Arthur B. Emmons at its head."[39] Emmons's cottage, Hillside, was located a short distance from Easton's Beach and had been completed in 1881.

The Peabody & Stearns–designed bathing pavilion at Easton's Beach was destroyed in the hurricane of 1938; its replacements were lost in the hurricane of 1954, and again in 1991. The current facility was constructed in 1993.

1.43. Bathing Pavilion, Easton's Beach, Newport, Rhode Island, 1906. Postcard, collection of the author.

1.44. Rough Point, street view. Courtesy of Memorial Library, Boston Architectural College.

1.45. Rough Point, water view. Postcard, collection of the author.

Rough Point

Newport, Rhode Island, 1889–1890

Frederick W. Vanderbilt, 1856–1938

The English manor-house of the time of Henry VIII
is revived in its purest and most abstract form; . . .
— RUSSELL STURGIS, "A Critique of the Work
of Peabody and Stearns" [40]

Rough Point is famous today because it was the Newport residence of the wealthy and reclusive Doris Duke, but it was originally built for Frederick W. Vanderbilt and his wife Louise "Lulu"

Holmes Anthony Torrance. The location at the Cliffs was the most dramatic of all of the Peabody & Stearns Newport residences: waves crashed on the massive rocks, sending spumes of white spray over the embankment, prompting Mrs. John King Van Rensselaer to describe the property: "At Rough Point the sea has beaten into the land with such fury that it has cut it sharply back in many places, leaving the old bones of the island bare in spots." [41] It was almost as if Rough Point had been constructed on an ancient burial ground.

Frederick Vanderbilt corresponded extensively with Frederick Law Olmsted to determine how to treat the Rough Point landscaping. Mrs. Vanderbilt wanted to retain the lush green lawns left from a pre-

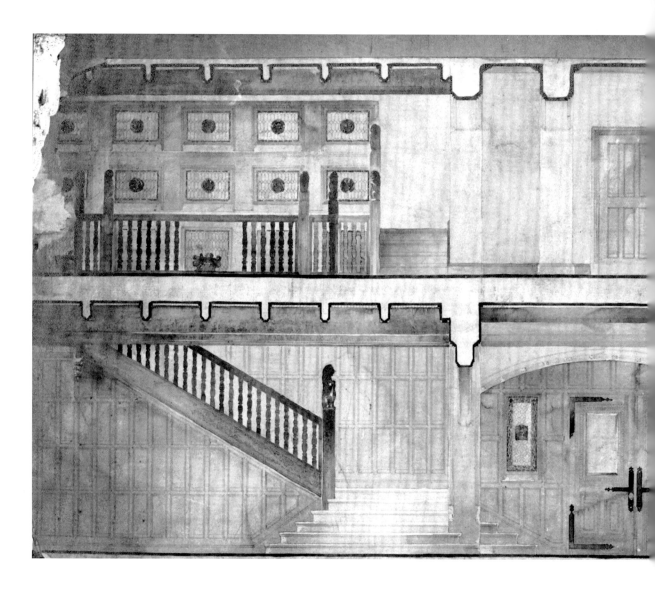

1.46. Rough Point,
interior sketch of the
Great Hall. Courtesy of
Memorial Library, Boston
Architectural College.

vious residence, but Olmsted was in favor of restoring "the original aspect of the ground on the sea front"— re-creating the rugged aspects of the land, which would be planted with hardy native bushes and vegetation. Compromises were made on both sides of the relationship.

Rough Point was constructed of locally quarried, rough-dressed Rocky Farm granite. Two balanced gabled projections with matching one-story hip-roofed verandah pavilions dominated the water side of the façade. Horizontal bands of unadorned and repetitious fenestration stretched across the face of the house, relieved only by a two-story octagonal bay situated between the gabled projections. Rough Point was large—it stretched 200 feet in length by 80 feet in width across the largely unprotected nine-acre site.

Little remains of the original interior. However, extensive descriptions existed in the contemporary press.[42] Entry was made into the vestibule and then into a massive oak stair hall and three-story Great Hall. The latter was finished with beamed ceiling, oak floor-

ing, and a fireplace so large that each of the steel and-irons within reportedly weighed one ton. The room was furnished with carved furniture; costly tapestries and rare silks hung on the fireplace wall. To the north of the Great Hall, folding doors led to a spacious oak and mahogany library that opened out to one of the 12-foot-wide covered verandahs. The adjoining draw-ing room's walls were hung with tapestries and plum-colored silk curtains, and the ceiling was decorated with yellow cloth, plaited in folds. A billiards room and the dining room were located to the south of the Great Hall. A coat room, toilet room, and room for the storage of Mr. Vanderbilt's guns and fishing tackle were situated off of the stair hall, while the kitchen, butler's pantry, and servants' hall completed the first-floor plan.

In 1895, Frederick and Louise Vanderbilt began work on a McKim, Mead & White–designed Italian Renaissance country house in Hyde Park, New York. Rough Point was rented out by the season and was sold in 1906 to William B. Leeds, the "tin-plate tycoon." Later, in 1922, American Tobacco Company millionaire James Buchanan Duke purchased the property and hired Phil-

adelphia architect Horace Trumbauer to enlarge and redesign the original Peabody & Stearns cottage. The verandahs were enclosed and the building was nearly doubled in length; although the alterations and addi-tions were masterfully executed, the cottage lost much of its picturesque attitude.

When James Duke died in 1924, his thirteen-year-old daughter became "the richest girl in the world" and inherited Rough Point as part of her father's estate. In later years she spent extended periods of time at Rough Point, often staying all summer and fall. Like Frederick Vanderbilt, she craved privacy; she even blocked off the Cliff Walk in front of the prop-erty. Her Newport legacy, however, was the creation in 1968 of the Newport Restoration Foundation "in order to preserve and restore the historic architec-ture of the eighteenth and early nineteenth centuries in Newport."

Rough Point is now a house museum owned and operated by the Newport Restoration Foundation. It has been preserved to reflect the period of Doris Duke's residency.

Althorpe

Newport, Rhode Island, 1888

John Thompson Spencer, 1841-1924

Peabody & Stearns created this Colonial Revival summer villa for John Thompson Spencer, a prominent Philadelphia attorney and a vice president of the Philadelphia Railroad Company. It was built on a three-and-a-half-acre corner lot with ocean view and bounded by Ruggles, Lawrence, and Victoria avenues in Ochre Point. Privacy was provided by a high privet hedge that surrounded the grounds. Mrs. John King Van Rensselaer described the cottage in *Newport, Our Social Capital:* "At this point of the Cliff Walk the pedestrian not only enjoys the ocean view, but, looking backward, catches a glimpse of Mr. John Thompson Spencer's colonial house standing on an eminence on Ruggles Avenue, secure of privacy but enjoying a lovely view.

It was here that Mrs. Spencer entertained the Comte de Turin, who was at the time heir to the throne of Italy."[43]

Visually, the house calls upon traditional American stylistic motifs. A 75-foot-long porch envelopes the first floor of the residence, recalling Henry James's remark that the porch was the "happiest disposition of the old American country-house."[44] The porch adds visual interest with Doric columns and carved balustrades to what might have become a strictly academic exterior façade. The *Newport Mercury* described its appearance in June 1890: "The house is painted a pale straw color relieved by white. It is adorned by the familiar piazza and stands in its own grounds. . . . One of the simplest—I speak relatively—of the new cottages that have sprung up by magic . . ."[45]

The second and third floors abound with Colonial Revival detailing. A Palladian window arrangement is centered over the front door. The main block of the house is distinguished by quoined corner blocks and a Classical dentil molding that encircles the eave

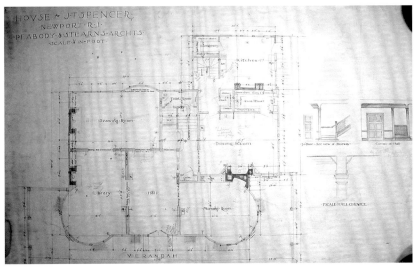

1.48. Althorpe, south elevation. Peabody and Stearns Collection, courtesy of the Boston Public Library Fine Arts Department.

1.49. House for J.T. Spencer, Althorpe, first floor plan. Peabody and Stearns Collection, courtesy of the Boston Public Library, Fine Arts Department.

line at the second floor as well as the porch roof. Four chimneys squarely mark the four corners of the main house, and dormers with alternating triangular and broken-scroll pediments relieve the severity of the steeply pitched hipped roof. The widow's walk with Chinese Chippendale railings perched on the top of the main block served to recall Newport's seafaring American heritage. Two rounded tower rooms soften the severity of the front corners, echoing the tower rooms of French Loire Valley chateaus, American Shingle Style and Romanesque resort homes, as well as the bow fronts of Boston Back Bay town houses.

The original interior plan was clearly designed for entertaining, but not on the same scale as at the Lorillards', the Wolfes', or the Vanderbilts'. Guests entered a large center hall that opened onto a drawing room with fireplace, large library with built-in mahogany bookcases, and spacious living and dining rooms. Rooms were arranged in a squared-off symmetrical floor plan that recalled the large homes of Newport's affluent past. Five large bed chambers, four baths, and a sitting room were located on the second floor for family and guests, along with one maid's bedroom and bath. Six more service bedrooms and a bath were situated on the third floor, while the maid's sitting room was tucked into the basement area next to the laundry.

John Thompson Spencer served as president of the Newport Reading Room and of the Newport Improvement Association, was a director of the Newport Casino and governor of the Society of Colonial Wars of Pennsylvania. His summer residence was named after the ancestral home of the English Spencer family, although his relation to them is dubious.

Althorpe was purchased by Salve Regina University in 1964 and converted to a student dormitory and renamed Founders Hall. The Spencer stables on Lawrence Avenue were designed and built by local Newport architect J. D. Johnson; renamed The Hedges by Salve Regina University, they, too, have been repurposed as residential space.

Bleecker's Box

Jamestown, Rhode Island, 1889

John Van Benthuysen Bleecker, 1847-1922

A summer cottage for Lieutenant J. V. Bleecker, U.S.N., is now being raised upon his lot on Raquet Road, Cottrell plat; Mr. Charles H. Burdick of Newport, builder; Peabody & Stearns of Boston, architects.

— *Newport Journal*, March 23, 1889

Across the bay from Newport, in the town of Jamestown, is one of the most unique of the summer cottages attributed to Peabody & Stearns. With a footprint of only 1,089 square feet, Bleecker's Box, or the Box, was a perfect shingled cube—reportedly 33 feet by 33 feet by 33 feet and thus the smallest summer cottage the firm is currently known to have designed. Period photographs and a postcard view show the hip-roofed cottage in a landscape of far larger and more elaborate cottages.

Jamestown occupies the whole of Conanicut Island, located between Newport and Narragansett in Narragansett Bay. The town was settled in the mid-1600s and remained primarily an agricultural community until the 1870s when a steam ferry service between Conanicut and Newport made it more accessible to development interests. Several hotels were constructed during the ensuing decades, and a handful of residential land developments were established, with varying degrees of success. When marine artist William Trost Richards built a cottage in the early 1880s, it apparently sparked the interest of his

fellow Philadelphians, and shortly thereafter Joseph Wharton built the spectacular stone and shingle cottage Horsehead. When Walcott Avenue connected Ocean Highlands to Jamestown Village in 1884, it provided an important impetus to the area's success; three years later the old Cottrell Farm property was platted for development, and the Bleeckers were not far behind with their plans to build their simple summer cottage.

John Van Benthuysen Bleecker was the grandson of Anthony James and Cornelia Van Benthuysen Bleecker, each from prominent New York families. He was a graduate of the United States Naval Academy and achieved the rank of rear admiral before his retirement in 1905. Bleecker's naval career may well have led to his interest in the summer community that was established on Jamestown. This commission, however, undoubtedly came through his wife, Lizzie Frances Stearns, who was the sister of John Goddard Stearns, Jr.

Bleecker's Box was built on a 16,760-square-foot water-view lot in the Ocean Highlands development area (now the Ocean Highlands–Walcott Avenue Historic District), which Lizzie Bleecker purchased in February 1889 for $760. The purchase included the use of "private bathing houses and for bathing and boating . . . at the Cottrell beach [now Green's Beach]." Thirteen years later Admiral Bleecker purchased an additional 12,505-square-foot lot adjoining the property. The land and cottage remained in the Bleecker family until 1945, when it was sold to the family in whose control it remains. The interior of the cottage was simply arranged: the living room and adjoining dining room were lined with windows overlooking the wide porch and the view of the water; both rooms featured corner fireplaces on the central chimney, with blue and white delft tilework surrounds. Kitchen and pantry space was located in the back half of the first floor. A small wainscoted staircase led up to four corner bedrooms arranged around the central hallspace; an upstairs bathroom may have been added at a later time. Woodwork and decorative details were minimal, as might be expected in a summer home of this size. As the current owner points out, the siting of the house, angled as it is into the prevailing summer afternoon southwest breeze, must have been influenced by a navy man, and it makes the Box a delightful retreat in the hot summer months.

As a final note, land speculation in Jamestown continued through the end of the nineteenth century. The final development at Shoreby Hill, a private enclave on the northern edge of the village, was masterminded by two St. Louis residents—James Taussig, and Ephron Catlin, the brother of Daniel Catlin, whose Dublin, New Hampshire, cottage Stonlea was designed and built by Peabody & Stearns in 1891.

Bleecker's Box (aka Brushwood) is privately owned.

1.50. Bleecker's Box.
Courtesy of the Jamestown Historical Society.

Rockhurst

Newport, Rhode Island, 1891

Mrs. H. Mortimer Brooks, d. 1920

... Mrs. Brooks recently had added to her palatial villa a
marvelously beautiful salon, the interior adornment of
which was sketched and accomplished by a corps
of Parisian artists, who received their commission a year
ago ... so much has been said of it and its richness that
society has been longing since early summer for an
opportunity to behold it. ...

— *Boston Daily Globe*, August 16, 1896

Mrs. H. Mortimer Brooks of New York
acquired the Gardner Brewer estate at
the southern end of Bellevue Avenue for a
reported purchase price of about $425,000, with the
expressed intention of tearing it down and building
a "new and elegant villa of more modern design."[46]
"Modern" at this point in Newport meant French.
Mrs. Brooks was looking for a more continental
appearance for her summer cottage than that of
many of the previous Peabody & Stearns residences,
including that of her neighbor at Rough Point.

The stakes were changing in Newport at the end of
the 1880s. Richard Morris Hunt constructed the cha-
teau-styled Ochre Court for Ogden Goelet from 1888
to 1891. McKim, Mead & White completed the Gordon
King house on Harrison Avenue (1887–88) in a deriva-
tive Loire Valley mode. Richard Morris Hunt's Breakers and Marble House were under construction at the

time. Competition was clearly an issue in the Newport
community. Mrs. Brooks planned the addition of the
Rockhurst ballroom in anticipation of her daughter's
coming-out in August 1896, which was the same week
that Miss Van Alen (daughter of James T. Van Allen of
Wakehurst, on Ochre Point Avenue) was introduced to
Newport society. The *Boston Globe* noted that "Mr. Van
Alen's ballroom, as it is called, is really nothing of the
sort, and might very truly be termed a tent."[47] The notation on the Peabody & Stearns plans for the addition
of Mrs. Brooks's ballroom was that "according to our
drawings Mrs. I.T. Burden's Ball room measures 35 x 38
x 14 high. Music gallery 10 x 18." Mrs. Brooks's addition
was meant to be larger, beyond a shadow of a doubt.

The exterior of the Brooks cottage was of local
Rocky Farm stone and shingle, with much decorative
bargeboarding and detail, and with pseudo-timber
framing which caused Russell Sturgis in the *Architectural Record* to comment unfavorably on the current
trend toward this kind of dishonesty in construction:
"It is hard to take such work seriously," he said. "As
architecture, it is not to be taken seriously."[48] However,
this deficiency did not prevent Sturgis from including four views of Rockhurst manor and gate lodge in
his article. The floor plan of Rockhurst incorporated
open-air terracing and porches into the interior plan
to a larger extent than perhaps any other design by
Peabody—fully half of the original square footage was
devoted to "covered verandah," although much of this
was later enclosed.

The porte-cochere and vestibule opened into a
small entry hall and a formal reception room; a narrow

1.51. Rockhurst, street
view. Courtesy of Memorial
Library, Boston Architectural
College.

FACING PAGE

1.52. Rockhurst, view from water. Courtesy of The Newport Historical Society.

1.53. Rockhurst, later known as Aspen Hall, John Aspegren's Residence. Postcard, collection of the author.

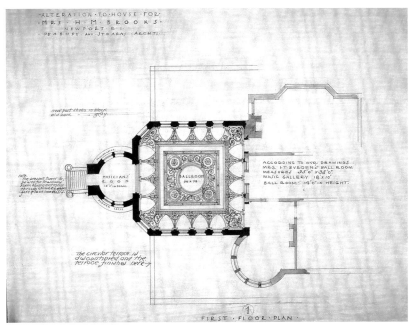

galley-type hall bisected the floor plan front to back and ran the entire length of the house. The drawing room and dining room were located on the water side of the house, in order to maximize the view, while the billiards room occupied the other tower flanking the entrance. The elegant ballroom addition was a two-story structure with a separate circular musicians' gallery and an equally large conservatory; a luxurious boudoir for Mrs. Brooks was added upstairs over the conservatory.

Henry Mortimer Brooks was engaged in the wholesale cloth-importing business in New York, a business and fortune established by his grandfather. He was a member of the Metropolitan and the Racquet clubs of New York, and of the Meadowbrook Hunt Club. Josephine Higgins Brooks, his wife (and the driving force behind Rockhurst), was the heiress to the "great Higgins carpet industry," having inherited about $6,000,000. The Brookses had three children: two daughters and one son, Reginald, Harvard Class of 1886.

Mrs. Brooks predeceased her husband in 1920 while at her summer home at Southampton, Long Island. Rockhurst was sold to John Aspegren and renamed Aspen Hall. It was Aspegren who hired the Olmsted firm to landscape his estate, including the requisite greenhouses, tennis courts, etc. His family enjoyed the cottage for ten years, hosting many entertainments for friends and family, including one historic event that presented the entire Ballet Russe on a stage set up on the lawn. After 1930 the property passed through several owners; in 1955 the main house was demolished; the gatehouse and gardener's cottage were restored and are private residences.

TOP

1.54. Rockhurst, aerial view after additions. Courtesy of Preservation Society of Newport County.

ABOVE

1.55. Ballroom alterations to house for Mrs. H. M. Brooks, Rockhurst. Peabody and Stearns Collection, courtesy of the Boston Public Library Fine Arts Department.

1.56. Shamrock Cliffs,
street elevation, 1895.
Courtesy of The Newport
Historical Society (P2691).

Shamrock Cliff

Newport, Rhode Island, 1895

Gaun McRobert Hutton, 1849–1916

... the entrance to the ivy-covered, turreted mansion was
enhanced with Newport's favorite shrub, the
blue hydrangea ...

— HARRIET JACKSON PHELPS,
Newport in Flower [49]

As the trend toward Neoclassicism strengthened
in the 1890s, Peabody & Stearns and their clients responded accordingly. More than perhaps
any other Peabody design in Newport, Shamrock Cliff
presents a mélange of architectural styles and details,
skillfully combined into what has been called Peabody
& Stearns's "ultimate achievement at Newport." [50]

Gaun Hutton was born in a small town near Belfast,
Ireland, in 1849. As a teenager, he moved to the United
States, where he lived with relatives in Baltimore who
groomed him for the Foreign Service. He served for a
time as vice-consul in the American embassy in Petrograd (St. Petersburg); there he met Celeste Winans, the
daughter of Thomas DeKay Winans (1820–1878), also

of Baltimore, a wealthy inventor who had been instrumental in the construction of a railroad from St. Petersburg to Moscow. Gaun and Celeste were married in
1883; in 1884, Gaun retired to society life in Baltimore
and Newport. Perhaps it is not coincidental that the
Newport Mercury reported in December of 1887 that
Miss [sic] Hutton, "daughter of Thomas Winans," was at
the time "one of the wealthiest Baltimore dames" with
"$20,000,000 or more." [51]

In 1887 the Huttons purchased the Katherine
DeKay Bronson estate on the Ridge Road section of
Ocean Avenue, not far from Celeste's childhood summer home at Castle Hill, and named it Shamrock Cliff
in acknowledgment of Gaun's Irish roots. By 1894 the
old estate house was just not elegant enough. An article
in the *Newport Mercury* informed: "Last year [Mr. Hutton] built a handsome lodge and otherwise improved
the entrance to the estate, and now he has contracted
with McNeal of Boston for the erection of a new villa
which shall be in keeping with Newport's more modern summer homes. The plans are by Peabody and Stearns of Boston. The estate, which adjoins Prof. Agassiz's
... is most beautifully situated." [52]

Unlike many of Peabody & Stearns's previous Newport commissions, built of brick, shingle, or native New
England stone, Shamrock Cliff was constructed of red

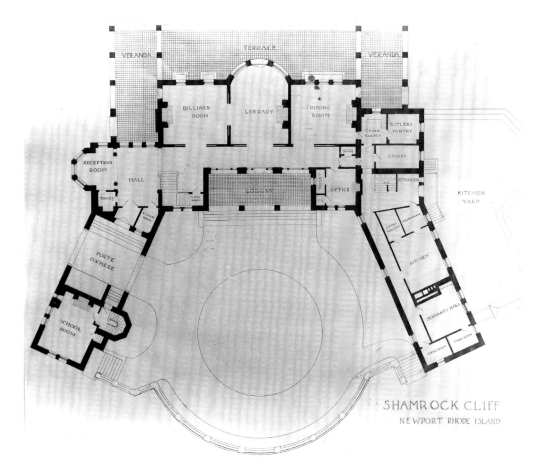

1.57. Shamrock Cliff,
water view, 1895.
Courtesy of The Newport
Historical Society (P2688).

1.58. Shamrock Cliff,
floor plan, 1895. Courtesy
of The Newport Historical
Society (P2687).

1.59. Shamrock Cliffs gateway and porter's lodge. Postcard, collection of the author.

granite and Mediterranean clay roof tiles, imported from Europe. The two main elevations were created in startlingly different styles: the street side presented a picturesque arrangement, while the water-view façade appeared to be more influenced by buildings of the Italian Renaissance. The primary decorative feature of the cottage was the ashlar of the granite; a series of light-colored belt courses encircled the exterior, elongating the design and helping to coordinate the two opposing façades.

In plan, Shamrock Cliff was decidedly Beaux Arts rather than English country house, with a hallway running the length of the house. While the large loggia centered on the streetscape façade allowed entry to the hall, the main entrance was through the grand arch of the porte-cochere, in the southern wing. A modest hall and reception room area greeted guests; the view from the hall was directed outside to the ocean view. Billiards room, library, and dining room were lined up across the face of the house, each allowing access to the terrace and covered verandahs that stretched the length of the cottage. The northern wing of the house was entirely devoted to storage and service: China closet, butler's pantry, storeroom, refrigerated room, cook's pantry, kitchen, housekeeper's room, cook's room, man's room (a room for a male servant), and servants' hall occupied fully a third of the first floor's usable square footage. The children's schoolroom was located in the square tower in the north wing, with entrance from the porte-cochere and from the central yard. The plan was surprisingly simple. No drawing room, morning room, or parlors complicated the plan, suggesting that this was, in fact, a summer home.

The property at Shamrock Cliff was landscaped by the Olmsted firm. A topographical map dated September 1895 indicates that J. P. Cotton was the local civil engineer and that the plans for the estate included the mansion, a stable, a play house, a pump, tennis courts, a workhouse–boardinghouse and cottage. A formal flower bed was centered in the circular driveway, and plantings continued around the various corners of the house.

Shamrock Cliff remained in the Hutton family until 1958. During the next two decades, it was used as an inn and a discothèque. In 1981 it was converted into a timeshare resort hotel and renamed Oceancliff. The waterfront façade has endured the addition of a ballroom of dubious architectural pedigree, but the street façade remains much as originally designed. Remnants of the original interior consist primarily of stone columns where porches and piazzas were located. The original gatehouse remains on the property.

Bleak House

Newport, Rhode Island, 1895

Ross R. Winans, 1850-1912

Mr. Ross R. Winans is having built on his Castle Hill estate a fine cottage, in addition to the one occupied by himself and his family.

— *New York Times*, February 22, 1893

Charles Dickens's popular novel *Bleak House* provided the name for three Newport cottages located in the Castle Hill neighborhood on Ocean Avenue; it was chosen perhaps for the windswept desolation of much of the shorefront property overlooking Pirate's Cove. The first was Thomas Winans's (1820-1878) cottage built in 1864. The second was a cottage built next door by his son Ross R. Winans in 1873, according to the *Newport Mercury*, "three stories with a Mansard roof.... a large carriage house and stable, the cost ... will be $60,000." This cottage was replaced by the third Bleak House, a fine Shingle Style cottage designed by Peabody & Stearns in 1895. Ross and his sister Celeste evidently loved this area of Newport where they spent their childhood summers because they both returned as adults: Celeste Winans and her husband Gaun Hutton built the nearby Shamrock Cliff.

Bleak House was unique in its simplicity of form and variety of floor plan. The cottage was two stories in height, with gently sloped hipped roofs on the main body of the house as well as numerous covered piazzas and walkways. The roofline, sprawling floor plan, and lack of attached ornament gave the design a decidedly Wrightian feeling of groundedness. The landscaping by the Olmsted firm extended the apparent footprint through use of terraced gardens and low stone walls.

The Winans maintained their permanent residence in Baltimore, where in 1882, they built a lavish home designed by McKim, Mead & White, which the *New York Times* referred to as the "finest private house south of New York."[53] Following the death of his wife Neva and their son Ross W. in England in 1907, Ross seldom left his Baltimore home. He sold Bleak House that year to Marsden Perry of Providence, Rhode Island.

Bleak House's exposed location made it vulnerable to the damaging 1938 hurricane, and the distinctive cottage was demolished in 1948. The property was purchased and later developed as a residential subdivision.

1.60. Bleak House, residence of Mardsen J. Perry (second owner). Postcard, collection of the author.

1.61. Beech Bound, preliminary study, water view. Courtesy of Memorial Library, Boston Architectural College.

Beech Bound

Newport, Rhode Island, 1895

William F. Burden, 1859-1897

Mr. William F. Burden . . . has purchased eight acres of land fronting on the harbor next adjoining E. D. Morgan's place, with fine marine view, and boat and yachting facilities. Mr. Burden . . . will at once build a palatial cottage on his new estate.

— *New York Times,* March 2, 1892

If William Burden was intimidated by E. D. Morgan's monumental McKim, Mead & White-designed cottage, Beacon Rock (1891), that abutted his property, he did not let on. The "palatial cottage" that Peabody & Stearns designed for Burden was so unlike Morgan's that no comparisons could have been drawn—and perhaps that was the point of the wonderful stone and brick castle that was constructed on the waterfront site overlooking Newport Harbor.

William Fletcher Burden was born in Troy, New York, where the extended members of the Burden family owned and operated one of Troy's most important industries, the Burden Iron Company. Burden's cousin was the influential I. Townsend Burden, whose cottage, Fairlawn, stands at the corner of Bellevue and Ruggles avenues in Newport, and for which Peabody & Stearns designed a later addition. Burden graduated from Williams College in Williamstown, Massachusetts, in 1879 and married Miss Daisy McCoy of Waterford, New York, in 1883.

The Burdens decided to build in Newport, and they purchased a fine piece of property just off of Ocean Avenue. When the cottage was completed, it was reported to have cost over $1,000,000—"one of the handsomest in that city of handsome homes."[54] It was named Beech Bound, presumably for the rows of beech trees planted along the boundaries of the property.

Beech Bound was "built after the style of an ancient Norman castle, with a banquet hall in the center."[55] The first floor was constructed of stone, with shingles on the upper floors. A crenellated stone tower stretched above the rooftop of the cottage and provided the signature feature of the property, especially as viewed from the water. The initial site planning was done by the Olmsted firm in 1893, but subsequent owners, Mr. and Mrs. Henry B. H. Ripley, were responsible for the lavish gardens planted on the grounds.

Burden was reported to be a "great lover of Newport" and spent much time there—he was "one of the first to arrive and one of the last to go."[56] The couple arrived early in May and stayed until November when the Horse Show opened in New York City. Unfortunately, they spent only two summers at Beech Bound, their years there cut short by William Burden's death in 1897. Daisy McCoy Burden received the bulk of her husband's estate, and she continued to spend summers at Beech Bound. She remarried in 1923, to Dr. Alexander S. Clarke of Paris, but they continued to visit the cottage.

During the late 1970s the Beech Bound cottage (now Beechbound) was subdivided into seven condominium residences, and the property was split to allow the construction of several additional homes. Few changes have been made to the exterior, which retains much of its original architectural impact. The property is private.

1.62. Beech Bound, street view. Courtesy of Memorial Library, Boston Architectural College.

1.63. Ridgemere, street view, c. 2006. Photograph by Annie Robinson.

FACING PAGE
1.64. House for Miss Foster, Ridgemere, front elevation. Peabody and Stearns Collection, courtesy of the Boston Public Library Fine Arts Department.

1.65. House for Miss Foster, Ridgemere, first floor plan. Peabody and Stearns Collection, courtesy of the Boston Public Library, Fine Arts Department.

Ridgemere

Newport, Rhode Island, 1898

Fanny Foster, 1852–1934

Just down the street from the Vinland farm buildings is Ridgemere, built for Miss Fanny Foster of Boston. It is an excellent example of the more modest cottages that Peabody & Stearns designed for many of their clients—distinctive and well suited to their use.

Ridgemere is an academic red brick cottage with green-painted ironwork trim. Upon closer inspection, it appears to be the very image of the earlier Althorpe, although constructed with different materials and on a smaller scale. The deep porch around the front and side and the imposing corner tower rooms are identical to those of the Spencer cottage. A number of details are repeated: the Palladian tripartite window motif above the front door; three Classical pedimented dormers top the second-story roof; even the Chinese Chippendale roof balustrade echoes the former Colonial-style cottage, this time worked in green-painted ironwork rather than white woodwork. The quoining

of Althorpe is re-created in the brick through the use of red mortar between the bricks, which contrasts with the gray mortar used for the rest of the construction. An enlarged pediment supported by Doric columns tops the porch at the front entrance and is repeated at the porte-cochere located to the side of the house.

Guests entered Ridgemere from either the front door or from the porte-cochere, stepping into the large entry hall with its staircase leading to the second floor. The parlor and the library were each located in one of the rounded turret rooms at the front of the house; the dining room was behind the library, with a view of the gardens through a curved wall of windows. The kitchen was located in the service wing to the rear of the house. It was a compact and well-conceived floor plan.

Fanny Foster was the daughter of John and Harriet Sanford Foster of Boston. Her father was an owner of the Foster & Taylor grocery business, which he dissolved in 1871 in order to pursue real estate investments; he was also a stockholder and director in the Exchange Bank and was generally regarded as an affable and generous "old-time merchant." He had purchased the property on Leroy Avenue in 1869. There, in a Stick Style cottage with mansard roof, Fanny and her parents spent the

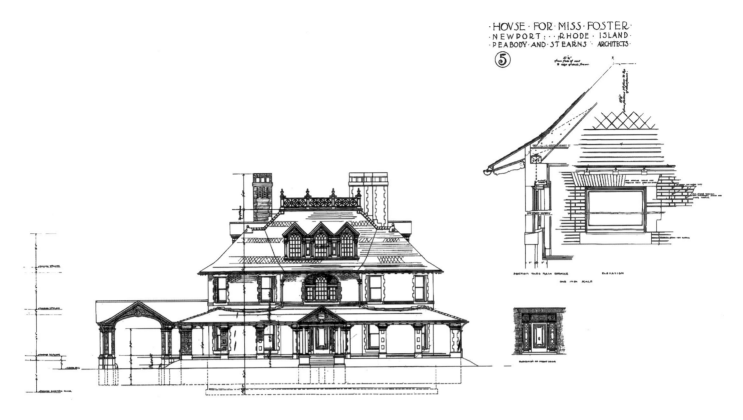

FRONT ELEVATION
ONE QVARTER·INCH SCALE

summers. After her parents died, Fanny had their cottage moved to Perry Street and commissioned Peabody & Stearns to design the house that we see now. She also hired Peabody & Stearns to design her new Boston winter residence in 1901 at 26 The Fenway, next door to Robert Peabody's own townhouse. She continued to split her time between the two residences until 1915, at which time she chose to live in Newport full-time. The Fenway residence is currently owned by the Boston Conservatory, a school for the performing arts.

Miss Foster also requested a stable–carriage house and two Lord & Burnham greenhouses for the Leroy Avenue property. Her interest in horticulture is confirmed by several articles in the *Boston Daily Globe* in the early 1900s in which it was reported that Miss Fanny Foster had taken high honors at the Newport Horticultural Society shows, for roses and for "palms, ferns and foliage plants."[57] Her competition was the likes of Mrs. Robert Goelet, Mrs. Perry Belmont, Mrs. Hamilton McKown Twombly, and Mrs. H. Mortimer Brooks. One of the original greenhouses and the pump house are extant. The carriage house was renovated as a separate residence in the late 1900s, and the property was divided.

Ridgemere is a private residence.

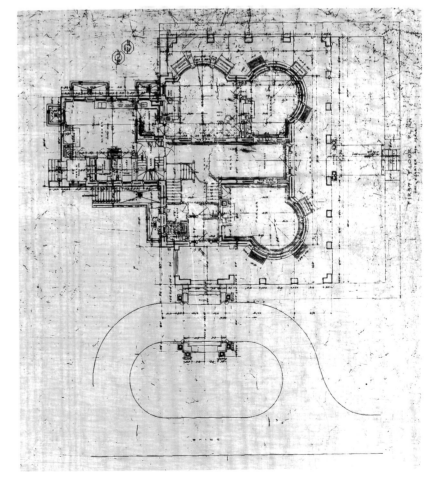

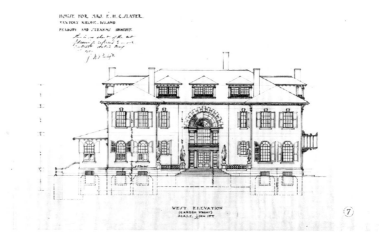

1.66. House for Mrs. E. H. G. Slater, Hopedene, west elevation. Peabody and Stearns Collection, courtesy of the Boston Public Library Fine Arts Department.

Hopedene

Newport, Rhode Island, 1898–1902

Elizabeth Hope Gammell Slater, d. 1944

In front of Hopedene Mrs. Slater maintains a small lobster industry, and all the fish food for the most part used on her tables is caught by one of the men on the estate, who is employed expressly for this duty.

— *Boston Daily Globe*, August 19, 1906

Hopedene is a splendid cottage. Constructed during the years 1898 to 1902, it was the fourth and last house to be built on the Ives-Gammell family compound overlooking the Cliff Walk. This brick Georgian mansion was commissioned by Mrs. Elizabeth Hope Gammell Slater, whose grandfather, Robert Hales Ives had first assembled the sixty-acre compound in the 1850s. Hopedene was widely written about: it was featured in articles in *Country Life in America* (1906), in Barr Ferree's *American Estates and Gardens* (1906), in *Architectural Review* (1908), and *The Brickbuilder* (1907), and in Mrs. Van Renssalaer's *Newport, Our Social Capital*. It was described variously as Colonial Revival, Georgian, or Italian Renaissance—a confusing juxtaposition of characterizations, to be sure. The *Architectural Review* described Hopedene as . . . "here England—and even Georgian England—provided the suggestion, although the house as developed has not altogether escaped that sense of pomposity, of striving for recognition, of pretension, that is so catchingly communicated from palace to palace, from the so-called "cottage" to "cottage" of Newport,"[58] while Barr Ferree characterized the house as "designed in a quiet Italian style, very subdued in treatment, but thoroughly good and homelike in character."[59] All agreed that it was large and self-possessed in stature.

The cottage was constructed of red brick with white trim, with a hipped roof and a program of fenestration of the Georgian influence. The round-roofed portico above the front door mimics the arched and keystoned windows on the first floor; the hipped roof dormer located directly above accentuates the positioning. The garden front has been substantially altered from its original disposition. Early photographs capture the two symmetrical wings that projected toward the garden with a large terrace between them. The striking element of the garden façade was the triple window enclosed under a large stone arch, a muscular, almost postmodern Palladian window arrangement. On the waterfront façade, a two-story semicircular porch covered a terrace with balustrades and steps. A story in the *Boston Daily Globe* dated August 19, 1906, described it: "On the cliff side of the estate is a large veranda, which is enclosed by a white and green painted canopy of heavy canvas. The tiled flooring is covered with matting and rugs, and the illumination is effected by electricity. . . . Mrs. Slater is a strong believer in outdoor dinners, and even during the most disagreeable weather some of her largest dinners have been given on this veranda."

Ogden Codman designed the interior, cataloged in Pauline Metcalf's book *Ogden Codman and the Decoration of Houses*. Although the house was designed to be occupied all year, Mrs. Slater reportedly "stays but little of her time on the cliffs during the colder weather, occupying her Washington home throughout the winter."[60]

Hopedene was surrounded by formal gardens, with views of Easton's Beach and the Atlantic Ocean. Although Frederick Law Olmsted had been called in by the Gammells in 1898 to determine placement of their new Peabody & Stearns cottage, Beatrix Farrand was the landscape architect for Hopedene's thirty-acre site.

Mrs. Slater continued to occupy Hopedene until her death in 1944. The house was sold at auction the following year. Subsequent owners included the Count and Countess Court Haugwitz Hardenberg Reventlow, and the Preservation Society of Newport County.

Hopedene is currently a private residence.

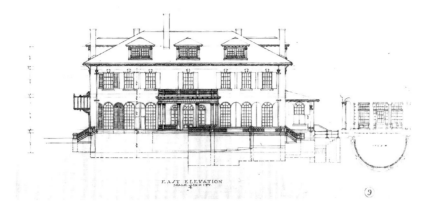

1.67. House for Mrs. E. H.
G. Slater, Hopedene, east
elevation. Peabody and
Stearns Collection, courtesy
of the Boston Public Library
Fine Arts Department.

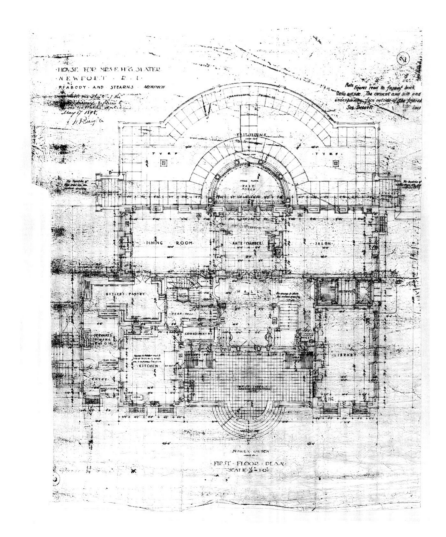

1.68. House for Mrs. E. H.
G. Slater, Hopedene, first
floor plan. Peabody and
Stearns Collection, courtesy
of the Boston Public Library
Fine Arts Department.

1.69. House for Mrs. E.
H. G. Slater, Hopedene,
west and east façades.
Brickbuilder, May 1907, vol.
16, no. 5, pl. 80. Courtesy of
Rotch Library, Massachusetts
Institute of Technology.

1.70. Residence of E.
G. H. Slater, Hopedene,
north façade. Postcard,
collection of the author.

1.71 Hopedene, dining
room. *Architectural Review*,
March 1908, vol. XV, no. 3.
Courtesy of the Boston Public
Library Fine Arts Department.

Massachusetts

The North Shore

...the lavish disposition of nature and the costly efforts of
art have together made of the Beverly shore a region that
approaches the ideal of an earthly paradise ..."
— OBER, *History of Essex County, Massachusetts* [61]

Moraine Farm

North Beverly, Massachusetts, 1880-1882

John Charles Phillips, 1838-1885

Moraine Farm is an outstanding example of collaboration between Peabody & Stearns and landscape architect Frederick Law Olmsted. The two firms produced a quintessential Peabody & Stearns Queen Anne country house set like a jewel in an intricately carved and filled Olmsted site plan.

In 1878, John Charles Phillips purchased several small, nonproducing farms in North Beverly to create a 275-acre site overlooking Wenham Lake. His plan was to combine the elements of a country residence, a working farm, and a managed forest, which could serve as an example of modern farming on marginal or poorly drained soil. Although this might fulfill John Phillips's desire for a country house, his wife did not necessarily totally concur. Their son, William Phillips recalled that "my mother often spoke of her love for the sea and her disappointment that her future Summer home was not to be on the coast near Manchester, where a fine wooded property was then for sale."[62]

Peabody & Stearns suggested a familiar Queen Anne motif for Phillips's country house. It was commissioned and constructed in 1878 for $79,222.67, but alterations and additions over the years totaled more than $280,000—certainly well over $6 million in today's currency. The exterior of the ground floor featured undressed stone with brownstone trim, while the upper floors were shingled. A cross gable with decorative half-timbering extended over the main entry to the house. Multiple levels of roof were punctuated by English chimneys and various dormers. Outside terrace areas and verandahs were protected and decorated with a variety of decorative screens and balusters, while an octagonally shaped gazebo with rooftop deck above extended out from the main footprint of the house, a familiar feature in Peabody's waterfront cottages.

1.72. Moraine Farm, street view. Courtesy of Memorial Library, Boston Architectural College.

1.73. Sketch, "On Wenham Lake", Moraine Farm, garden view. Courtesy of Memorial Library, Boston Architectural College.

The first-time visitor entered the front door of Moraine Farm with no idea that the breathtaking vista of the lake awaited him—the views of the lake were hidden from the carriage roads leading to the house. The entry hall extended through the house to the terrace beyond, bypassing a massive staircase decorated with spindle fanlight screens. The floorplan included a parlor, library, hall, dining room (with a bay window for a view of the lake), and a children's room on the first floor. The angled wing contained kitchen and service areas.

Frederick Law Olmsted was hired in 1880 to create a master plan for what scholars consider to be "the most significant forerunner of the two extensive estates he planned for members of the Vanderbilt family in the early 1890s, Biltmore Estate in North Carolina and Shelburne Farms in Shelburne, Vermont."[63] Residential, agricultural, and forestry areas were all separated by natural dividers and by the path of the carriage-road system that led into the property. Olmsted designed a massive terrace for the garden façade of the house in order to raise the house and to establish a platform from which to view Wenham Lake as well as specialized sunken gardens and garden rooms.

John Charles Phillips was born in Boston, the son of a Congregational clergyman and the nephew of Wendell Phillips, the social reformer. He attended Phillips Academy in Andover, Massachusetts, and was an 1858 graduate of Harvard University. He became involved in the shipping and import business, ultimately in his own partnership, Mackay & Phillips, and later John C. Phillips & Co., Boston, in which he remained active until just a few months before his death. The year before his purchase of Moraine Farm, Phillips had commissioned Peabody & Stearns to design a town house at 299 Berkeley Street, at the corner of Marlborough Street. This French Renaissance–influenced was demolished in 1939 (fig. 1.74).

Moraine Farm is now covered by conservation and preservation restrictions under the guidance of

the Trustees of Reservations and the Essex County Greenbelt Association. The Peabody & Stearns country house was altered and modernized in the decades following 1930, and in 1978 it was reduced to one story; this compromised its original picturesque façade but maintained the original footprint and relationship to the view of Wenham Lake. The house and gardens with approximately seventy surrounding acres are owned by Project Adventure, a nonprofit organization that provides leadership in the expansion of adventure-based experiential programming. The 1913 home site of John Charles and Anna Phillips's son, William Phillips, consists of 85 acres of the original property, which is now managed by the Beverly Conservation Commission as a public passive-recreation preserve. An additional 110 acres, including the agricultural buildings and areas, is privately owned.

1.74. John C. Phillips' house on Berkeley Street, Boston, Massachusetts. Peabody & Stearns, 1878. *The American Architect and Building News*, March 31, 1888, no. 640. Collection of the author.

1.75. Spouting Horn, water view, c. 2006. Photograph by the author.

Spouting Horn

Nahant, Massachusetts, 1881–1882

Thomas Motley, Jr., 1847–1909

1.76. Spouting Horn, street view, c. 1900. Courtesy of Nahant Historical Society.

Spouting Horn was built on a spectacular property on Spouting Horn Road for Thomas Motley, Jr., at the same time that Peabody & Stearns was creating the cottages on Swallows Cave Road for the Grant and the Guild families. The breathtaking views of Egg Rock and the open ocean have not diminished with time.

Thomas Motley, Jr., was a Boston merchant who was active in Nahant and Boston community issues. His family was well placed in Boston society and was well acquainted with the Sears family, the Lodges, as well as the Grants and the Guilds. Motley was among the founding members of the Nahant Club in 1888, along with Richard Sears and Samuel Eliot Guild.

Spouting Horn is a fine example of a Queen Anne cottage, with panels of plain and patterned shingles as well as clapboards and half-timbered gable ends. Large porches wrap around the first floor of the two-and-a-half-story cottage; over time, some areas of the porch have been glassed in to provide a respite from the direct ocean breezes. The interior floor plan is organized around a massive central carved staircase that reaches to the top floor, alongside an originally installed elevator. Entrance is made to a large living hall with fireplace. Most unusual is the sgrafitti floral frieze that decorates the upper walls of the living hall and the adjacent dining room. The rooms are large and open on to one another, providing excellent views of the water from nearly every room. The second floor is comprised of a large stair hall off which are four large chambers and three smaller rooms, and an entrance to a large open porch. The third floor contains five chambers. The kitchen, laundry, and service areas are were originally located in the daylight basement. Peabody & Stearns's records indicate that the initial construction cost of $12,209.51. Unlike many other clients, no further alterations or additions were listed. A stable was constructed in 1894 by local builder J. T. Wilson, the same who built the original cottage.

Spouting Horn remained in the Motley family until at least 1942. It is now a private residence.

Patrick Grant Cottage

Nahant, Massachusetts, 1882

Patrick Grant, 1809–95

The house overhung the water close to Swallow's
Cave, and its piazza was rarely without a breeze
in the hottest weather.
    — Robert Grant,
        Fourscore, an Autobiography, p. 164 [64]

Charlotte Rice, the widow of Henry G. Rice of
Beacon Hill, purchased a large summer property on Swallows Cave Road in 1850. It was
here that the families of her two daughters, Charlotte
Bordman Rice Grant (Mrs. Patrick Grant) and Elizabeth Henderson Rice Guild (Mrs. Samuel Eliot Guild),
summered. When Mrs. Rice died, her house was torn
down and two Peabody & Stearns–designed cottages
were built on adjoining lots for the two families.

Patrick Grant was born in Boston and lived most of
his life on Beacon Hill. Through his mother, Susannah
Powell Mason Grant, he was first cousin to many of
the leading Boston families, including the Parkers, the
Warrens, the Searses, and the Parkmans; through his
wife he had connections to Harrison Gray Otis and
John Bates. He graduated from Harvard in the Class of
1828 and, after graduation, worked as a commission
merchant. Patrick Grant was a successful Bostonian
merchant in the way that Bostonians had of being
prominent without being obvious: "A singularly quiet
gentleman, he has always avoided public positions of
any sort, his name never appearing as connected with
Boston institutions or enterprises."[65]

Patrick Grant's first wife, Elizabeth Bryant, died in
1843, leaving him with a two-year-old daughter, Anna
Mason. They reportedly lived with his mother and aunt
at 53 Mount Vernon Street, and spent summers in Newport. In 1850, Grant married Charlotte Bordman Rice of
Boston. Their oldest son, Robert, became a well-known
judge and the author of numerous fictional satires on
Boston society, including *The Confessions of a Frivo-
lous Girl*, *The Chippendales*, and in 1934, *Fourscore,
An Autobiography*.

During the summer months when the family was
in Nahant, Grant set out for Boston on the reliable
steamboat *Nelly Baker* every morning at eight o'clock
and returned at three forty-five, in time for dinner. His
son described the routine of a typical summer day
in Nahant: His grandmother would see that breakfast
was served at seven-thirty for the men who were traveling to Boston, and that another was served at nine
for the ladies and "any children who lay abed." A light
luncheon of fruit and cake was served at noon, which
was followed by dinner at four. The dinner menu might
include lobster, tinker mackerel, scrod, partridge or
squab, accompanied by local vegetables and fruit. High
tea was served at seven-thirty. The days were spent vis-

iting with neighbors and friends and playing lawn tennis (a new phenomenon), while the children played
and swam. Evenings were social, with guests that
included friends and family as well as notables such as
the poet Henry Wadsworth Longfellow and the scientist Louis Agassiz. Among the Grants's friends were the
parents of Thomas Motley, for whom Peabody & Stearns designed Spouting Horn in Nahant in 1881.

In the fall of 1881, Robert Peabody recorded in his
diary several meetings with the Guilds regarding the
design of their cottage, at least two of which included
Mr. Olmsted's services. Presumably, he met with the
Grants at the same time.

The Grant cottage appears to have had less of the
Queen Anne influence in design than the neighboring Guild cottage, with a simpler roofline, a squared
tower roof, and a long sloping roofline on what was
presumably the kitchen wing. The Peabody & Stearns
drawings archive does not include plans for the Patrick
Grant cottage but does include a list of specifications
for the construction.

Charlotte Grant died before the completion of the
Peabody & Stearns cottage. Her husband and children
summered there for two years and then leased it out.
The Grant cottage was sold after Patrick Grant's death
to Dr. Francis P. Sprague, and it later became known as
the Sprague-Lowell house. It was demolished in the fall
of 1941 by the next owner of the property in order to
build a new cottage, Cas-el-ot.

1.77. Patrick Grant
House (later Lowell/
Sprague House), street
view, c. 1900. Courtesy of
Nahant Historical Society.

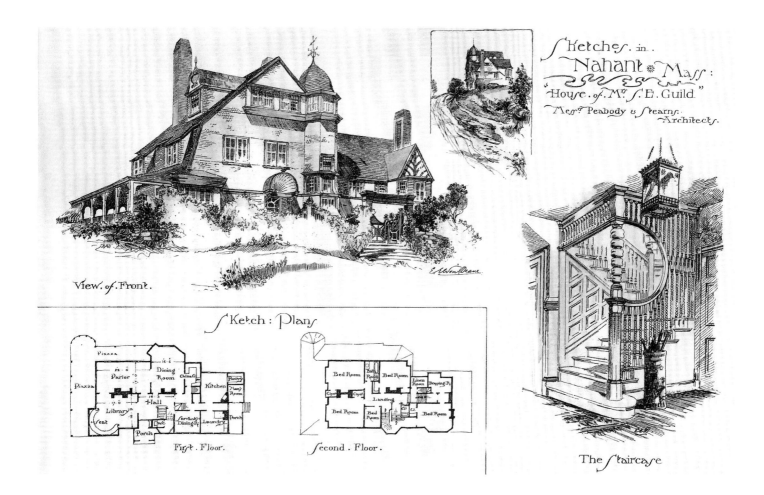

1.78. Sketches in Nahant, Massachusetts, house of Mrs. S. E. Guild, Guild Cottage, E. Eldon Deane, delineator. *The American Architect and Building News*, September 5, 1885, no. 506. Collection of the author.

FACING PAGE
1.79. Guild Cottage, watercolor sketch, street view. Courtesy of Memorial Library, Boston Architectural College.

1.80. Guild Cottage, street view, c. 1933. Courtesy of Nahant Historical Society.

Guild Cottage

Nahant, Massachusetts, 1882

Mrs. Samuel Eliot Guild

Took the children to the Swallows' Cave after breakfast. A delightful stroll ... on the cliff, watching the sails in sunshine and in shadow, and our own shadows on far-off brown rocks.

— HENRY WADSWORTH LONGFELLOW,
Life of Henry Wadsworth Longfellow [66]

As with the Grant cottage, this cottage was built by one of Charlotte Rice's daughters on her property overlooking Swallows Cave. Elizabeth Henderson Rice married Samuel Eliot Guild in 1847; he died at Nahant in 1862, at the age of forty-three. Twenty years later Elizabeth had this cottage built for herself and their two children.

The Guild cottage presents a combination of Queen Anne and Colonial Revival elements, remarkable for the interaction of hooded doorway, stair tower, and timbered gables. The plan for the interior of the cottage appears somewhat unremarkable until one realizes that it was built on four levels serviced by several flights of stairs. [67] The first floor contained a large hall opening in to a dining room that overlooked the L-shaped piazza, a large library with curved window seat, and a parlor. Stairs led up to five bedrooms and

one bath on the second floor. Service areas included kitchen, laundry, and servants' dining room on the first floor. The cost of the cottage was computed by Peabody & Stearns to be $14,741.89.

The Guild cottage was well published, in the *American Architect and Building News* (September 5, 1885), and in *Building* magazine (February 12, 1887), as well as in the *British Architect* (September 17, 1886). One of the most striking interior details was the main staircase, which was enclosed by a screen of balusters reminiscent of the staircase designed for the nearly contemporaneous Merrywood in Lenox, Massachusetts. Another important comparison can be made with Kragsyde, the Shingle Style masterpiece designed by Peabody & Stearns at about the same time for a site in nearby Manchester-by-the-Sea. Kragsyde utilized several of the same details, including the use of multiple living levels and the combination of exterior details.

Landscape plans for the property were drawn by the Olmsted landscaping firm. Robert Peabody included a notation in his diary for Friday, October 21, 1881, that he went to Nahant with Mr. Olmsted and that he made a rough sketch for the house that evening; on November 28 they returned to stake out the footprint of the house with Mrs. Guild.

The Guild cottage remained in the family until 1927; like the Grant cottage, it was demolished in 1938–39 in order to make way for the garage and caretaker's cottage for Cas-el-ot.

Kragsyde

Manchester-by-the-Sea, Massachusetts,
1882–1884

George Nixon Black, Jr., 1842–1928

For beauty of situation, Mr. G. N. Black's villa, at Manchester-by-the-Sea, is almost unrivaled. Standing on a craggy height beside the ocean, surrounded by wild shore-effects and charming landscape-gardening, . . . the roar of the breakers at its feet, . . . this noble villa could scarcely be more happily located. Nor has the peculiarity of the situation been lost sight of by the architects, Messrs. Peabody and Stearns, in preparing the design. On the contrary, the design is a logical outgrowth of the structural necessities of the situation.

— GEORGE SHELDON,
Artistic Country-Seats [68]

Kragsyde was and is arguably Peabody & Stearns's most talked-about and most-published residential commission. In its own time it was included in Sheldon's *Artistic Country-Seats,* in Russell Sturgis's "Critique of Peabody and Stearns," and in the *Inland Architect and News Record* (1889); the *American Architect and Building News* included a full-page illustration of the house in plan and in sketches by Eldon Deane (1885). In more recent years it was included in Vincent Scully's *The Shingle Style and the Stick Style* (1955:1971), and in numerous other articles and architectural survey books. All agree that the house was an inventive and picturesque solution to a difficult but striking piece of property overlooking Lobster Cove. "If there is a more successful attempt of its kind anywhere about Boston, the writer has failed to discover it. The house seems to belong just where it is; and the irregularities, the ups and down, the angles in the wind and the dip of the driveway, all are warranted by the natural conditions and are a logical adaptation of the necessities of the plan to an irregular site, the picturesque results being none the less satisfactory, in that it appears to be spontaneous and unstudied."[69]

Black purchased the property for Kragsyde in October 1882 from Cyrus Bartol and spent over $58,000 over the next three years building his cottage. Landscaping on this unique property was designed by Frederick Law Olmsted. A conversation between Olmsted and Robert Peabody recorded by Charles Eliot, an Olmsted employee, illustrates Olmsted's personal philosophy regarding the appropriateness of natural landscaping:

> Noticed many ridiculously incongruous attempts at gardening about the houses on Gales Point. Several Proprietors have seen fit to "smooth up" all their land that they possibly could and here lawn mowers and hose are to be seen—also ribbon beds of coleus and other foliage bedding plants—with circles of geraniums scarlet, and other such abominations. Said Mr. O to R.S.P., "I wish Mr. Black would put his place into my hands, and let me show these people that a satisfactory result can be obtained without resorting to these 'public garden' things." "Why, what would you do?" "I would not attempt to change the very pleasing natural character.—I would take this present character and work it up.[70]

The carriage-road approach to Kragsyde kept the house nearly hidden on the drive in. Then, the iconic image of the cottage, the archway over the drive, came into view. The main entrance to the cottage was located underneath that archway, through heavy double doors into a small vestibule. A short flight of wide stairs led to the main hall, which was finished with wood paneling, a heavy beamed ceiling, and a substantial fireplace with seats. The dining room was located to the right of the hall, and the parlor to the left, with access to a wide, covered piazza extending out nearly to the edge of the water. On the second floor, four bedrooms connected by a gallery, and a "Boudoir Library" located above the arch, made up the accommodations for owner and guests. The kitchen was located in the basement of the house, and was connected via dumbwaiter to the butler's pantry next to the dining room. The cottage encompassed about 5,000 square feet. It seemed larger due to the use of many living levels connected by short flights of stairs, and to the abundance of windows and porches and verandahs.

George Nixon Black, Jr. (known to family and friends as Nixon) was born in Ellsworth, Maine, in the family homestead known as Woodlawn, a Federal brick home of 1820. In 1860 the Blacks moved to a house on Pemberton Square on Beacon Hill in Boston, perhaps so that Nixon could begin at Harvard College. He did not stay long at his studies, however; instead, he traveled in Europe for a year and then reluctantly settled in to work in his father's commercial real estate empire. Nixon was active in the Boston community and maintained friendships with many artists as well as prominent citizens such as Isabella Stewart Gardner; he was a generous benefactor of the Museum of Fine Arts and he commissioned the New Jerusalem window at Trinity Church in Boston from John La Farge in memory of his father and his older sister. He also remained interested in the family property in Ellsworth—he remodeled the library and decorated a model "Colonial" kitchen, and collected a variety of furnishings that reflected his interest in the

1.82. Sketch of Kragsyde, American Seashore Residence. *The Builder*, January 21, 1888, p. 47. Courtesy of the Boston Public Library Fine Arts Department.

1.83. House at Lobster Cove, Kragsyde, side view. *Architectural Record*, July 1896, p. 86. Courtesy of the Boston Public Library Fine Arts Department.

1.84. Sketches at Manchester-by-the-Sea, Kragsyde. *The American Architect and Building News*, March 1885, vol. 17, pl. 480.

Colonial Revival. Years later, the citizens of Ellsworth learned that he had donated Woodlawn, along with its furnishings, to the city to be used as a museum.

Nixon died in 1928 at his home on Beacon Street. Kragsyde was sold, and the new owners demolished the Peabody & Stearns cottage in order to make room for a more contemporary summer house named La Tourelle. Incredibly, Kragsyde was recreated in the 1980s on a remarkably appropriate rocky site on an island off the coast of Maine. This reproduction of Peabody & Stearns' iconic cottage is a private residence. The original carriage house in Manchester-by-the-Sea was converted to a residence in 1991 and is privately owned.

Brinley Cottage

Magnolia, Massachusetts, 1891

Charles A. Brinley, 1847-1919

Magnolia is . . . the most attractive summer resort
between Salem and Gloucester. It boasts every
variety of attractions. . . .
— *The North Shore of Massachusetts Bay*, 1881[71]

Magnolia is a village in the town Gloucester,
named for the magnolia shrub that is found
in Massachusetts in its wild state only in the
small geographical area known as Magnolia Point.[72]

Charles A. Brinley commissioned Peabody & Stearns to design his cottage in 1891, having purchased
nearly three acres of land in the spring of that year.
The cottage was completed by the following year,
according to town records—it was taxed on a land
value of $2,500 and a house value of $8,000 in May
1892. Records in the architects' office indicate that
his expenditure for the cottage was $14,524.98. Plans
show that the house was designed in the Shingle
Style for a sloped site that allowed the basement area
to be partially exposed to daylight. The main block of
the house measured approximately 40 feet wide by
27 feet deep; a 25-foot service wing doglegged forward on the left side of the front elevation. Together
with the two-story extension that housed an office
on the ground floor, the two extensions formed a
courtyard area in the front of the cottage. Two turret-topped dormers on the main block of the house were
echoed by the stair tower on the front of the service
wing. The presentation-drawing elevation suggests a
wishbone detail in the end gable of the wing and diamond-shaped window detailing.

Peabody planned a wide covered porch at the
main entry. An 11-foot-wide stair hall ran the full
depth of the residence. To the right was the parlor
and Brinley's office. The parlor, a modest room of
about 18 by 20 feet, showed double doors opening
out onto the large covered verandah that wrapped
around the room (later partially enclosed). The largest
room was the dining room, which ran the full depth
of the house, with a bay window and window seat at
the farthest end of the room. Notations made on the
plans indicate that the dining room fireplace was
made of mottled Perth Amboy brick, with a hearth
of unglazed gray tiles. The pine mantel was painted
to match the room. In the parlor the fireplace was of
gray Perth Amboy bricks, again with a pine mantel. A
letter dated May 15, 1891, from Brinley at 247 South
16th Street in Philadelphia addressed to Peabody &
Stearns, reads in part: "The verse which the people
tinseling in gilt on Library mantelpiece runs as follows: In returning and rest shall ye be saved; in quietness and in confidence shall be your strength. Isaiah
30th-15th verse."[73] The second floor contained four

chambers, including "Mr. B's" and "Mrs. B's," a bathroom, and three servant rooms. A later owner of the
house indicates that there were a dozen Brinley children, suggesting that the chambers on the third floor
were well used!

Landscaping of the property included a tennis
court below the house and a garden area in the front.
A small stable at the driveway entrance was reportedly converted to a garage by a later owner; it included
chambers for staff on the second floor.

Charles A. Brinley was born in Hartford, Connecticut. He attended Yale University and graduated from
Yale's Sheffield Scientific School in 1869, where he
spent three more years doing postgraduate work in
chemistry and metallurgy. He worked at Midvale Steel
in Nicetown, Pennsylvania, for ten years; it was here
during Brinley's tenure that efficiency expert Frederick Winslow Taylor developed his "techniques to raise
the efficiency of production throughout the plant."
Brinley then managed a sugar refinery in Philadelphia
until the early 1890s, and later became managing
director and president of the American Pulley Company, a position that was later taken over by his son,
Charles E. Brinley.

The Brinley cottage exists in altered form as a private condominium residence.

1.85. House for C.
A. Brinley, first floor
plan. Peabody and Stearns
Collection, courtesy of the
Boston Public Library Fine
Arts Department.

1.86. House for C.A.
Brinley, presentation
drawing, front elevation.
Peabody and Stearns
Collection, courtesy of the
Boston Public Library Fine
Arts Department.

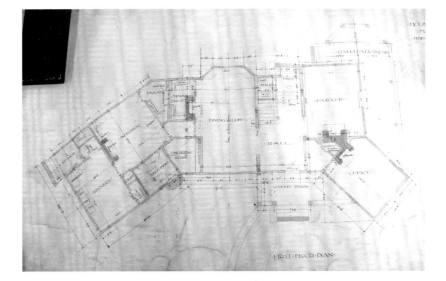

The Knoll

Marblehead, Massachusetts, 1896

George Howe Davenport, 1851–1932

In the meantime, in 1895, Mr. and Mrs. George H. Davenport bought the adjoining hilltop and built their house.... After a while Mr. Davenport bought the Chandler Farlow house and tore it down and established the bowling green on the site.

— ROBERT E. PEABODY, "Peach's Point, Marblehead" [74]

George Davenport purchased a lot that measured approximately two and a half acres with frontage on Doliber's Cove, in the midst of the Crowninshield and Peabody family's territory—Peach's Point. Robert Peabody designed the Peach's Point Club stable, which was built on the small Crowninshield lot that separated the two families.[75] The summer house that Peabody designed for his neighbor was small in comparison to many of the cottages of the period—only 1,500 square feet on the first floor—but it was well designed for its purposes.

Plans indicate that there was an ample covered porch at the front door. From there, a short run of stairs led up to a large verandah that stretched from the front entrance all the way around the living room to the water side of the cottage. The building was raised on a stone foundation, with a Dutch gambrel roof and leaded diamond window detailing. Inside, the floor plan was simple but functional. The entry hall was divided into levels by several small groupings of stairs. The living room dominated the floor plan, with fully 40 percent of the square footage of the first floor. Detail drawings indicate that the walls of the

living room and dining room had wood wainscoting. The living room fireplace was large, with inglenook benches on either side of the fireplace wall suggestive of a Colonial interior. The water-view dining room, a kitchen with china closet, and pantry service areas made up the remainder of the first floor. Evidence that this was a summer home in keeping with the times? Bicycle storage was planned for underneath the main staircase.

Notations on Peabody's drawings indicate that the exterior trim of the house was to be white, but that the interior was to be "Cypress stained brown." Window sashes and the front Dutch door were to be "white outside and brown inside." The "screen door to have Spring on it."

That George Davenport's cottage was smaller than those of many of the other North Shore summer residents is not surprising—he was not a Harvard University graduate, New York industrialist, or railroad company director. He was a successful businessman, however. Davenport graduated from the Roxbury Latin School in Boston and then entered the wholesale lumber business with the George H. Peters Company. After the company fell on hard times, it was later revived as the Davenport, Peters Company. Its successor firm is considered today to be the oldest continuous wholesaler of lumber in the United States. Davenport remained with the company for sixty-five years, retiring as its president in the summer of 1932 at the age of eighty-one years. When he died a few months later, he was survived by his wife, Camilla Chace Davenport, their daughter Dorothea, who was the wife of William T. Aldrich, a Boston architect who had spent some time working in the offices of Peabody & Stearns, and three grandchildren.

The Knoll is a private residence.

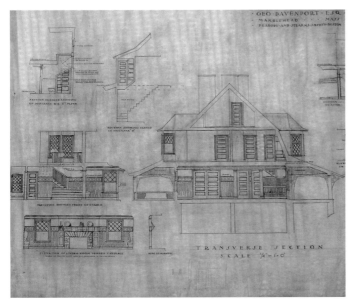

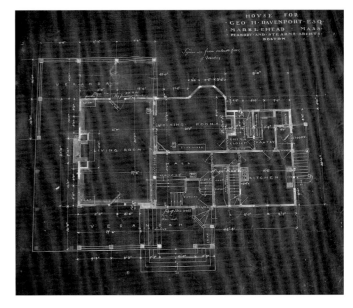

1.88. House for Geo. H.
Davenport, The Knoll,
southeast elevation.
Peabody and Stearns
Collection, courtesy of the
Boston Public Library Fine
Arts Department.

1.90. House for Geo. H.
Davenport, The Knoll,
transverse section and
details. Peabody and Stearns
Collection, courtesy of the
Boston Public Library Fine
Arts Department.

1.89. House for Geo. H.
Davenport, The Knoll,
northwest elevation.
Peabody and Stearns
Collection, courtesy of the
Boston Public Library Fine
Arts Department.

1.91. House for Geo. H.
Davenport, The Knoll,
first floor plan. Peabody
and Stearns Collection,
courtesy of the Boston Public
Library Fine Arts Department.

1.92. Peach's Point
Drive, Marblehead,
Massachusetts. Postcard,
collection of the author.

Peabody Family Cottage

Marblehead, Massachusetts, 1887–1923

As nearly as I can ascertain, the development of Peach's
Point as a summer resort began in 1871–72 when Francis
B. Crowninshield built the large house at the end of the
Point now occupied by the Hammonds.
— ROBERT E. PEABODY, "Peach's Point, Marblehead"[76]

Like their affluent clients, both Robert Swain Peabody and John Goddard Stearns had summer
cottages. Peabody's was located on a diminu-
tive outcropping of Marblehead on the North Shore,
and Stearns's was in Duxbury, on the South Shore. It is
interesting to see how the architect created his own
cottage retreat.

Robert Swain Peabody and his wife, Annie Putnam
Peabody, purchased a preexisting cottage on Peach's
Point in 1887. According to an account written by their
son, Robert Ephraim Peabody, the cottage had been
built by Benjamin W. Crowninshield in the late 1870s
for his widowed mother, Mrs. Francis B. Crowninshield,
but it was soon enhanced to accommodate the Peabody family. Son Robert Ephraim Peabody noted, "My
father . . . an architect, kept adding new rooms to the
house over the years until it gradually became twice as
large as originally."[77]

The Peabody cottage is a ramble of a house—the
old and new elements fit together like mismatched
jigsaw puzzle pieces, and yet the composition works

wonderfully. Understandably, there are no extant
building documents for the Peabody cottage, so it is
hard to know which additions came first and which
later. Rooms and porches were apparently added as
they were needed; the total effect is of a charming,
eclectic, and homey cottage. On the first floor the old
house opens out into a large Peabody-designed family room with a vaulted ceiling and a fireplace wall.
Each of the windows features a leaded-glass insert of
a pseudo-Viking vessel, perhaps an idea left over from
the building of Vinland. Outside, over the door to the
addition, a ship's figurehead of Tamerlain greeted
guests—it was one of a sizable collection of figureheads amassed by Robert Peabody that otherwise
were displayed in the walled garden next to Castle
Joyous, the playhouse he designed for the children.
These figureheads were later donated to the Peabody
Essex Museum in Salem, where several can be seen
on the walls of East India Marine Hall.

Several years after Peabody's death, the Peabody
cottage was sold to Mr. Thomas Hill Shepard. Robert E.
Peabody purchased land on Beacon Street in 1928 and
built a cottage for his own family, not far from where
he had summered since he was four months old. The
Shepard family used the Peabody cottage until the
late 1960s, when it was sold to the current owners.
Although Peach's Point was primarily a summer resort
until the mid-twentieth century, there are now numerous year-round residents.

The Peabody cottage is a private residence.

1.93. Tamerlain. Ship's figurehead, installed over the door of the Peabody & Stearns addition to the Peabody Cottage on Peach's Point. Courtesy of Historic New England.

The Cove

Beverly Cove, Massachusetts, 1897-98

Henry Francis Sears, 1862-1942

Emily Sears and Henry Cabot Lodge, Jr. tie[d] the knot at an event of "national interest" at the Sears home, The Cove … on July 1, 1926.

— Dorothy Wexler,
Reared in a Greenhouse [78]

The Cove overlooked the ocean at Patch Beach in Beverly. Dark shingles, deep eave overhangs, and natural fieldstone porch columns gave it a look of permanence, with no hint that it would be gone in less than fifty years.

Dr. Henry F. Sears was born in Boston, the son of David Sears III and Emily Esther Hoyt. His family members relate that he had searched for years for a summer place of escape and had bought land at various times in Topsfield, Boxford, and Ipswich;[79] the proximity of relatives in Beverly Cove is what perhaps induced him to build the cottage on a twenty-one acre site at Hale Street and Brackenbury Lane in Beverly.

Plans for The Cove indicate a gracious stone entry flanked by large planters on the north side of the house. Visitors entered a tiled vestibule and the Great Hall and were greeted with a view through the combined dining room and living rooms to the terraced lawn and the ocean beyond. Doors opened out to give access to the large open piazza that stretched across the face of the building; it was flanked by covered porches that provided a sheltered view of the water. A spacious library with large fireplace and built-in window seat was located to the right of the hall; it opened to a covered porch that included a fieldstone fireplace for cool evenings. The main staircase led upstairs from the hall, and the large mid-stair landing was illuminated by an elegant arched, leaded diamond-paned window.

Henry Sears graduated from Harvard College in 1883, and subsequently from the Harvard Medical School. He worked as a pathologist at Boston City Hospital until 1894, when he retired and devoted his life to philanthropy and his love of the outdoors. Following the death of Emily Sears, he and his brother moved to 420 Beacon Street, the large town house that Peabody & Stearns designed in 1892 for their sister. In 1904 he married Jean Struthers of Philadelphia, in a wedding ceremony in Vevey, near Lake Geneva, where the guest list included Mary Cassatt and Henry Sears's cousin Frederick Sears Grace d'Hauteville, whose Newport cottage had been designed by Peabody & Stearns in 1871. Jean's parents belonged to the newly formed Jekyll Island Club in Georgia. Henry and Jean were frequent visitors to the Struthers's Moss House at Jekyll Island and joined in 1905.

From the open-air piazza on the water side of the house, two sets of grand stairs led down to the formal

TOP
1.94. The Cove, water view. Courtesy of Henry Sears Lodge.

MIDDLE
1.95. The Cove, view of cottage and garden. Courtesy of Henry Sears Lodge.

BOTTOM
1.96. House for Dr. H. F. Sears, The Cove, elevation towards street. Peabody and Stearns Collection, courtesy of the Boston Public Library Fine Arts Department.

1.97. The Cove, stable. Courtesy of Henry Sears Lodge.

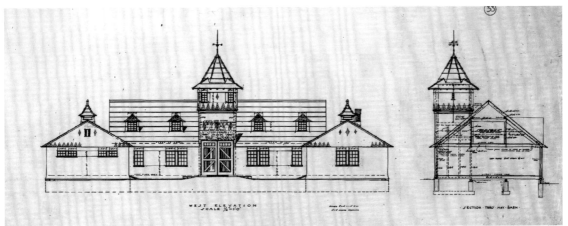

1.98. West elevation of farm barn for Dr. H. F. Sears in Topsfield, Massachusetts. Peabody and Stearns Collection, courtesy of the Boston Public Library Fine Arts Department.

1.99. House of Miss Sears, 420 Beacon Street, Boston. *American Architect and Building News,* May 20, 1899. Collection of the author.

semicircular grass terrace. These stairs were probably well used; Joseph Garland relates in *Boston's North Shore and Boston's Gold Coast* that the spacious Sears lawn was the site of "games, folk dances and 'stunts' designed to teach chicks [children under the age of six] to be 'real true sports.' " One suspects that there was much laughter mixed in with the lessons of the day.[80]

The Cove was constructed at an approximate cost of $43,000. According to the Peabody & Stearns project record card, alterations and additions continued on an almost yearly basis until 1908, including two small cottages, a new stable, and a new library. In 1901, Dr. Sears commissioned Peabody & Stearns to design his farm in nearby Topsfield. Although little documentation of the farm survives, the Boston Public Library archives include a few plans. The project record card indicates "two groups of farm buildings" in Topsfield in 1901, for a total cost of $60,245.00

The Cove was bequeathed in 1942 to the Sears' older daughter Emily and her husband, the Honorable Henry Cabot Lodge. A few years later the house was torn down. A new cottage was constructed just in front of the old building site and utilized stonework from the original piazza areas for the walls of a sunken garden. The Peabody & Stearns stables have been converted into a residence that reflects much of its original design.

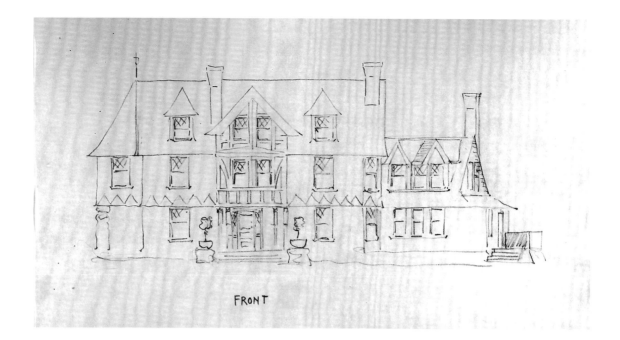

FRONT

1.101. House for
Miss Mary F. Bartlett,
architect's sketch.
Peabody and Stearns
Collection, courtesy of the
Boston Public Library Fine
Arts Department.

Bartlett Cottage

Manchester-by-the-Sea, Massachusetts, 1898

Mary F. Bartlett, n.d.
Nelson Slater Bartlett, 1848–1921

Mary F. Bartlett of Boston purchased property in the Old Neck section of Manchester at Masconomo and Sea streets in 1897. Peabody & Stearns designed a large two-and-a-half story shingled cottage for the site, with ample porches from which to view the surrounding landscape. Here Miss Mary Bartlett and her sister Fanny spent their summers, joined occasionally by their brother, Nelson, who owned property nearby on Smith's Point.

The *Manchester Cricket* reported on October 9, 1897, that Mary Bartlett had purchased the Bower estate at the corner of Masconomo Street and Old Neck Road and that the existing house and stable were to be removed. This was immediately accomplished, for the report in the October 30 paper stated that the "Bower Cottage has been moved . . . and a new residence will be built on the old site this winter."[81] Plans indicate that the cottage featured a large living hall that extended the full depth of the house and turned at a ninety-degree angle for a large stair hall. Guests entered the hall through a large covered porch and could turn right into the dining room or left into the cozy parlor with its corner fireplace and opposing built-in corner seat. The parlor

opened into the large library, which also had a fireplace; from there one could step out onto an uncovered piazza that ran nearly the length of the library, or to a smaller covered piazza with wood floor and built-in seat. Beyond the dining room, the service wing included the requisite china pantry, kitchen, and servant's dining room. On the second floor, four bedrooms and two baths amply accommodated the Bartlett sisters, along with two bedrooms and a separate bath for the servants. The attic was comprised of two chambers and a bath, a maid's room, a sewing room, and a trunk room. Total cost for the cottage was $18,598.29, with later alterations that included a bay window. A photograph in the 1912 Directory of the North Shore pictures the house with a few changes from the original elevation, with the circular drive and mature plantings presenting a totally appealing view.

The Misses Bartlett resided in Boston during the winter, in a Back Bay townhouse designed by Peabody & Stearns in 1884, commissioned by their brother, Nelson S. Bartlett. Both Mary and Nelson may have contributed to the cost of the town house, as the property record card indicates that Mary paid $23,660.04 in August of 1884; a confusing entry indicates that Nelson paid $45,633.72 for the "orig house." In 1893, Nelson had been staying in "The Brown Cottage on Sea Street," but two years later he purchased a cottage from the Merrill family on Smith's Point that had been constructed in 1880 as a summer rental. Peabody & Stearns designed a stable for Bartlett in 1899, and it was presumably for this property.

The Bartlett cottage is a private residence.

1.102. House for Miss Mary F. Bartlett, south elevation. Peabody and Stearns Collection, courtesy of the Boston Public Library Fine Arts Department.

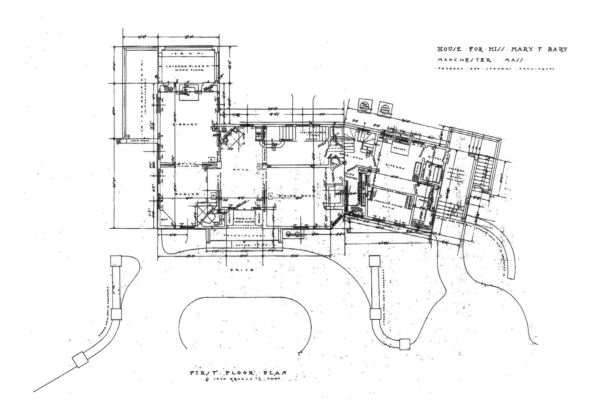

HOUSE FOR MISS MARY F BART
MANCHESTER MASS
PEABODY AND STEARNS ARCHITECTS

FIRST FLOOR PLAN
¼ INCH EQUALS 1 FOOT

1.103. House for Miss Mary F. Bartlett, first floor plan. Peabody and Stearns Collection, courtesy of the Boston Public Library Fine Arts Department.

Cochrane Cottage
Manchester-by-the-Sea, Massachusetts, 1902

Colonel Hugh Cochrane, 1848–1904

The Cochrane Cottage is a fine, formal clap-boarded cottage overlooking Singing Beach in Manchester-by-the-Sea. Colonel Hugh Cochrane purchased land at Cobb Avenue and the beach from Mary Cobb in 1899 and 1901, on a spur of land next to the Cobb homestead. Shortly thereafter, Peabody & Stearns prepared the design for Cochrane's cottage, and local builders Roberts & Hoare began construction. The cottage was completed and occupied in the summer of 1902, but Cochrane used the residence for only two summers—he died of stomach complications at his residence at the Hotel Tudor in Boston in January 1904.

The plans were drawn for a two-and-a-half-story four-square, hip-roofed residence, with a decorative widow's walk at the peak. Windows are six-over-ones throughout; a notation on the plans dated January 31, 1901, indicates, "Mr. Cochrane said leave the glass as drawn and specified, i.e. plate in large lights . . . ,"[82] thus providing excellent views from the interior spaces. The east elevation of the cottage faced the water view and featured a deep covered piazza with a full open deck above. A formal entrance porch on the west elevation was graced with a semicircular porch supported by columns and topped with a Colonial Revival balustrade. An imposing tripartite arched top window was centered over the front door, and provided light and formality to the main staircase, located just inside. Guests were admitted to a vestibule and then into the hall. A spacious reception room was located to the left; from there guests might enter the large den, which was lighted by a spacious bay window facing Cobb Avenue and heated with a large fireplace opposite. The formal covered piazza that faced the view of Singing Beach opened off of both the den and the adjoining dining room. A small service wing was located at the west elevation of the cottage and contained a kitchen, a china closet, and ample back porches. The second floor included four chambers, one with dressing room, and two baths; an additional chamber and servants' accommodations of four bedrooms and bath were located on the third floor. Records indicate that the cottage was built at a cost of $21,241.05.

Hugh Cochrane was born in Scotland, but his family moved to Billerica, Massachusetts, shortly thereafter. Both Hugh and his older brother Alexander worked in the family chemical business. Alexander had a summer cottage on the North Shore—his Queen Anne-style summer residence, designed by William Ralph Emerson, was built in Prides Crossing in 1881. It is to be pre-

1.105. House for Hugh
Cochrane, first floor plan.
Peabody and Stearns Collection,
courtesy of the Boston Public Library
Fine Arts Department.

1.106. House for Hugh
Cochrane, west elevation.
Peabody and Stearns Collection,
courtesy of the Boston Public Library
Fine Arts Department.

1.107. House for Hugh
Cochrane, east elevation.
Peabody and Stearns Collection,
courtesy of the Boston Public Library
Fine Arts Department.

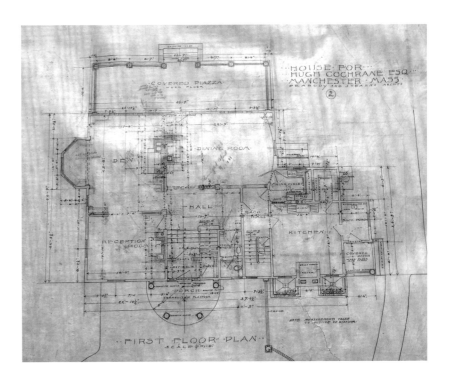

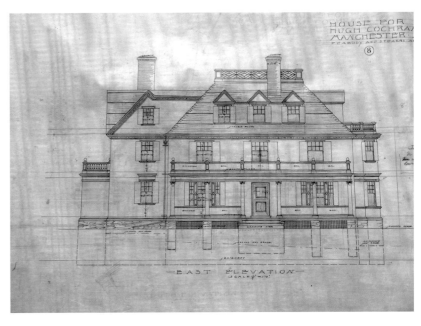

sumed that the colonel began to visit the North Shore at this point. The colonel and his wife had one daughter, Nellie (Eleanor M.), who married Richard Dudley Sears (a cousin of Dr. Henry Sears, whose summer cottage, the Cove, was located in nearby Beverly) in 1891 in what the *New York Times* called "a blue-blood wedding in Trinity Church. . . . Dr. Brooks officiated."[83] At about this time it was noted in the *Boston Daily News* that Colonel Hugh Cochrane of Boston had become "a familiar figure on the streets" of Manchester. He became active in the yachting community—he was a member of the New York Yacht Club and the local but prestigious Eastern Yacht Club—and had several custom yachts built during the 1880s and 1890s. Cochrane was also a member of the Essex Country Club, the Algonquin Club, the Union Club, the Country Club, the Papyrus Club, the Boston Athletic Association, and the Exchange Clubs, all in Boston.

Colonel Cochrane's cottage was featured in the 1910 edition of *Who's Who Along the North Shore*. Following his death, the cottage passed to his daughter, Mrs. Eleanor M. Sears, who sold it in 1906. The residence still stands, in remarkably original condition, although a few dormers have been added over the years, and almost all of the decorative balustrades have been removed.

The Cochrane Cottage is a private residence.

NORTH EAST ELEVATION
SCALE ¼" = 1 FOOT

1.108. House for Dr. R.
H. Fitz, The Mountain,
northeast elevation.
Peabody and Stearns
Collection, courtesy of the
Boston Public Library Fine
Arts Department.

The Mountain (Bartol's Mountain)

Manchester-by-the-Sea, Massachusetts, 1903

Dr. Reginald Heber Fitz, 1843-1913

Beautifully situated among the trees on the "Mountain,"
on the West Manchester Road is the picturesque new
residence of Dr. R. H. Fitz of Boston, which has also been
completed this winter. Set on the crest of the hill, it commands a fine view of the ocean, and the broad piazzas in
the rear suggest an enhancing view of the country back.
The house is built in the Queen Anne style. It is reached
from the main road by a winding avenue. At the base of the
knoll, in the rear, is the stable, which has accommodations
for 6 horses.

— *North Shore Breeze*, May 21, 1904 [84]

It is noteworthy that Dr. Fitz, his wife (the former
Elizabeth Loring Clarke), and the Mountain were a
frequent topic of interest in the pages of the *North
Shore Breeze*. Dr. Fitz was a renowned Boston pathologist who is credited with the discovery of appendicitis.
Born in Chelsea, Massachusetts, and educated at the
Chauncy Hall School and at Harvard College (B.A.,
1864; M.D., 1868), he was known internationally for
his research, writings, and abilities as a lecturer.

Dr. Fitz purchased a cottage in Beverly in 1874, above
the west end of West Beach. After he sold that property
to Henry H. Moore, he purchased property in 1902 on
Norton Mountain in Manchester from Elizabeth Bartol
(hence the alternate name Bartol's Mountain). He then
commissioned Peabody & Stearns to design his Queen
Anne–style cottage and stable for the hilltop site. High
ceilings and generous room dimensions distinguish the

1.109. House for Dr. R. H. Fitz, The Mountain, southeast elevation. Peabody and Stearns Collection, courtesy of the Boston Public Library Fine Arts Department.

Mountain's interior. The main level included a parlor, a den, and a dining room, the last of which was to be fitted out with buffet, fireplace, and bookcase, all in white wood. Service areas included kitchen, pantry, servant's dining room, china closet, and dedicated flower room. On the second floor was Dr. and Mrs. Fitz's bedchamber, along with rooms for their son, two daughters, a guest chamber, three baths, and servants' rooms: six bedrooms, a bath, and a sewing room. The accompanying stable building measured a roomy 50 by 50 feet and included a large stable area, carriage house, harness room, and seven stalls. On the second level were a man's room, workroom, bathroom, and grain bin. The buildings were constructed by the local firm of Roberts & Hoare, for a sum of approximately $40,000.

The 1912 Directory for West Manchester indicates that Dr. Fitz's winter residence was 18 Arlington Street in Boston. He was a close friend of Francis Greene (Green Acres, 1902), whose bequests of "a selection" of "horses, carriages, harnesses, paintings, silver and plate, ornaments, furniture and personal articles to his friends Dr. Reginald H. Fitz of Boston and Charles B. Barnes of Brookline"[85] indicate the network of his Boston connections with the firm of Peabody & Stearns.

The Mountain is a private residence.

Massachusetts

The Berkshire Hills

Of Newport, of Bar Harbor, of the North Shore, and of
Lenox, the last is the only one without the sea, and this,
of course, is the chief characteristic in which it differs
from the others...."

— GEORGE A. HIBBARD, "Lenox,"
Scribner's Magazine, October 1894

Merrywood

Lenox, Massachusetts, 1882

Charles Bullard, 1857–1911

The annual outing and field day of the Berkshire Historical
and Scientific Society was held in Lenox on the north
shore of Stockbridge Bowl on Thursday, Aug. 2 [1900]. The
gathering was on the land of Charles Bullard of Boston in
a fine grove of maples, beneath the high slope on which
stood, until 1890, the "Little Red House," where Nathaniel
Hawthorne lived and wrote from 1850 to 1852.

— *New York Times*, August 5, 1900

Merrywood was a charming Colonial Revival
cottage set on a fifteen-acre site with views
of Rattlesnake Mountain and the Stockbridge
Bowl. Renderings of the original façade and plans suggest a cottage more in keeping with the nearly contemporaneous Charles William Eliot cottage in Northeast
Harbor, Maine (Blueberry Ledge, 1881) (see fig. 1.172)
than the larger Queen Anne structures that Peabody
& Stearns was designing in Lenox at about the same

time for Charles Lanier (Allen Winden) or John Barnes
(Coldbrook). This similarity is not surprising: owner
Charles Bullard probably had more in common with
the Cambridge academics in Northeast Harbor than
with the captains of industry in New York and Lenox.
His mother, Louisa Norton Bullard, was a sister of
Charles Eliot Norton. His father, William Storey Bullard,
had been an East India merchant in Boston, and had
summered both at nearby Highwood in Lenox (built in
1846, but altered by Peabody & Stearns in 1899–1900)
and on North Haven Island, Maine. Charles attended
the Bussey Institute in Jamaica Plain, which had been
established by Harvard University with the bequest of
Benjamin Bussey for instruction in agriculture, horticulture, and related subjects.[86]

Many comparisons can be made between Blueberry
Ledge and Merrywood in terms of general massing,
rooflines, and Colonial Revival detailing. Both residences
have the additive qualities of early homes: a two-story
main core with a gambrel roof was supported by an
addition with a long sloping shed roof. Multiple dormers punctuated the shingled roof, and a few important
details are complementary—the broken-arch pediment
above the adapted Queen Anne stair tower, a rejected

1.110. Merrywood,
entrance façade. Courtesy
of The Berkshire Eagle.

Palladian window, a hooded roof sheltering a second-
floor window. Bullard's cottage had an uncomplicated
floor plan like Eliot's, although slightly larger. The main
entrance in both cases was a wide Dutch door leading
into the hall. Merrywood had a small hall that opened
into the parlor and a separate dining room; while Eliot's
cottage had just a living hall and dining room, the use of
space was similarly simplified. The service wing set at an
angle on Bullard's Lenox residence provided a servant's
room in addition to the large kitchen and related pantry
and china-closet areas.

Merrywood was completed in 1882. Bullard was by
all reports a loner, perhaps considered to be somewhat
eccentric, and he moved to his cottage as a full-time
resident in 1884. He lived there for the remainder of
his life. Following his death in 1911, Merrywood was
sold; it was eventually purchased by Clark Voorhees
(1871–1937), an American Impressionist painter, who
added two wings to the house and with his wife and
family used Merrywood as a summer cottage for many
years. Later use as a summer camp again changed the
look and floor plan of Merrywood. The original structure survives, however, as a residence.

Merrywood is privately owned.

Allen Winden

Lenox, Massachusetts, 1882

Charles Lanier, 1837-1926

The gardens here were bright with summer flowering
plants and the groups of coniferous trees were especially
interesting.

— *Massachusetts Horticultural Society,* 1913

Allen Winden, the massive, eclectic cottage
designed by Robert Peabody for Charles Lanier
in 1881, was the firm's first major commission
in Lenox. It appeared as one of a number of transitional
designs in which Peabody explored the vocabularies of
summer architecture, linking and layering a confluence
of Queen Anne, Tudor, and Colonial Revival elements.

Charles Lanier was, like many of his fellow cottagers, intricately involved with both banking and the
development of the railroads in the United States. He
entered the family banking establishment in 1859 and
never left it until the time of his death. He was a business associate and good friend of J. Pierpont Morgan,
who reportedly stayed with the Laniers when visiting
Lenox, despite the fact that his sister Sarah and her
husband, George Halle Morgan, owned nearby Ventfort
Hall. Lanier was a member of Morgan's exclusive Corsair Club, and was a founding member and president
(1897-1913) of the Jekyll Island Club. He socialized
with many other Peabody & Stearns clients, including
Pierre Lorillard (the Breakers at Newport), and Mr. and
Mrs. Carlos M. De Heredia, who later lived in the nearby
Peabody & Stearns–designed Wheatleigh. Lanier was

the president of the Pittsburgh, Fort Wayne & Chicago
Railway, as well as the Massillon & Cleveland Railroad;
he was a trustee of the Central Union Trust Company
and a director of the Southern Railway. He belonged
to the Metropolitan, Union League and Knickerbocker
clubs, and was a member of the New York Yacht Club.

Unlike many of his financial peers, Charles Lanier
had an impressive ancestral genealogy in addition to
his business accomplishments, claiming kinship with
no less than George Washington. This, combined with
his success in business and his reputation as a gentleman, most certainly recommended him to Miss Sarah
Egleston of Lenox, to whom Lanier was married in the
late 1850s. Her family introduced Lanier and his father,
James, to what would become prime resort home sites
for the Gilded Age. James Lanier purchased several
properties in Lenox, including the two-hundred-acre
parcel on which Allen Winden was constructed beginning in 1881.

Robert Peabody and landscape architect Ernest
Bowditch sited Allen Winden on the top of the windy
knoll that inspired the cottage's name. A report by a
committee of the Massachusetts Horticultural Society
that visited Allen Winden in 1913 commented favorably
on the "extensive views of the noble Taconic range of
mountains across the intervening valley."[87] The cottage
was constructed of brick, shingles, and half-timbering, in an eclectic mix. The brick stepped gable on the
northern, entrance façade drew visitors into the ivy-
covered porte-cochere, the second story of which was
a porch framed by Japanese-inspired latticework and a
bonnet-topped gable with urn decoration—for all the
world looking as if a massive Colonial-era highboy had
been perched atop the porte-cochere roof. This struc-

ture was balanced by a double Queen Anne shingled gable that sloped downward to a recognizable shed-style roof. On the lawn façade, two half-timbered gables on the west end transitioned back to a simpler duo of shingled dormer and gable. First- and second-story piazzas and balconies abounded in order to take in the magnificence of the view. The activity and variety of the façades at Allen Winden are reminiscent of the slightly earlier Newport Breakers; the later addition of the Tudor-influenced gables reflected the tastes of many of the Lenox cottagers. The original construction of the cottage in 1881 cost just under $30,000. Peabody & Stearns was called back to Allen Winden on numerous occasions for alterations and additions, including a cow barn that was built across the Old Stockbridge Road in 1888 as part of a larger farm complex; the ensuing additions and alterations for the house alone totaled $70,000. Charles Lanier also commissioned the firm to design an addition to his town home at 30 East 37th Street in New York City in 1895-96 and to design the choir room at Trinity Church in Lenox (1899).

The interiors of Allen Winden were designed by Richard Codman. During this same period of time Codman was working on the interior at Catherine Lorillard Wolfe's Arts and Crafts–inspired cottage, Vinland, in Newport, R.I. He later assisted the William Sloanes in the decorating of Elm Court in Lenox.

Peabody & Stearns's first major commission to be built in Lenox was the first to be demolished. Several years after Lanier's death, the property was divided and the "windy" site on the Old Stockbridge Road was sold. The Henry Seaver–designed Georgian-style brick dwelling that replaced Allen Winden is now part of a condominium complex.

Coldbrook

Lenox, Massachusetts, 1882

John Sanford Barnes, 1836–1911

On the Lee road, Captain John S. Barnes, United States navy, of New York, has his "Coldbrook Farm." He built the house in 1882, and added thereto in 1885.

— *The Book of Berkshire* [88]

John Sanford Barnes seems an unusual client for Peabody & Stearns in Lenox. He was a naval officer during the Civil War, an accomplished naval historian, an avid collector of Revolutionary War and War of 1812 naval memorabilia, and the author of an autobiography entitled *My Egotistigraphy*. He was also, however, an attorney and a knowledgeable railroad businessman, and many of his friends and social contacts (Joseph Choate and Morris Jesup among them) summered in Lenox. Lenox was far removed from the oceanfront resort that we might anticipate for him because of his sailing background, but it was close to Springfield, Massachusetts, where he grew up.

Coldbrook was designed and constructed at the same time as Charles Lanier's nearby Allen Winden. The view from Beecher's Hill was of sloping lawns, neighboring farmland, and in the distance, Laurel Lake. Coldbrook began as a large shingled cottage, similar in many respects to Allen Winden. Long and low, its asymmetrical façade and rooflines presented a pleasing picturesque massing. Across the garden façade, a long covered porch provided access to the view and to Ernest Bowditch's landscaping. Colonial Revival details abound—a broken pediment above the porch door is topped by a narrow central gable with a Palladianesque window and sculpted relief work in the gable pediment. Later remodelings added fan motifs above the windows, a large two-story rounded tower with turret roof, and a sizeable service wing. On the façade, an ivy-covered porte-cochere greeted guests, with a shaped gable, second-story decks, and gallery railings to add to the eclectic mood of the cottage. Inside, a large living hall with fireplace opened into the music room and library complex, and later a sunken reception room with imaginative curved stairs and railing framing the large Colonial brick fireplace. The boxed stair to

the left of the entrance is enclosed by a screen composed of turned staircase ballisters with elliptical cutouts. The dining room, pantry, and kitchen areas completed the original first-floor plan.

John Sanford Barnes was born in 1836 at West Point, New York, where his father, James Barnes, was an instructor at the military academy. His family moved to Springfield, Massachusetts, where John attended school at the Springfield Public High School. He was a member of the first graduating class of the newly reorganized United States Naval Academy, Annapolis, and sailed the Atlantic and the Caribbean for seven years. After serving in the Civil War, he worked at the investment firm of J. S. Kennedy & Company and in 1880 purchased his own seat on the New York Stock Exchange. He commissioned Peabody & Stearns to design a business building for him at 18 Wall Street in 1883.

Barnes retired from business in the early 1900s to pursue his interests in naval history and collecting. He edited and published two books—*The Logs of the Serapis-Alliance-Ariel, Under the Command of John Paul Jones, 1779-1780*, and *Fanning's Narrative; being the Memoirs of Nathaniel Fanning, an*

Officer of the Revolutionary Navy, 1778-1783—in addition to writing the article "With Lincoln from Washington to Richmond in 1865," which recounted his experiences escorting President Lincoln to Richmond immediately after that city's surrender, and which appeared in *Appleton's Magazine* in May and June of 1907.

Barnes married Susan Bainbridge Hayes in 1863. She was the granddaughter of Commodore William Bainbridge of "Old Ironsides" fame; when her brother, Captain Richard Somers Hayes, died in 1905, many of the commodore's memorabilia, including a pair of pistols presented to Commodore John Barry by John Paul Jones, were added to Barnes's already sizable collections.[89] These collections of books, manuscripts, and memorabilia would later constitute the collection of the Naval History Society, which John Barnes founded in 1909.

Coldbrook was owned by members of the Barnes family until the 1920s, when it was purchased along with John Sloane's Wyndhurst for use as the Berkshire Hunt and Country Club. It later served as St. Joseph's Hall for the Cranwell School, and is now Beecher's Hall, part of the Cranwell Resort, Spa, and Golf Club.

1.116. Coldbrook, garden view. *Lenox*, East Lee, Massachusetts, 1886. E.A. Morley, photographer.

1.117. Elm Court, garden view before expansions. *Lenox*, East Lee, Massachusetts, 1886. E.A. Morley, photographer.

Elm Court

Lenox, Massachusetts, 1887–1900

William Douglas Sloane, 1844–1915
Emily Thorn Vanderbilt Sloane, 1852–1946

Most visitors at Lenox, Massachusetts, consider Mr. William D. Sloane's magnificent new villa the most important architectural attraction of the place.

— GEORGE SHELDON, *Artistic Country-Seats* [90]

Elm Court was a veritable "moving target" of a country house for many years. From the time of its conception in 1885 until Emily Vanderbilt Sloane White's death at Elm Court in 1946, this cottage underwent multiple additions and alterations, at a cost of hundreds of thousands of dollars. What began as a "modest" country cottage for Mr. and Mrs. William D. Sloane and their young family topped out at ninety-four rooms in 1900 and was called the largest Shingle Style house in America. In 1887 when George Sheldon inventoried Elm Court, there were a mere eleven upstairs bedrooms plus a first-floor guest room, a main hall that he considered to be the most comfortable "sitting room . . . on this side of the Atlantic," a library, a dining room, a drawing room, a billiards room, and seemingly endless service rooms (including thirteen servant's bedrooms). Despite its size, however, the house retained its sense of domestic scale, thanks to the careful, though eclectic, design of Robert Peabody.

William Douglas Sloane was born in New York City, the son of a Scottish carpet weaver who emigrated to the United States and founded the William Sloane Company in 1843 to sell carpets; in 1852 his brother, John, joined as a partner and the firm changed its name to W. & J. Sloane. Their firm was extremely successful and expanded numerous times to include furniture and other interior furnishings in several United States locations. At William's death in 1879, his sons, William Douglas, John (Wyndhurst, Lenox) and Henry T. (Dupee-Sloane Cottage, Islesboro, Maine)—took over the partnership and continued its successful operation providing carpets and interior decoration to patrons in the United States and abroad.

Elm Court was remarkable before its many expansions. Its original Shingle Style exterior was a mixture of Colonial Revival features—gambrel roof, overhanging gables, bay windows and decorative details—all incongruously constructed on a white marble foundation, which was locally quarried and therefore an inexpensive building material. Sheldon noted that even the barn foundations were made of marble. The shingles were painted in the signature Vanderbilt maroon, highlighted with a yellowy orange trim. Repetitions of details visually tied the various façades and later additions together—the plan, although basically an L shape, is difficult to discern from the exterior. Entrance from the circular main drive was made through the porte-cochere into the spacious main living hall. Although it was trimmed with painted pine (as were many of the rooms), its magnificent carved brownstone fireplace dominated the entrance and set the tone for the rest of the house. The leather-covered walls of the library were trimmed with cherry woodwork and a painted frieze, while the dining room's quartered oak trim made it a sumptuous place to dine.

The Sloanes spent winters in their elegant residence at No. 642 Fifth Avenue and summers at Lenox, with spring or autumn trips to Europe and other destinations. A reading of daughter Florence Adele Sloane's diary for 1893 gives a taste of their schedule. She arrived at Elm Court on June 4, and spent the next month riding, driving, and walking, both alone and with a variety of visitors. On July 14 she traveled to the Adirondack Mountains to spend ten days at her Uncle Seward Webb's camp Pine Tree Point; July 23–30, she was at Elm Court, then the family was off to Bar Harbor for two weeks, with time in Newport, Rhode Island, and in Beverly on the North Shore of Massachusetts with friends and family. She returned to Lenox for September and October, and then traveled to New York for November and presumably the beginning of the winter season there.

Location and landscaping of the estate was of great importance to Elm Court, which was named for the massive elm tree that was located on the property. George Sheldon described the setting: "It has, besides, an unusually commanding site on the slope of a hill, with a noble view of the Stockbridge Bowl and the surrounding mountains." The landscaping for Elm Court was planned by the Olmsted firm; in a letter dated September 21, 1886, J. C. Olmsted wrote to Mr. Sloane that he had given Mr. Peabody a plan showing "where the farm buildings should be located." A later landscape sketch contained the remark to "keep bldg less than 20` ± to keep view of mountains & valley open." Over 900 acres were gathered into the estate at one point. In addition to 40 acres of manicured lawns, the property included 23 greenhouses (covering 2 acres of property), capable of producing the 700 roses and

250 carnations a week that might be required by the Sloanes in either their Lenox or their New York home. In 1910 the property was divided—a large parcel, High Lawn Farm, was given to the Sloanes' daughter Lila and her husband, W. B. Osgood Field. Later, under the stewardship of the Fields' daughter Marjorie and her husband, Colonel H. George Wilde, the farm was developed into the largest Jersey-breeding enterprise in the Northeast.

Elm Court's *first* "fifteen minutes of fame" came in 1919 when Emily Sloane and her second husband, Ambassador Henry White, were hosts to delegates for the Elm Court Talks armistice meetings, which resulted in the treaty of Versailles. However, following Mrs. White's demise in 1946, the property foundered. Her daughter and her daughter's husband, the Wildes, operated a seasonal inn in the historic villa for a period of several years, which coincided with the beginning operations of Tanglewood, the summer home of the Boston Symphony Orchestra. Their attempts to maintain the cottage failed, however, and Elm Court descended into ignominy for four decades. In 1998, the great-grandson of the original owners and his wife rescued the property, and for the grand old building's *second* moments of fame, the cottage was repaired, restored, and refurnished, filmed all the while for Bob Vila's television show *Home Again*. Now painted a creamy white that blends with the original stonework, the property was reborn as a beautiful bed and breakfast, reclaiming the grandeur of the old rooms with many pieces of family furnishings and restoring many aspects of the original landscaping.

Elm Court remains in private ownership. It is listed in the National Register of Historic Places.

1.118. Elm Court, view from lawns after several expansions. From the Collections of the Library of Congress (LC-D4-72958).

Wheatleigh

Stockbridge, Massachusetts, 1893

Henry Harvey Cook, 1822-1905
Carlos M. and Georgia de Heredia

I am thinking of making a purchase of several acres of land near Lenox with a view of improving it. Before doing so, I would like to be informed whether or not it has all the requisites for making a fine place.

— HENRY H. COOK to FREDERICK LAW OLMSTED,
October 11, 1892[91]

1.123. Wheatleigh, garden view. Postcard, collection of the author.

FACING PAGE
1.124. Wheatleigh, courtyard. Courtesy of Memorial Library, Boston Architectural College.

1.125. Wheatleigh, side view. Courtesy of Memorial Library, Boston Architectural College.

Henry H. Cook subsequently bought the two-hundred-acre Gideon Smith farm in Stockbridge; with the guidance of the Olmsted landscape firm and architects Peabody & Stearns, he built Wheatleigh at the top of the hill facing south over lawns and gardens and the shoreline of Lake Mahkeenac (Stockbridge Bowl). Olmsted designed a terraced formal garden to the east of the house, as well as a more informal rock garden. These gardens, plus the farm buildings and actively cultivated fields that surrounded the property, created an appropriate setting for the splendid Italian villa that the Cooks and later their daughter and son-in-law Georgia and Count de Heredia enjoyed for over fifty years.

Wheatleigh is an obvious deviation from the usual Shingle Style, Colonial Revival, and Queen Anne designs that are generally associated with Peabody & Stearns; indeed, it was reported by the *New York Times* in 1894 to be "different in many respects from any in Lenox."[92] It appeared as if an Italian villa had been transported to western Massachusetts—that this was the intention of the architects is suggested by the sketched terracotta details in the *American Architect and Building News* of April 1902, which were isolated and arranged on the page as if they were archeological fragments (fig 1.126) Years later, Robert Peabody would remark that there was nothing unusual in the idea that a "rich American" might find a model in the buildings of ancient Rome, for adaptation to modern uses.[93] When

the *American Architect and Building News* published views of Wheatleigh in 1902, it included the five different sketches for Wheatleigh that had been under consideration for the Cook's cottage—each a different style, such as English country house, French château, Scottish baronial, and Italian villa.[94] Many years later, an article published in the *Springfield Republican* documented that although "slight tentative sketches in various styles were made when this house was first talked of . . . all . . . agreed that the broad surfaces and horizontal lines found in an Italian villa were best suited to the beautiful rolling country and the shore of the lake where the house was to be placed."[95]

Wheatleigh was constructed of cream-colored brick with exterior moldings and detailing of light-colored terra-cotta. On the garden side the two-story hip-roofed central block anchored what appear to be two symmetrical connected tower buildings. Arched windows and Ionic columns dominated the façade. Twin classically pedimented porticos extended out onto the piazza, which stepped down to the lawn and toward the lake. Entry was made from a winding driveway that passed through two large gateposts and on into a formal circular courtyard with marble fountain. An ornate glass and iron canopy was flanked by the service wing on one side and by a smaller, columned pavilion and summerhouse on the other. Visitors entered the main hall, which stretched through the building to the piazza and the striking view of the Stockbridge Bowl. The hall bisected an open plan of reception rooms; living room, library, and dining rooms with decorative wooden ceilings and intricately carved beams were stretched across the garden façade. Two matched Tiffany windows adorned the staircase. The mood was grand, but simple, and was certainly influenced by the villas that Peabody had seen while abroad for several months in 1892. The main villa was constructed at a cost of $165,000; the extensive farm building complex, lodge, and pump house brought Cook's expenditure for Wheatleigh to over $237,000. A fountain, balcony, and water tower were later added in 1899.

Henry Harvey Cook was born in Bath, New York, the son of a judge. He married Mary E. McKay, also of Bath; one of their daughters, Georgia, inherited Wheatleigh and entertained there for many years. Cook was a merchant and bank president, but became truly wealthy only after he moved to New York City in 1875 to become involved in railroad construction and the financial backing of that industry, as well as "other enterprises."[96] It has been suggested that the Cooks planned Wheatleigh as a gift for their daughter, who married a Cuban aristocrat, Carlos M. de Heredia; this is perhaps borne out by the de Heredias' involvement in the planning process of the villa. Henry Cook soon divided his time between Wheatleigh and his home in Manhattan, which he shared with his wife, his daughter and her husband, and a staff of eleven. He died at Wheatleigh in October of 1905, after four years of ill health.

1.126. Terra cotta details from Wheatleigh. *The American Architect and Building News*, April 5, 1902. Courtesy of the Boston Public Library Fine Arts Department.

The de Heredias were active in the Lenox social scene, and the society columns frequently carried notices of dinners, balls, and entertainments held by them at Wheatleigh. The farms and gardens of Wheatleigh also made the news—the de Heredias hosted the Massachusetts Horticultural Society on its visit to Lenox in 1913 and were the recipients of many prizes in the Lenox Horticultural Society's flower and vegetable competitions.

Wheatleigh's gatehouses are now private homes, and the farm buildings have been adapted for condominium residences. The main villa was purchased in 1981 and renovated in 1997 as a member hotel within the organization of Small Luxury Hotels of the World.

1.127. Five tentative sketches for Wheatleigh. *The American Architect and Building News*, April 5, 1902. Courtesy of the Boston Public Library, Fine Arts Department.

Wyndhurst

Lenox, Massachusetts, 1893

John D. Sloane, 1834–1905

The English manor-house of the time of Henry VIII is revived in its purest and most abstract form; incongruous additions are taken away, inharmonious excesses are toned down. If in this process, the picturesque, the playful, and the unexpected are all too much ignored, and the resulting buildings are somewhat cold and lack interest, that result is one which might have been looked for.
— RUSSELL STURGIS, 1896 [97]

Wyndhurst, the castellated Tudor cottage built for mega-merchant John D. Sloane, was not the largest or the most lavish of the Lenox cottages, but it was frequently featured in articles about Lenox written during the cottage era, including *Munsey's Magazine, Boston Daily Globe, American Architect and Builders News,* and *Country Life in America.* It was sited on the top of Beecher Hill, named for its most celebrated property owner, Henry Ward Beecher. Beecher's cottage, Blos-

som Hill, had been moved from its site in 1869 by General John F. Rathbone, a prosperous stovemaker from Albany, who built his own residence atop the hill. This was the first Wyndhurst. When John Sloane purchased the property in 1893, Robert Peabody and Charles Eliot of the Olmsted firm both advised him to demolish Rathbone's cottage to make way for the new Wyndhurst. Construction began in 1893; in May of 1894 the *New York Times* reported that more than one hundred men were at work on the mansion, and it was completed in the fall of that year. The grounds of Wyndhurst were variously reported to have comprised between 200 and 350 acres, and included a forty-acre English lawn and garden as well as a full complement of Peabody & Stearns-designed Shingle Style farm buildings constructed the year after the main house was completed.

The entire cottage was constructed of mottled ochre Perth Amboy bricks, each approximately one foot long, trimmed with cast stone arched windows and doors, which produced a smooth, simplified façade. The main house measured in excess of two hundred feet long by seventy-five feet wide (a footprint of over fifteen thousand square feet). The two-story crenellated tower was

1.128. Wyndhurst, porte-cochère. Courtesy of Memorial Library, Boston Architectural College.

Residence of J. W. Sloane, Lenox, Mass.

1.129. Wyndhurst, side view. Postcard, collection of the author.

1.130. John Sloane's garden. Postcard, collection of the author.

a defining element of the Wyndhurst façade, appearing from a distance as a separate dominant element. According to a story in the *New York Times*, May 27, 1894, the tower offered one of the finest views in the Berkshires, reaching from the Green Mountains in Vermont to the hills of Salisbury, Connecticut and encompassing five New England states.

The Great Hall of Wyndhurst was entered from the porte cochere on the north side of the building. The massive hall was constructed of oak with oak paneled ceilings embellished with dyed and stamped leather inserts. It was bisected by a hallway on axis, allowing circulation to the dining room, a fine music room "finished and furnished throughout in the Louis XV style,"[98] and to a conservatory that accessed the two-story billiard room in the tower. The floor plan was arranged to allow all public rooms on the main floor to be opened into one space for balls and social occasions.[99] Much of the house interior was English Renaissance in design. Rich marbles, terra cottas, and faience tiles finished the fireplace surrounds. Beam ceilings and wood-

work accentuated the general theme. The Sloanes, however, requested that the dining room be "white in [the] Colonial Style with cornice and a stucco wreath ceiling, like [the] Hancock House."[100] Evidently, they could not resist the temptation to reference the great Chicago World's Columbian Exposition, which was running concurrently with the construction of their cottage, and the Peabody & Stearns-designed Massachusetts State Building, which was based on the famed John Hancock House of Boston. The entire residence was illuminated by electricity provided by a plant in nearby Lee (a reference in Peabody's diary in August 1893 noted that if Barnes [his neighbor at Coldbrook] could get electric lights, then no gas would be desired at Sloane's. Wyndhurst was completed for a breathtaking $185,728 in 1894. The next year, the Sloanes spent an additional $46,000 for their Peabody & Stearns-designed farm buildings.

The Sloane family fortune was somewhat remarkable in that it was derived not from railroads or banking, but from merchandizing. John D. Sloane was born

1.131. Wyndhurst,
garden front, c. 1899.
*American Architect and
Building News*, December 25,
1899, no. 1252. Collection of
the author.

in Edinburgh, Scotland and came to the United States with his family in 1853. The carpet store that his father established in New York flourished, and grew into the carpet, furniture, and design firm of W. & J. Sloane Company, which Sloane later ran with his younger brothers, William Douglas Sloane (Elm Court, Lenox) and Henry T. Sloane (Dupee-Sloane House, Islesboro, Maine). Despite the fact that the Sloanes were considered by some of the New York 400 to be of a slightly questionable status (they were, after all, "in retail"), they were fully accepted in many of the same pastimes. Sloane was a director of a number of financial institutions and was a member of the Metropolitan, Union League, Century, and New York Yacht Clubs, as well as a member of the prestigious Jekyll Island Club. In May of 1898 the *New York Times* reported that the popular French painter Carolus-Duran was at Wyndhurst while Mrs. Adela Sloane and her daughter Evelyn each sat for their portraits. One June 4th the *Times* further reported that Carolus-Duran was still in Lenox, where he was working on portraits of the younger daughters of William D.

Sloane, and that it was probable that he would spend the summer in Newport, where he had been urged to paint several portraits.

While the Sloane cottage was certainly the setting for many elaborate dinner parties, perhaps the most widely reported was in September of 1897 when Mr. and Mrs. Sloane hosted President and Mrs. McKinley for dinner and a reception. Decorations for the event were decidedly patriotic. Strings of red, white, and blue electric lights illuminated the grounds and a massive mechanized American Eagle constructed of hundreds of American Beauty roses adorned the dining table.[101] Other local Peabody & Stearns clients were listed among the dinner guests.

Wyndhurst was sold by the Sloane family following Mrs. Sloane's death in 1911. It served as the Berkshire Hunt and Country Club for a short time in the 1930s, and later was the home of the Cranwell School for Boys. Today, the Cranwell Resort Spa and Golf Club occupies Wyndhurst, as well as the neighboring Barnes cottage, Coldbrooke.

Massachusetts

Cape Cod and the South Shore

Forbes Cottage

Naushon Island, Massachusetts, 1871

William Hathaway Forbes, 1840-1897

We began the house March 1—finished cellar April 1 and the house was completed and ready for occupation June 30. the architects were Peabody & Stearns and the Builder Barker of Boston....

— William H. Forbes Journal, 1871 [102]

Peabody & Stearns designed a wood-frame cottage for William Hathaway Forbes very early in the firm's career—at the same time that it was working on the Matthews cottage in Newport, Rhode Island. Forbes's father, John Murray Forbes, had purchased Naushon Island as a summer retreat in 1842 with a business associate, William W. Swain. It is the largest of the Elizabeth Islands located just southwest of Cape Cod and northwest of Martha's Vineyard, and so close to Woods Hole that William Forbes was prompted to write to his father in January of 1871: "... the result was that we fixed upon the Harbor Hill as the only practicable place ... although Bob and all were charmed with the Weepeckit Bay—the smell from the Guano works at the Harbour nearly took the roof of my head off—"[103] William was eager to get the project underway, and in the same letter indicated that "Bob [Peabody] & Stearns are to give us sketches at once."

The cottage was built on the ridge to the west of Hadley Harbor, angled "so that the south west wind will blow, not square on the end but will bear somewhat on the south face of the house."[104] There the family spent sixteen summers. A sketch of the east elevation in the collection of the Forbes family shows a simple two-story cottage with a deep porch surrounding the first floor. One French window and one smaller window open out onto the covered space; the columns supporting the porch roof are simply edge-chamfered and undecorated. The only bit of whimsy in the drawing is a lightly penciled oriel window located on the second floor. A letter from Robert Peabody to William Forbes dated July 12, 1871, indicates that the house was completed and that the accounts were tallied and ready for Forbes's approval. The total billing was slightly higher than Peabody had originally estimated—they had thought that "$12,000 would cover the house but ... it cost $12,182.85 + the cellar." Peabody adds, "I hope you will find the house just so much better than you had expected...."[105]

In 1885, Forbes and his wife, Edith Emerson Forbes (daughter of the writer Ralph Waldo Emerson), decided to replace the wood-framed cottage with a larger one built of stones from the property, designed by architect W. Ralph Emerson and constructed and heated for cold-weather use. The Peabody & Stearns–designed cottage was partially dismantled in the spring of 1886, part was moved for use as a boardinghouse for the construction crew. The stone house was built on the original site.[106]

Naushon Island is currently owned by the Naushon Island Trust and continues to be the summer haven of the Forbes families.

Tanglewood

Falmouth, Massachusetts, 1878

James Arthur Beebe, 1846–1914

Travellers were attracted by the many beautiful shore resorts at Woods Holl, Falmouth Heights, Quissett, Menauhant, and other localities within the town limits, and began to build summer homes, so that now some of the most beautiful and elegant summer residences in southeastern Massachusetts are found scattered about the town. Prominent among them are "Tanglewood," the fine summer home of M. Arthur Beebe of Boston and "Highwoods," the summer residence of the late J. M. Beebe." [*sic*]

> — *The Celebration of the 200th Anniversary of the Incorporation of the Town of Falmouth* [107]

1.132. Tanglewood, side view. From E. G. Perry's *A Trip Around Buzzards Bay Shores*, 1976, p. 358. Collection of the author.

In tennis circles J. Arthur Beebe is best known as the first importer of the game of lawn tennis to the United States. Legend has it that Beebe gave a boxed set of *sphairistike* (lawn tennis racquets) to his father-in-law, William Appleton. Fred Sears and James Dwight discovered it at Appleton's summer house in Nahant and played the first games on the lawn there in 1874.[108]

However, in Falmouth, Massachusetts, Beebe is known as the son of one of the founders of the summer colony in that town, James Madison Beebe (1809–1875), who came to Falmouth in 1872 with his wife Esther and purchased a summer residence. They continued to buy property and become more involved in town affairs. St. Barnabas Church was dedicated by the Beebe family in 1890 to James and Esther Beebe.

J. Arthur Beebe commissioned Peabody & Stearns to design his summer cottage, Tanglewood, in 1878. Peabody & Stearns's property record cards indicate that the cost for the house and stable totaled $12,530.04 in 1879, with an additional $6,000 billed in 1894, and additional alterations in 1905 that totaled over $10,000. When completed, the cottage was an elegant two-and-a-half-story hip-roofed, clapboard residence in the Colonial Revival style. The main block of the house featured covered porches on either side with a large piazza that wrapped around the end of the house. An imposing double Dutch dormer dominated the façade. Formal decorative elements included a fine balustered roof balcony and Ionic pilasters at the corners and midpoint of the house. The service ell appeared as a Colonial house that had been moved and attached to the original, in a very vernacular and additive fashion. Exterior landscaping was designed by Ernest Bowditch, who later worked on the Woods Hole projects of the Fay family. Outbuildings on the property included a gate lodge, a caretaker's house, a barn, and an observation tower.

Edward Pierson Beebe (1843–1926), J. Arthur Beebe's older brother, had built a summer manor

house in Falmouth in 1876. Highfield Hall was originally a gracious Queen Anne Revival cottage but was given a two-story Greek Revival façade in the early 1950s. Although the original architect of the cottage is not known, there are many similarities that suggest that Peabody & Stearns may have been the architectural firm. The stable and carriage house complex is extant as the current Highfield Theatre, while the main house has recently undergone major restoration under the ownership of the Town of Falmouth. Property record cards indicate that E. Pierson Beebe had hired Peabody & Stearns to design an apartment house in Boston in 1882 and to remodel the St. Barnabas rectory in 1903, while J. Arthur commissioned a town house on Beacon Street (1880–81), with renovations in 1905.

J. Arthur Beebe was predeceased by his wife, Emily Appleton Beebe (d. 1912) and by two of his three children. Tanglewood was left to Harvard University at his death. Years later, it was sold, along with Highfield, to a series of owners who ran a succession of businesses, including a hotel and a health spa. When subsequent owners considered a subdivision of the land for a residential development, Josephine and Josiah K. Lilly III bought the combined properties and donated parcels to a variety of community organizations. Three hundred eighty-three acres became the present Beebe Woods, owned by the Town of Falmouth. Tanglewood and Highfield Hall with twenty-six surrounding acres were given to the Cape Cod Conservatory of Music and Arts. While Tanglewood was used for a period of time, it was ultimately demolished in 1977. Several of its outbuildings survive, including the gate lodge, which is now used as an office. The carriage house is still owned by the Cape Cod Conservatory, as is Highfield Hall, which has undergone extensive renovation.

1.133. The Larches, after remodeling. Courtesy of Woods Hole Historical Collection, Judith Lang Day, photographer.

The Larches

Woods Hole, Massachusetts, 1879

John M. Glidden, n.d.

The house ... was a fairly plain example of the Shingle Style. It sat on a hill overlooking Nobska Pond with Vineyard Sound in the distance.

— SUSAN WITZEL, "Gardeners and Caretakers of Woods Hole" [109]

The Larches was commissioned at about the same time that Peabody & Stearns was working with the Beebes and the Fays in Falmouth and Woods Hole. It was built on Long Neck, later Penzance Point, for Mr. John M. Glidden, a man with an unfortunate history in the area.

Glidden was the treasurer of the Pacific Guano Company, an enterprise that converted fish oil, nitrates, and bird guano into plant food. This process produced an objectionable odor as a by product to the fertilizer and was therefore unpopular with the neighbors. The company experienced financial difficulties and declared bankruptcy in 1889; an investigation found that while there had been "errors of fact" in the firm's accounts and annual reports, there had been "no misuse of Pacific Guano funds." [110] However, Mr. Glidden disap-

peared from Woods Hole at that time, and the Larches remained empty from that year until it was purchased in 1923 by Eugene Nims of St. Louis, Missouri.

Nims preserved the original Peabody & Stearns structure, but removed the shingles and stuccoed the exterior. This, combined with faux half-timber detailing, gave the house a distinctive English cottage feel. As the stucco aged, it took a decidedly pink cast, and the house was known locally as "the pink house." [111] Mrs. Nims was an experienced gardener and with the help of assistants transformed the abandoned landscape into a delightful country garden landscape.

Just prior to Nims's purchase of the Larches, Newcomb Carlton had purchased a five-acre parcel of the Glidden estate that included the stone water tower; this tower was the butt of many Viking jokes at the time and was a popular tourist attraction. Architect Welles Bosworth incorporated it as the entrance and stairway of the eclectic Carlton summer house, in a picturesque design that certainly would have resonated with Robert Peabody.

As a final note, the land once occupied by the Pacific Guano Company was subdivided and developed as residential properties in the 1940s, with a considerable increase in value.

The Larches is a private residence.

Edgewood

Woods Hole, Massachusetts, 1882

Joseph Story Fay, Jr., 1847–1912

Fay Farm

Alterations and Additions, 1889

Henry H. Fay, 1848–1920

Father had bought Nobska Point in 1878 and had
built a house there, . . . very ugly but Peabody and
Stearns' best."

       — *For My Children*, n.d.[112]

Joseph Story Fay, Jr., his brother Henry, and their
father, J. S. Fay, Sr., all had connections to Peabody
& Stearns. The Fay family was important in the
developing resort town of Woods Hole, and their various commissions parallel in some respects the building projects of another prominent family in nearby
Falmouth, the Beebes.

Edgewood, the Joseph Story Fay, Jr. cottage, was
constructed on a hilly lot overlooking Little Harbor.
Photographs suggest a compact shingled cottage with
a porch and piazza overlooking the water view; a picturesque square tower completed the elevation. The
cottage was built at a cost of $28,812.00. Sizable altera-
tions to the main residence in 1888 included a basement, at which time the kitchen and servants' dining
room were relocated. A new nursery and a playroom
that were added next to the old dining room suggest
that the family was growing—it then consisted of Mr.
Fay and his second wife, his two sons, and a daughter.
A handsome two-story stable constructed in 1882 contained four stalls, a carriage area, and a harness room.
The Olmsted firm served as the landscape architects
for this house, and their inventory records indicate
that Ernest W. Bowditch of 60 Devonshire Street of
Boston was the engineer and landscape gardener for
the project

Edgewood was sold out of the Fay family following
the death of their daughter, in about 1940. The house
and land was then purchased by architect E. Gunnar
Peterson in 1952, and the property was subdivided.
The land to the east of the cottage is currently the site
of the Dome restaurant, a geodesic dome designed
by Peterson and Buckminster Fuller, and the Nautilus
Motor Inn.

Edgewood is a private residence.

1.135. Edgewood, garden view. From Arnold W. Dyer's *Residential Falmouth: An 1897 Souvenir for the Sojourner Brought Up to Date*, Falmouth Historical Society, 1995, p. 61.

Joseph Story Fay, Jr.'s brother, Henry H. Fay, commissioned a summer house at the Moors in Woods Hole in 1879—the year of his father's town-house commission in Boston—but not from Peabody & Stearns. The architect of record was A. C. Martin of Boston. According to George Moses, a well-known Cape Cod newspaper columnist, Henry Fay purchased a large farm at the Moors, where he "had a sizable dairy herd of Guernsey cows grazing over all the land now occupied by gracious homes and spacious grounds."[113] Located on the land north of Nobska Light, it was originally a simple house—in Mrs. Fay's words, "without any ell and only one bathroom."[114] Job cards indicate that Peabody & Stearns was commissioned to do slight alterations to the house in 1880, and then more substantial ones in 1889, resulting in a final count of twenty-three rooms. Photographs capture a rambling shingled cottage, two-and-a-half stories, with steeply pitched roofs and hints of Stick Style detailing. A large verandah faced the water view, and a glass-enclosed room

was thrust out from the main house into the green lawn beyond. Service areas, including kitchen and servants' quarters, would have been located in the large ell that jutted off the rear of the residence. Landscaping on the property was designed by Ernest Bowditch and later in 1885 and 1886 by the firm of Frederick Law Olmsted.

Two houses, perhaps caretaker's houses, were added to the property by the firm in 1885, totaling $21,772.00. Plans for a house and water tower are dated 1900–1901. In addition to the Woods Hole properties, Peabody & Stearns designed the stable for Fay's 330 Beacon Street residence in 1888. The Henry H. Fay cottage was demolished in 1947, following the death of Mrs. Fay and the subdivision of the property among members of the family.

The Honorable Joseph Story Fay, Sr. (1812–1897) did not commission Peabody & Stearns to design his resort cottage. He was, however, a client of the firm and an

important influence in the summer retreat of Woods Hole. He was engaged in the shipping of timber and cotton in Boston and New York, as well as in the financing of whaling boats in New Bedford. Financial reversals sent him to Savannah, Georgia, in 1835 to work in his brother's cotton brokerage firm.

While it has been speculated that Fay went to Woods Hole to visit his friend John Murray Forbes (1813-1898) of Milton, who had purchased property on nearby Naushon Island in 1843, a diary entry documents that he had traveled to Woods Hole in order to take the boat to New Bedford. While waiting for the ferry, he became interested in the town and purchased his summer home there in 1850. That cottage, the Homestead, is now the Challenger House, owned by the Woods Hole Oceanographic Institution.

Fay donated the land and the funding for the construction of the Church of the Messiah in Woods Hole (1889) and gave a seventy-acre tract of land to the town of Falmouth as "Goodwill Park."

Like Newport, Rhode Island, the Falmouth area had its share of Viking history aficionados. The village at Great Harbor was alternately spelled "Woods Hole" or "Woods Holl"—the Peabody & Stearns drawings for the Fays use the latter spelling. This confusion was evidently the work of Joseph Fay, who proposed that Norsemen had visited the Cape Cod area centuries before and taught the Native Americans the term "holl," the Norse word for "hill."[115] Fay even petitioned the United States Post Office to officially change the spelling of the name of the town. Although that initiative failed, the Viking stories proliferated. The stone tower on the nearby J. M Glidden property was rumored to be a Viking tower—à la the Stone Tower of Newport—but was actually a nineteenth-century structure that held the water tanks for the Glidden household.

The senior Fay commissioned Peabody & Stearns to design his winter residence in Boston at 169 Commonwealth Avenue in 1879.

1.136. Henry Fay Cottage, Peabody & Stearns alterations and additions. From *Residential Falmouth: Homes, New and Old*, Falmouth-by-the-Sea, Massachusetts, Board of Industry, 1897, p. 40. Collection of the author.

The Stone House

Cataumet, Massachusetts, 1896-98

William Ellery Channing Eustis,

1849-1932

The house . . . was built when carpenters spent five or six years learning their trade and they received 25-50 cents an hour.

— Elmer Watson Landers,
From Pocasset to Cataumet [116]

The Eustis Mansion was reported to be the "most palatial estate" built in Scraggy Neck—an uninviting place name for a beautiful and quiet location in Cataumet, Massachusetts. It was the perfect location for a man whose main interest was yachting—an avocation that Eustis pursued until he was in his eighties.

William Ellery Channing Eustis was the grandson of General Abraham Eustis, U.S. Army, on his father's side and of religious leader William Ellery Channing on his mother's. Frederic Augustus and Mary Channing Eustis lived in Milton, Massachusetts, where young William "followed the path of the privileged boy of his day." [117] Like Robert Peabody, he attended the Dixwell School and later graduated from Harvard College (Class of 1871). Eustis received a degree in metallurgical engineering from the Lawrence Scientific School and made his fortune in the business of mining and ore smelting; a Cape Cod source referred to him as "the Copper King." Following the death of his wife, he divided his time between his home in Readville near the Blue Hills of Massachusetts, his cottage in Cataumet, and the Canaveral Club in Florida.

Eustis reportedly bought all of the land that makes up Scraggy Neck for $40,000 in 1890—approxi-

1.140. House for W. E. C. Eustis, Stone House, north elevation. Peabody and Stearns Collection, Courtesy of the Boston Public Library Fine Arts Department.

1.141. House for W. E. C. Eustis, Stone House, south elevation. Peabody and Stearns Collection, Courtesy of the Boston Public Library Fine Arts Department.

mately 382 acres with almost three miles of shore frontage. He cleared a site on the highest point of land, with a sweeping view of Pocasset Harbor, leaving an old farmhouse and barn in place. The large stone mansion that Peabody & Stearns designed was constructed of native and imported stone, both of which were also used to build the stone walls that enclosed the property. Little is known of the original landscaping of the property, other than a notation by a former caretaker that sheep were kept to maintain the grass.[118]

The understated northern elevation stretched long and low along the landscape. The first story was all stonework, while the intersecting gables and dormers on the second floor were dark shingled. A covered piazza dog-legged out from the main footprint of the house, looking north to the far end of Bassetts Island. The southern elevation was alive with intricately carved bargeboards and stonework

of outstanding quality. A two-story round tower in the center of the façade was totally stone construction, as were the walls and columns that supported the deep porch overhang. Construction was done by a local contractor, Moses Waterhouse of Bourne, who was also responsible for the nearby Parkinson house. The cottage was completed for an additional $40,000. Family members remember that there were four large bedrooms as well as six servant's chambers. The house and outbuildings—barn, boathouse, sail loft, blacksmith shop, and boat pier—were all wired for electricity, which was still something of a rarity on Cape Cod at the time; power was produced by a generator in the basement of the house.

The Stone House burned in the mid-1940s.

The Plainfield
Barn & Water Tower at Rocky Point,
1898–1900

Bourne, Massachusetts

John Parkinson, 1843–1918

When the house was built, there was only one tree on the field . . . so that the owners thought of naming the place "Single-Tree." They did name it "Plainfield."
— CHARLES W. ELIOT,
Charles Eliot, Landscape Architect [119]

The summer residence of John Parkinson at Monument Neck in Bourne commanded an impressive expanse of land overlooking the Back River from Rocky Point Road. Photographs show a long, Dutch-gabled cottage with a two-story tower, later removed when the house was extended by approximately a third of its original length. A note on the back of one photograph indicates that the house was constructed in 1898 by Moses Waterhouse of Bourne, the builder of the nearby Eustis cottage in Cataumet. Peabody & Stearns's design for this cottage is unsubstantiated, although the firm did design the small farm complex, consisting of a picturesque barn and water tower, for the property. The barn and tower are documented by a rare perspective drawing and plans in the Peabody & Stearns archives—it was perhaps this drawing that Parkinson referred to in his letter dated January 3, 1898, addressed "Dear Bob," stating that he had "received the sketch . . . and it looks very attractive" and instructing Peabody to "go ahead and build as [he] thought best." Later alterations to the cottage were designed by the firm and carried out by Waterhouse in 1905.

The Parkinson family purchased the land with an existing central-hall farmhouse built in 1825 for Captain Peter Storms, a well-known shipowner who had amassed more than three hundred acres that included Rocky Point and the area known as Gray Gables in the Monument Beach area of Bourne. Gray Gables later received national attention as the location of Grover Cleveland's summer White House. The farmhouse was certainly altered several times over the years, and Peabody & Stearns may have been involved in one of the later expansions.

The barn is a picturesque Queen Anne and Shingle Style structure with the foundation and first floor constructed of fieldstone. The upper floors of the barn are of shingle. A hooded gable and large windows face what was once the water view, providing light and breezes for the upper floor of the barn. A two-story ell intersects the barn, with a further one-story ell jutting off from that. A note in the Peabody & Stearns files for the Henry Sears farm in Topsfield indicates that in May 1912, Peabody had "a print made of Dr. Sears Hen House" for John Parkinson, suggesting that a henhouse might have been added to the Parkinson farm buildings at that time.

Landscaping of the property was done by Charles Eliot, son of Peabody's brother-in-law, Charles William Eliot. It was young Eliot's first private design commission. The property was described in his biography: "The house was already built close to the shore, and about it was a bare, wind-swept, sandy field. . . . Charles planted at various distances from the house . . . masses of small Willow, Maple, Linden, cork-barked Elm, Poplar, and sumac, with some Stone Pines; but reserved about three acres between these detached groups for an open lawn." [120]

John Parkinson was born in Jamaica Plain in 1842. In 1866 he became a founding member of the brokerage firm of Parkinson & Burr, which later located its offices in the Peabody & Stearns–designed building at 53 State Street in Boston; Parkinson was the oldest living member of the Boston Stock Exchange when he retired from banking in 1914. He and his wife Gertrude Weld (1844–1904), the cousin of Stephen Minot Weld (Indian Neck, Wareham) and the sister of Cora Weld (who married Robert Peabody's brother, Francis G. Peabody), lived at 160 Beacon Street in Boston, which they had commissioned from Peabody & Stearns in 1901.

The main cottage at the Plainfield burned in 1994; the windmill–water tower had been lost in the hurricane of 1938. The charming barn and the original farmhouse still stand and are privately owned.

1.142. View from the north. Stable and water tower for John Parkinson, Peabody & Stearns sketch. Peabody and Stearns Collection, courtesy of the Boston Public Library Fine Arts Department.

NORTH · ELEVATION
SCALE 1/8 = 1.

1.143. Barn for John Parkinson, north elevation. Peabody and Stearns Collection, courtesy of the Boston Public Library Fine Arts Department.

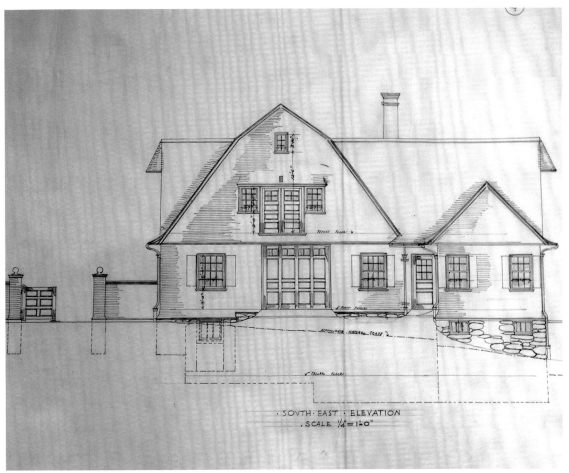

SOVTH · EAST · ELEVATION
. SCALE 1/4 = 1-0"

1.144. Stable for John Parkinson, southeast elevation. Peabody and Stearns Collection, courtesy of the Boston Public Library Fine Arts Department.

1.145. Greene Acres, street view. Courtesy of the Holy Cross Fathers.

Greene Acres

Dartmouth, Massachusetts, 1902

Francis Bunker Greene, 1844-1911

Greene Acres is one of only a few Peabody & Stearns Neo-Georgian designs intended for seasonal use. The façade is reminiscent of the John Hancock house of Boston, memorialized by Peabody & Stearns in the Massachusetts State Building at the World's Columbian Exposition in 1893, with gambrel roof, decorative balustrades, and a grand oversized two-story pedimented entrance. For this reason as well as its location in the farming community of Dartmouth, Massachusetts, Greene Acres was not a typical resort cottage. Greene and his wife spent approximately eight months a year at Green Acres, and the remaining months at their residence at 182 Beacon Street in Boston.

Francis Bunker Greene was born in New Bedford in 1844, the son of David R. Greene, a wealthy whaling mer-

chant. He graduated from Harvard University with the Class of 1865 (one year before Robert Peabody), where he was reportedly the "strong man of the class," being the first credited with lifting a ton—probably something of an exaggeration, and an accolade Greene himself doubted. After law school he returned to New Bedford, where he practiced law and business and involved himself in local politics.

Greene purchased approximately eighty acres of farmland in 1901 from his friend, neighbor, and colleague, Oliver Prescott. He then commissioned Peabody & Stearns to design a house and stable for the property. The finely detailed Neo-Georgian residence was completed the next year for the approximate cost of $66,100; the stable and a greenhouse were added later.

Greene Acres has clapboard siding and heavy corner quoining The exterior was richly detailed with dentil molding, several Palladian-style tripartite windows, and an oculus window in the pediment (later replaced by a rectangular opening window). The delicate balustrade that trimmed the lower ridge line of the gambrel roof echoed that of the Hancock House; unfortunately, it was damaged in a hurricane in later years and removed.

1.146. Greene Acres, street view. Postcard, courtesy of Marcelle Woodhouse.

Entrance was made into an enclosed vestibule and into a large hall that traversed the house to double doors and an open terrace with views of the rear of the property. A formal parlor to the left of the hall opened out to a hip-roofed piazza with stairs leading down to the lawn; the library, with its walk-in bow window, shared the piazza area and the striking views of the Paskamansett River. To the right of the hall, the formal dining room mirrored the parlor. Unlike the Massachusetts State Building, whose auxiliary spaces were constructed behind the main block of the house, the service wing of Greene Acres stepped back from the front façade and stretched along to the north. It included a china closet, pantry, and kitchen, and a large coat closet, a storeroom, and the servants' dining room in the rear, plus a laundry and drying room.

In addition to Greene Acres, the Greenes also commissioned Peabody & Stearns to design a monument at Mount Auburn Cemetery and a memorial window for the Arlington Street Church (1908), which was executed under the supervision of Louis Comfort Tiffany.

On their honeymoon in Cairo the Greenes stayed at Giza in a large tent decorated with colorful appliqués. They brought the tent home with them, and years later it was used as a playhouse by their neighbors' children. When Francis Greene died, the tent was donated to the Semitic Museum of Harvard University, where it is set up every year for commencement festivities. His will also included a large gift to Radcliffe College, and the bequest of a selection of Greene's "horses, carriages, harnesses, paintings, silver and plate, ornaments, furniture and personal articles" to his friends Dr. Reginald H. Fitz of Boston and Charles B. Barnes of Brookline, both Peabody & Stearns clients.

Dr. Holder Crary Kirby purchased Greene Acres in 1914 for use as a health clinic. He sold it in 1934 to the order of Our Lady of Holy Cross as a seminary and residence for the Eastern Mission Band. With this acquisition the Eastern Province of the Holy Cross Community was established; it later expanded to its current location in North Easton, Massachusetts. The order currently uses the main house as a retirement home for priests, while the stable has been renovated for use as a chapel.

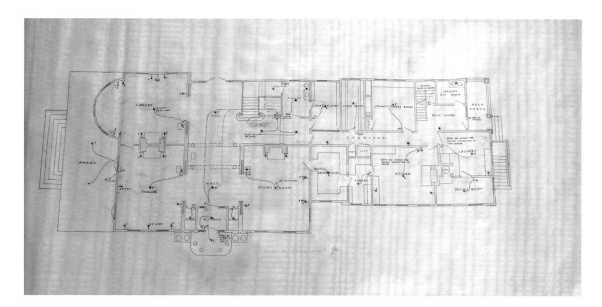

1.147. House for Francis
B. Greene, Greene Acres,
first floor plan. Peabody
and Stearns Collection,
courtesy of the Boston Public
Library Fine Arts Department.

1.148. House for Francis
B. Greene, Greene Acres,
front elevation. Peabody
and Stearns Collection,
courtesy of the Boston Public
Library Fine Arts Department.

1.149. House for Francis
B. Greene, Greene Acres,
rear elevation. Peabody
and Stearns Collection,
courtesy of the Boston Public
Library Fine Arts Department.

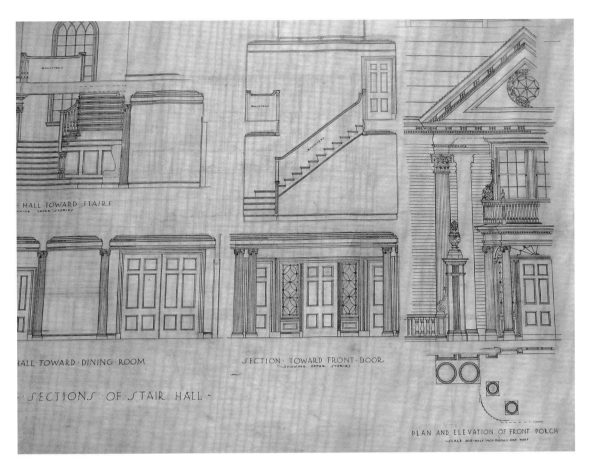

HALL TOWARD STAIRS

HALL TOWARD DINING ROOM

SECTION TOWARD FRONT DOOR

SECTIONS OF STAIR HALL

PLAN AND ELEVATION OF FRONT PORCH

1.150. House for Francis B. Greene, Greene Acres, details and cross sections of stair halls. Peabody and Stearns Collection, courtesy of the Boston Public Library Fine Arts Department.

SOUTH ELEVATION

1.151. House for Francis B. Greene, Green Acres, stable, south elevation. Peabody and Stearns Collection, courtesy of the Boston Public Library Fine Arts Department.

1.152. Cliff Beach Bath House, sunbathers at Jetties Beach, Nantucket Island. Courtesy of the Nantucket Historical Association (F6427).

Cliff Beach Bathhouse

Nantucket, Massachusetts, 1904

Clifford Folger, n.d.

There is comparatively little of the ostentation and display characteristic of most fashionable summer resorts to be found here, and the social life is quite simple and unaffected, though many of the regular cottage colony are people of wealth and social standing.

— William F. Macy, *The Story of Old Nantucket* [121]

A newspaper article dated May 14, 1904, in the collection of the Nantucket Historical Association describes the plans for a "fine public bathing place" that was under construction for Clifford Folger of South Framingham at the Cliff Bathing Beach on Nantucket. The article was accompanied by a sketch for "Casino and Bath-Houses" signed by "Peabody and Stearns, Archts." The reporter describes the project as consisting of a main building or casino, constructed of North Carolina pine, with hard pine floors, two stories, measuring about 40 by 20 feet, with a large covered piazza on the water side of the building. The first floor of the building contained an office and a counter where soft drinks and snacks could be purchased, as well as a sitting area that could be used by all visitors, "whether patrons for bathing or not." The second floor contained four apartments to be occupied by the janitor and his family.

Three hundred changing rooms divided between two wings (one for men and one for women) were accessed through the main casino building. Each section consisted of two rows of rooms facing a double aisle, and a room containing three showers, toilet stalls and lavatories, and "all the up-to-date accessories of a modern bathing pavilion." Bathing suit rentals were available at the bathhouse, and facilities were provided for patrons to care for their own suits, or to have the management care for them "free of expense."

The bathhouse was built upon property owned by the town of Nantucket and leased to the proprietors of the bathhouses. The Peabody & Stearns property record cards indicate that the Nantucket bathhouse for Mr. Folger was constructed in 1904 for a total cost of $5,263.30.

With this project, Clifford Folger became involved in the hospitality industry on Nantucket Island for a number of years. In addition to the bathhouses, that same year he commissioned Peabody & Stearns to plan unspecified alterations for the Sea Cliff Inn (1887, by architect Robert H. Slade), where he served as treasurer. Three years later, in May of 1907, Folger and William D. Carpenter purchased the Sea Cliff Inn, which they continued to own and operate through good times and bad. In 1933, the property was repossessed and sold to a new owner, John O. Wilson of Bourne, Massachusetts.[122] The inn continued in operation, with at least one additional owner, until 1972, when it was razed in order to develop the land into building lots.

Folger sold the Cliff Beach Bath House in May 1924 to Leon Royal, who had won the bid for the beach property lease from the town. The Cliff Beach Bathhouse is extant and was recently the subject of intensive research by the University of Florida's Preservation Institute: Nantucket. The building is open to the public.

1.153. Cliff Beach Bath House, bathing suits behind the bath houses, Jetties Beach, Nantucket Island. Courtesy of the Nantucket Historical Association (P12535).

1.154. Cliff Beach Bath House. Postcard, courtesy of the Nantucket Historical Association (P17902).

· DIRECT · ELEVATION · OF · NEW · PORTION ·
SCALE 1/4"=1'-0'

Indian Neck

East House, 1904
A Farmer's Cottage, 1905
West House, 1918

Wareham, Massachusetts

Stephen Minot Weld, Jr., 1842–1920

Indian Neck is a large spit of land across the Narrows from the center of Wareham. The fact that Wareham's town motto "Nepinnae Kekit" is the Wampanoag term for "summer home" suggests that the Native Americans had discovered the area as a summer retreat long before the influx of visitors from Boston in the late 1800s.

Families from Boston began buying property in the Wareham area after the Civil War. According to family history, the Codmans came to Wareham in 1872. The entire family (without maids) would move down to Wareham from Boston just after July 4 and stay until the first week of September, living a simplified and carefree lifestyle. When friends of the Codmans came to visit, "one by one they too succumbed to the charm of the Bay." Stephen Minot Weld is one of the friends listed—he purchased "land a little further West."[123]

This Codman recollection agrees with the Weld family lore, which states that in 1881, Weld and his cousin William Minot purchased property at Indian Neck in Wareham; the parcel became a summer family compound, with six separate houses. Weld built a house that he shared with his wife Eloise Rodman Weld until her death in 1898. He constructed a private eighteen-hole golf course on the property in order to indulge his love of the sport, which was reported to be "the pastime of the smart set of Boston today.... it is no exaggeration to say that today thousands of golf players maybe found in New England."[124] After Eloise died, Weld married Susan Edith Waterbury, former governess to his younger sons.

Like many of Peabody & Stearns's clients, Weld was a Harvard graduate. Not "just" a Harvard graduate, though, but one of the so-called "Welds of Harvard Yard."[125] He was the son of Stephen Minot Weld, for whom Weld Hall at Harvard was named. His cousin, George Walker Weld, donated the funds to build the Weld Boathouse, a Peabody & Stearns design. His cousin, Cora Weld, as mentioned earlier, married Francis Peabody. The connections are extensive. Weld joined the Army of the

Potomac while in law school and earned the rank of brigadier general; thereafter he was referred to as "the General" by the members of his family.

There were a variety of structures on the Indian Neck property. One of Wareham's original residences dating to the late 1700s, the Bourne Cottage, had been rebuilt on the land. Indian Neck house was the first Weld residence, which was followed by East House and West House, along with a series of outbuildings—the Farmer's Cottage, Cove House, a gardener's cottage, the hunter's cottage, the gamekeeper's cottage, and finally, Cannon Cottage. Of these, three were designed by Peabody & Stearns.

East House

Weld constructed East House from 1904 to 1906 for his second wife, Susan Edith Waterbury. Erected on a large lot overlooking Buzzards Bay, the cottage was clad in wood shingles over a stone foundation. The two-story, L-shaped residence supported a gable roof and a cross-gable bay at the intersection of the wings. A verandah (now enclosed) stretched across the water façade of the house, and ended in an octagonal room at the west end (known to family members as the Pagoda), a famil-

iar motif in Peabody's cottages of the time. The end gables were heavily decorated.

Visitors entered a spacious stairhall with fireplace placed on a diagonal. A double doorway led to the living room; the woodwork was adorned with a carved heart design, perhaps to commemorate the fact that it was built for Weld's new wife. A large dining room with fireplace could be accessed from either the living room or the hall; the kitchen and service rooms were located off the dining room in a small ell.

One year after East House was completed, Peabody & Stearns was commissioned to design a porte-cochere with a formal bedchamber above. This was completed with two dormers and an oriole window, and was always referred to as the "Coolidge Room" in honor of a friend who had helped Weld out of financial difficulties.

Formal gardens on the west side of the house were designed with the help of landscape architect Martha Brookes Hutcheson (1871–1959), one of the first professionally trained American women landscape architects. A family member remembers the gardens:

> The garden was shielded from the strong salty prevailing southwest wind by a high cement block wall

1.156. East House.
Courtesy of Kitty Benton.

1.157. East House, wedding in rose garden. Courtesy of Kitty Benton.

1.158. East House, fountain. Courtesy of Kitty Benton.

masked by fir trees. The upper level garden were beds of fragrance—heliotrope, fuchsia, daphne, phlox, sweet William, miniature carnations and mimosa—arranged in patterns separated by green paths radiating out from a fountain with a slim bronze statue of a young nude girl contemplating a butterfly on her arm. The lower level contained a formal rose garden. . . . .[together] they required a full-time gardener and two subordinates.[126]

When the General died in 1920, Susan Waterbury Weld inherited East House. She continued to use the house until her own death in 1960, at which time it passed to Weld's only surviving son, Philip Balch Weld. East House has changed hands several times since, and remains a private residence.

Farmer's Cottage, 1905

While the country houses and summer cottages of the Peabody & Stearns clientele are the principle focus of this book, the farm buildings and auxiliary buildings such as this cottage are another interesting study and in many cases provide a simplification of the design genre of their larger neighbors.

The Farmer's Cottage was built in the same year as the Coolidge addition to East House, for the man who

1.159. West House.
Courtesy of Kitty Benton.

tended the cows, mowed the hay, and performed other similar farm duties on the land. It is a snug, shingle-sided cottage with picturesque detailing and diamond-paned windows. A recessed porch opened into the stair hall. Pocket doors led the visitor to the left into a small parlor and then to the octagonally shaped living room. Alternatively, from the hall one might enter the dining room. There is no indication of fireplaces in the rooms, although there are flues and chimneys, suggesting that freestanding stoves must have been used to heat the rooms. A china closet opened off of the dining room, but unlike cottages where service staff would have been employed to carry meals from the kitchen through a butler's pantry and/or china closet, it was merely a storage area. The kitchen opened off the hallway separating the living room and dining room, and had room for a range, a large farm sink with drain board, and a walk-in pantry. The back hall had room for a refrigerator-ice box, and attached to the back porch were plans for the "earth closet," or privy.

West House, 1918

General Weld commissioned this cottage for his family and friends to occupy when they visited. Both Robert Peabody and his partner, John Stearns, had died during the previous year, so the commission would have been completed by their successor firm, Appleton & Stearns. The property abutted that of East House, and had an equally compelling waterfront view. The cottage itself was much simpler—in floor plan and in construction. It had a plain shingle exterior, highlighted by a Richardsonian arch that enclosed the doorway from the street entrance. The first floor contained a large kitchen, a dining room, and a living room in a linear floor plan, to provide all rooms with ocean views and breezes. Interior walls and woodwork were originally dark rustic paneling, but later this paneling was painted white. Upstairs a series of bedchambers stretched along the water side of the cottage, each opening off of a common corridor. On the third floor, built-in storage lined one side of the hall, and a series of small storage and service rooms lined the other.

The property that Weld purchased and developed as a family compound survives intact and is a rare example of such a property in today's landscape. Family members and later owners have placed the meadow that abuts most of the properties into a land trust, preserving the beauty and tranquility of this area of Indian Neck for future generations. East House, West House and the Farmer's Cottage are all private residences.

Cottage and Stable

Duxbury, Massachusetts, 1905–6

William Hill Young, 1867–1960

William Hill Young's cottage commissions straddled the transition of Peabody & Stearns to Appleton & Stearns. Financial records indicate a house and stable at King Caesar and Russell roads in Duxbury in 1905 and 1906, with alterations and additions done by W. Cornell Appleton and Frank A. Stearns in the years 1919 to 1922.

Duxbury's history followed that of many other towns along the southern coast of Massachusetts. It was first a farming community that then became a prosperous shipbuilding port. An economic decline in the 1850s was reversed in the 1870s when Duxbury was discovered as a resort town—the Duxbury & Cohasset Railroad brougvht visitors from Boston for $1.50 for a round trip, and boardinghouses and summer cottages were built. Because Young also owned a residence in Brookline, we assume that the house on King Caesar Road was used as a summer cottage. He was involved in the community, though, as he served as treasurer of the Duxbury Free Library, and of the Duxbury Beach Association. His hobby during the winter months was the building and rigging of model boats—perhaps a way of keeping his summer interests alive all year long.

According to the plan, the original house was approximately 42 feet across the front by 30 feet deep, with an ell to the rear. A piazza ran across the full front façade. The façade was simply styled, with a hipped roof. Windows were six-over-two and a simple railing outlined the piazza. The pedimented one-story entrance featured a large fifteen-light door with two large sidelights, recessed 7 feet into the volume of the house. Entry was made into a large hall with a coat closet and stairs to the second floor along the back wall. A modest living room (16 by 18 feet) with fireplace was to the right of the hall, with a chamber behind. A similar-sized dining room to the left of the hall was connected to the kitchen and shed ell by a large china closet and pantry with built-ins. A back stairway connected the service areas with the upstairs chambers. Cost of construction of the cottage was approximately $6,700, with an additional $1,000 for the stable, while the alterations in 1919 totaled $8,500.

Young was a graduate of Roxbury Latin High School and a member of the Harvard University Class of 1892. After graduation he was employed as a real estate officer in the firm of W. B. P. Weeks, and later worked in the office of trustees handling investments.

No photographs of the William Hill Young cottage are known to survive and its existence is uncertain.

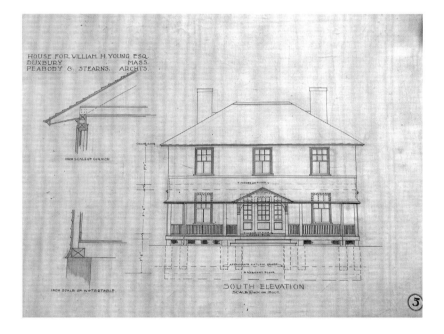

1.160. House for William H. Young, first floor plan. Peabody and Stearns Collection, courtesy of the Boston Public Library Fine Arts Department.

1.161. House for William H. Young, south elevation. Peabody and Stearns Collection, courtesy of the Boston Public Library Fine Arts Department.

Cottage and Garage

Hull, Massachusetts, 1914

James Ripley Hooper, 1855-1934

Little is known about the Peabody & Stearns commission in the town of Hull, located on the narrow Nantasket Peninsula jutting out into Massachusetts Bay at the entrance to Boston Harbor.

James Ripley Hooper was president of the National Bank of Boston and the New England Trust Company. He and his wife, Gertrude Williams, had a permanent residence at 478 Beacon Street in Boston, and built a summer cottage and garage in Hull in 1914. Drawings in the Peabody & Stearns archives show a modest cottage with a covered entrance on the gable end of the cottage. A bay window and two triple double-hung six-over-nine windows separated by a rose arbor, along with eyebrow windows in the roof, gave the street elevation a country cottage appearance.

The location and condition of the Hooper cottage are unknown.

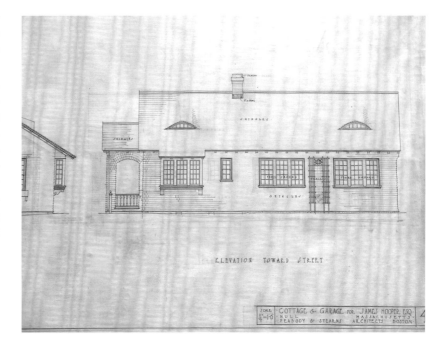

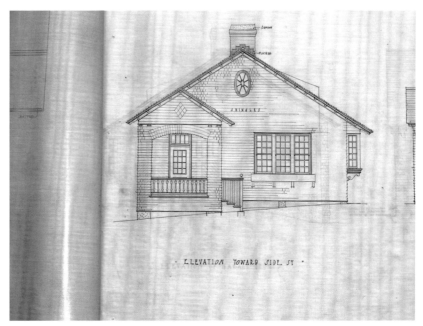

1.162. Cottage and garage for James Hooper, elevation toward street. Peabody and Stearns Collection, courtesy of the Boston Public Library Fine Arts Department.

1.163. Cottage and garage for James Hooper, elevation toward side street. Peabody and Stearns Collection, courtesy of the Boston Public Library Fine Arts Department.

Massachusetts

Other Locales

Holbrook Hall

Newton Centre, Massachusetts, 1875

William Sumner Appleton, Jr., 1840–1903

This estate covers 340 acres, bounded for a long distance by the Charles River, and beautifully diversified with wide lawns, sequestered glens, and bits of forest. The house is a spacious Gothic building, on a broad and sunny upland, with park-like surroundings of great symmetry and grace.

— Moses Foster Sweetser,
King's Handbook of Newton [127]

Holbrook Hall was located in Oak Hill, an area of Newton Centre that consisted of open fields and farmland. Appleton's country house was the earliest of three large estates constructed in the locale; guidebook author Moses Sweetser described it as a "baronial domain." Appleton and his wife (Edith Stuart Appleton) resided at 39 Beacon Street in Boston and built Holbrook Hall as a country estate four years after their marriage.

Holbrook Hall represents a transitional design. An early photograph features a large, boxy country house with the curved and carved detailing of the Stick Style type—it can be compared in many ways to the Nathan Matthews and Francis D'Hauteville cottages in Newport, which Peabody & Stearns had completed only a couple of years earlier. Large windows, coupled with the elevation of the house at 125 feet above sea level, provided superb views of the surrounding landscape. The estate was "set near a beautiful little pond named for Appleton's brother-in-law, Henry Wadsworth Longfellow and surrounded by green lawns, meadow, and woodlands."[128]

Holbrook Hall's floor plan reflected the influence of the burgeoning interest in the Queen Anne styling in the prominence of the living hall. Entrance to the house was through double doors from the front verandah, into the large living hall that bisected the house. A large fireplace warmed the area in the winter, while the cross ventilation between the front and rear doors and the shade of the verandahs cooled the house in the summer. Large French windows with quatrefoil-design stained-glass detailing allowed access to the verandahs from the dining room, the morning room, and the painted-pine parlor, all located to the right of

the living hall and all providing public spaces for the Appletons. To the left of the hall, a large ash-finish dining room with an octagonal sitting room welcomed dinner guests. Mr. Appleton's study and billiards room were located to the rear of the house. The billiards room featured a round clerestoried roof area above the center of the room that would have provided exceptional light above the billiards table, and a charming glow at night from the outside of the house. Many of the rooms included built-in details such as window seats and a recessed sideboard in the dining room and window seats and bookcases in the library.

On the second floor the plan provided four chambers with dressing rooms, plus an additional chamber, a bedroom (a smaller-sized chamber), one bathroom, and a nursery suite consisting of bedroom, bathroom, and large playroom. The attic included three "chambers for guests," seven additional chambers, one maid's chamber, a servants' hall, and linen and storage closets. Storage areas included a 16-by-22-foot wine room and a large root cellar. All in all, Holbrook Hall comprised approximately 4,000 square feet per floor—or almost 12,000 square feet of living space. The Peabody & Stearns job card indicates that the cost of construction in 1875 was $30,181.12.

William Sumner Appleton was the son of Nathan Appleton (1779–1861), a Boston businessman and politician whose wealth was derived from the textile business, and his second wife, Harriot Coffin Sumner. His older stepsiblings included Thomas Gold Appleton (1812–84), and Frances "Fanny" Appleton, the wife of poet Henry Wadsworth Longfellow—it was a family with many connections in the Boston community. Appleton's own son, William Sumner Appleton, Jr., was the founder of the Society for the Preservation of New England Antiquities in Boston, which has been a significant force in the regional and the national preservation movements since its inception in 1910. Now known as Historic New England, it is the custodian of thirty-seven historic houses as well as collections containing over 100,000 objects and an archive cataloging 1,000,000 photos, prints and engravings, architectural drawings, books, manuscripts, and ephemera.

Holbrook Hall was demolished to make way for the residence of Robert Gould Shaw II, a cousin of the Civil War hero. The property was acquired by Mount Ida College in 1939.

1.164. Holbrook Hall.
Courtesy of Historic New
England.

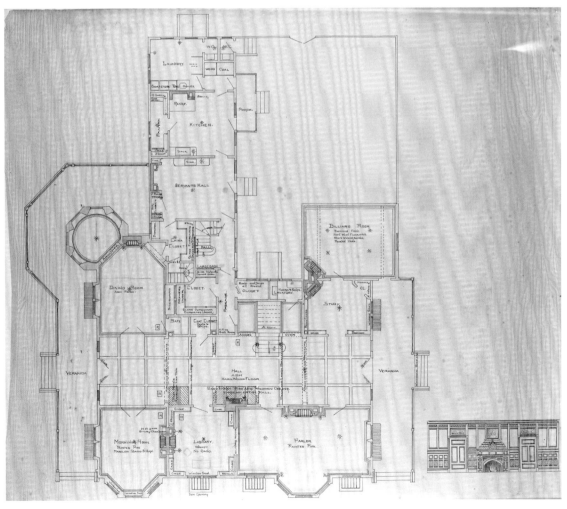

1.165. Holbrook Hall,
first floor plan. Courtesy
of Historic New England.

Battle Lawn

Concord, Massachusetts, 1878

Colonel Edwin Shepard Barrett, 1833-1898

At this time [1877] he bought a lot of land,
near the North Bridge, and built a very fine mansion
on the very battlefield of April 19, 1775,
calling the estate "Battle Lawn."
— FRANCIS H. BROWN, M.D.
"Edwin Shepard Barrett" [129]

Edwin Shepard Barrett was the great-great-grand-son of Colonel James Barrett, the commander of the Colonial troops at the historic battle at the North Bridge in Concord.[130] Edwin Barrett was intense in his interest in our country's historical heritage and belonged to numerous societies, including the Society of Mayflower Descendants, the Society of Colonial Wars, and served as president of the Massachusetts Society of the Sons of the American Revolution. So, when the hillside property that commemorated the battle at the North Bridge became available, he purchased it as his personal commemorative site and as the site of his Pea-body & Stearns–designed Queen Anne cottage. In addi-tion to Battle Lawn, Barrett built a stable and a small cottage on the property, and erected a stone marker noting the roles of his ancestors Colonel James Barrett and Captain Nathan Barrett on April 19, 1775.

Plans for Battle Lawn have not survived in the Pea-body & Stearns archives. However, three "Preliminary Sketches for a Country House" were published in the *American Architect and Building News* in November 1878, with the notation that the "house for E. S. Barrett, Esq., Concord, Mass. Messrs. Peabody & Stearns, Archi-tects," was being built "in the main like the large sketch . . . ,"[131] thus documenting the firm's role in its design. The country house had brick and wood siding, with stylized Tudor detailing in the multiple gables and dor-mers of the design. An oriel window with stained-glass detailing marked the stair hall. On the interior, Barrett incorporated an oak post from the old North Bridge into the dining room mantel. Lines from Emerson's "Concord Hymn" were carved alongside a decorative frieze.[132] Peabody & Stearns's design for the exterior might have been considered lackluster at the time, causing the author of a manuscript in the Concord Library to remark that Battle Lawn was "disappointing" on the outside; however, he hastened to add that the interior was "the handsomest in town."[133]

Edwin Barrett was born at his old family home-stead in Concord, where he attended school. He was employed in the leather business in Boston and later in a brokerage house in New York City. He had an interest in the Concord artillery unit that served in the Civil War and was an observer of the battle of Bull Run; his firsthand account of that battle was widely published during his lifetime. Barrett died in December 1898 following a fall from a window of his country house. The Battle Lawn property was sold and the house was substantially remodeled under the direction of Frank Chouteau Brown, staff architect for the Society for the Preservation of New England Antiquities and chief of the Massachusetts division of the Historic American Buildings Survey. Battle Lawn was torn down in 1953. Several years later the property overlooking the North Bridge was incorporated into the Minute Man National Historical Park.

1.166. Battle Lawn, street view. Courtesy of Concord Free Public Library.

1.167. House for E. S. Barrett: Preliminary Sketches for a Country House. *American Architect and Building News*, November 23, 1878, vol. 4, no. 152, p. 172. Courtesy of the Frances Loeb Library, Graduate School of Design, Harvard University.

1.168. Acorn Hill, street view. Photograph by Sarah Lawrence Brooks. Courtesy of Massachusetts Historical Society.

1.169. Acorn Hill, view of garden and pond from Acorn Hill. Photograph by Sarah Lawrence Brooks. Courtesy of Massachusetts Historical Society.

Acorn Hill/Brooks Manor

West Medford, Massachusetts, 1880

Shepherd Brooks, 1837–1922

He had . . . a beautiful estate in the western part of Medford, where he indulged his tastes for rural life and raised extensive crops of the highest quality. The Brooks estate was one of the show places of Medford, and was famed throughout the East.

— *New England Historical and Genealogical Register*, 1915 [134]

Acorn Hill was constructed by Shepherd Brooks on property that his family had owned in Medford since the late seventeenth century. His brother, Peter Chardon Brooks III had constructed his summer home, Point of Rocks (designed by Calvert Vaux) on the highest point of the same property in 1859; Shepherd created his own vistas by excavating Brooks Pond between 1884–1889, and sculpting a landscape view for his summer estate out of the surrounding countryside.

Although Acorn Hill is constructed of red brick in a Queen Anne style that had quickly become associated with the firm of Peabody & Stearns, it is difficult to find other cottages to compare to it. The core of the house is a two-and-a-half story hip-roofed structure, extended and enhanced on each façade by eclectic and picturesque detailing. The main façade, or east elevation, is dominated by the three-story projecting bay and attached porte-cochere. The west elevation features a two-story porch, and faced the vista across Brooks's property to his brother's estate. Steep chimneys, classical details, and assymetrical massing did indeed make the manor house one of the "show places of Medford." The exterior was detailed with brownstone sills and dark green windows and trim, while the granite for the

1.170. Acorn Hill, sketch of front façade. *American Architect and Building News*, July 17, 1877. Courtesy of the Frances Loeb Library, Graduate School of Design, Harvard University.

foundation was retrieved from the historic Middlesex Canal. The accompanying one-story carriage house was sympathetically styled, with a hip roof and eclectic details.

Inside, the floorplan was arranged around a broad central hall that runs the width of the house and contains a handsome carved butternut staircase. To the left, the parlor and library faced the southern exposure, while the dining room, an office, and the kitchen were located across the hall. Four large chambers on the second floor, three with dressing rooms, provided bedrooms for the family. Servant's chambers and storage areas were located above the kitchen and on the third floor.

Shepherd Brooks died in 1922, and although his wife, Clara Gardner Brooks, attempted to preserve Acorn Hill and the Brooks Manor Estate through the creation of a nature preserve, her death in 1939 left it unprotected. The property was sold to the city of Medford in 1942, and the house was used for a variety of residential purposes for forty years, with decreasing amounts of maintenance and supervision. Even though the house was nominated for inclusion in the National Register of Historic Places in 1975, the property continued to deteriorate. In 1998, fifty acres of the Brooks Estate, along with Acorn Hill and the carriage house were placed under the protection of a Conservation and Preservation Restriction and the refurbishment of this nineteenth-century gentleman's farm was begun. Today the property is owned by the city of Medford, Massachusetts. The projection and restoration of the Brooks Estate (some 50 acres surrounding the house and carriage house) is under the direction of the Medford-Brooks Estate Land Trust (M-BELT), a non-profit organization. The grounds are open from dawn to dusk for walking, fishing, birding, and other passive recreation. The house is open only for selected open house events.

1.171. Weld Boathouse,
Harvard University.
Courtesy of Memorial Library,
Boston Architectural College.

Weld Boathouse

Cambridge, Massachusetts, 1906–07

Harvard University

Besides the University, there are a number of other crews at Harvard. In 1879, class crews were formed, and the class races, rowed every spring on the Charles, have served to develop oarsmen for the "Varsity."
— *Official Guide to Harvard*, 1907 [135]

The author of the *Guide* went on to surmise that rowing was perhaps the oldest of athletic sports at Harvard, which shared a long-standing rivalry with the rowers of Yale University.

George Walker Weld, Harvard class of 1860, built and equipped a boathouse on the east bank of the Charles River "for the especial benefit of students not rowing on the University or class crews." [136] College publications pointed out that Weld was not personally a rower—in fact, he had disabilities which prevented his participation in active sports—but so strongly did he feel about the importance of the undergraduate athletic programs at Harvard that he funded the first boathouse in 1890, and left money in his will to pay for a new Weld Boathouse, built in 1907.

The boathouse was constructed of brick and concrete, with a red tile roof, and stood two-and-a-half stories high. The President of the University's Report of 1906 described the amenities planned: "a repair shop, offices, locker rooms, bath and rubbing rooms, and a club room." It measured 158 feet by 78 feet, and included "the latest improvements for run-ways, exits, and floats." [137] Photographs and plans of the boathouse were published in *The Brickbuilder* in 1907.

Several years earlier, Peabody & Stearns had also received a commission to design the Newell Boathouse, located on the opposite side of the Charles River, close to the development of the university's athletic facilities at Soldiers Field. Historian Bainbridge Bunting remarked on the use of a roofline inspired by Japanese architecture and the similarities in its silhouette to the nearby H. Langford Warren-designed Carey Cage (1897). The Newell, or University Boathouse, was named in honor of Marshall Newell, of the class of 1894, who was an oarsman as well as a popular member of the football team.

Both the Weld Boathouse and the Newell Boathouse are extant, and used by members of the Harvard University rowing community.

The Coast of Maine

Maine! The very name inspires a deeper breath and longing.

— WALLACE NUTTING, *Maine Beautiful* [138]

Archer had tried to persuade May to spend the summer on a remote island off the coast of Maine (called, appropriately enough, Mount Desert), where a few hardy Bostonians and Philadelphians were camping in "native" cottages, and whence came reports of enchanting scenery and a wild, almost trapper-like existence amid woods and waters.

— EDITH WHARTON, *The Age of Innocence* [139]

Sunshine/Blueberry Ledge

Northeast Harbor, Maine, 1881

Charles William Eliot, 1834-1926

…there is general agreement that during the last part of his life Eliot was one of the most influential of contemporary Americans; and many acute appraisers of character have proclaimed that he was for years not only the greatest of university presidents, but also the greatest of all our living private citizens.

— THEODORE W. RICHARDS, "Charles William Eliot" [140]

Peabody & Stearns's first Maine cottage was designed for the sitting president of Harvard University, Charles William Eliot. Eliot was a leader in American education and culture and was a leader in the summer community of Northeast Harbor as well.

Eliot and his family had sailed and camped in the Northeast Harbor area for a number of years. In 1880 he purchased about 120 acres owned by Augustus and Fred Lincoln Savage, opposite Bear Island. The land consisted of hay fields that were beginning to be overtaken by "fragrant patches of spruces, birch trees, prostrate juniper and blueberry bushes."[141] Unlike the carefully manicured lawns and planned landscape gardens of Newport and many in neighboring Bar Harbor, the natural setting of Eliot's home was not disturbed. The cottage was sited about 100 yards from the shore, on a hillside where it was integrated into the natural landscape and had views of the channel between the mainland and the island.

The silhouette of the Eliot cottage on paper made it appear less picturesque than later Northeast Harbor

cottages, appearing as a main block with few extensions to anchor it to its hillside site. At the time of construction, with few trees on the property, it appeared almost as a house on stilts, lifted above the rocky soil by columns and porches. The kitchen roofline, which sloped sharply from the third story down to the first-floor porch, effectively countered the house's verticality, and the floor of an addition to the attached piazza was actually sited nearly 10 feet below the main level and embedded in the hillside, helping the streetside silhouette of the house to flow down the slope.

Peabody incorporated exterior and interior decorative elements of the Colonial Revival to a greater extent here than in later Northeast Harbor cottages. Sunshine was sided with clapboard on the first floor, with shingles on the upper floors. The use of overhanging gables and patterned shingles in the Eliot house foreshadowed the more decorative Shingle- and Queen-Anne-style houses that Peabody & Stearns would later design for Northeast Harbor and the coastal communities of Massachusetts.

Entry to the house was made from the portico into a large hall. The main staircase in the hall featured gracefully curving steps at the bottom; at the mid-flight turn, a landing with window seat was lighted by the three large windows that dominated the north elevation. The hall originally led straight through the house, opening onto a piazza that overlooked the cove. Entertaining in the house would have been simple, according to the floor plan, with family and guests sharing the multipurpose living hall and dining room; Eliot's modest library was to the west of the hall. No other specialized spaces were necessary for the rusticator lifestyle of early Northeast Harbor. Eliot's son Samuel recalled, "The summer life of the decade 1880-1890 was very

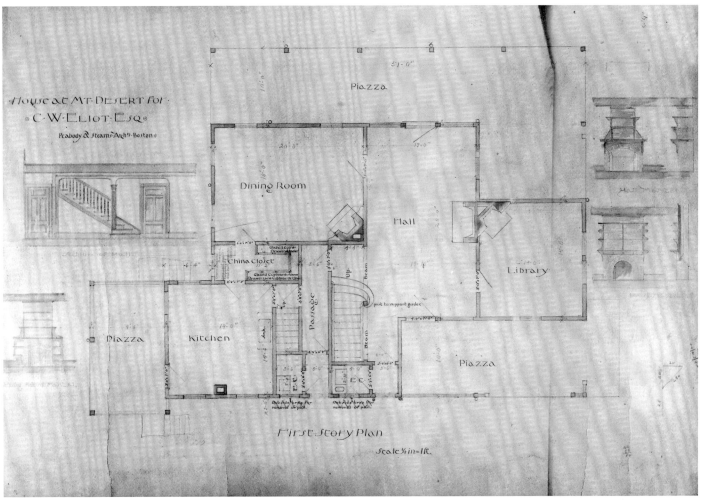

House at Mt. Desert For
C. W. Eliot. Esq.

Peabody & Stearns Arch.ts Boston

Piazza

Dining Room

Hall

Library

China Closet

Passage

Up

Piazza

Kitchen

Piazza

First Story Plan

Scale ¼ in=1ft.

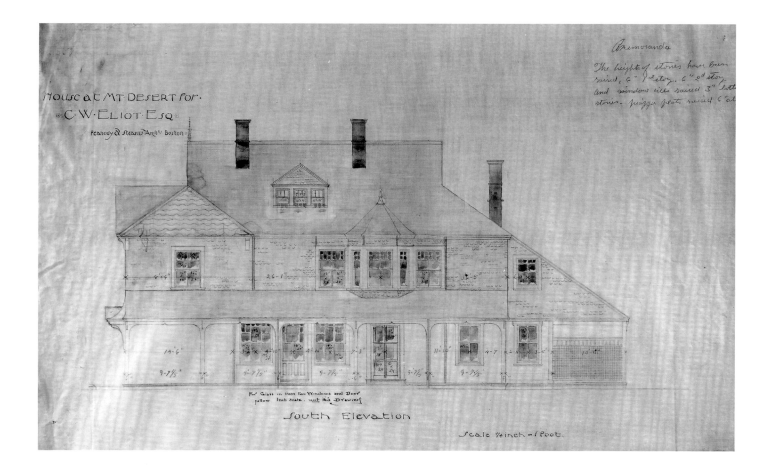

In the drawing:

HOUSE at MT DESERT for.
C.W.ELIOT Esq.

Peabody & Stearns Archt. Boston

Memoranda
The heights of stones have been
raised, 6" 1st story, 6" 2d story
and window sills raised 3" both
stories. piazza plate raised 6" &c

SOUTH Elevation

For Glass in these few Windows and Door
follow Inch Scale . . . mark this Drawing.

Scale 1/4 inch =1 Foot.

1.174. Sunshine, south elevation. Peabody and Stearns Collection, courtesy of the Boston Public Library Fine Arts Department.

FACING PAGE
1.175. Sunshine, north elevation. Peabody and Stearns Collection, courtesy of the Boston Public Library Fine Arts Department.

1.176. Sunshine, aerial photograph, c. 2001. Courtesy of the Knowles Company.

simple. . . . We swam in the ocean, caught our own fish, cut and stored our own ice, kept our own cow, picked our own berries and cut our own wood."[142]

The house did not contain extensive service areas, in keeping with the simplified life of a university president "getting away from it all" in the woods. A passageway separated kitchen and backstairs from the public areas of the house. On the second floor four of the five bedrooms enjoyed water views. There were no provisions indicated anywhere for bathrooms or water closets. The third floor—lit by small windows in two offset pedimented dormers—was divided into a number of low-eaved sleeping chambers.

As an aside, it was probably during the construction of Eliot's cottage that Peabody became acquainted with the young Fred Lincoln Savage, son of Augustus Savage, the original owner of the property. Savage had trained as a carpenter-craftsman before he apprenticed with Peabody & Stearns during the years 1884–1886; he then returned to Northeast Harbor to design many local homes and cottages under his own name.

Charles William Eliot graduated from Harvard College, where he studied mathematics and chemistry. He taught at Harvard and at the Massachusetts Institute of Technology, and became well regarded for his under-

standing of contemporary educational issues. In 1869 he was invited to assume the presidency of Harvard University, a position he held for forty years. On a personal level, however, he endured much sadness. His 1858 marriage to Robert Peabody's sister Ellen ended with her untimely death in 1869, just days before his nomination to the Harvard presidency. Their oldest son, Charles, died at the age of thirty-seven from spinal meningitis. Eliot remained a close friend and companion of both Robert and Francis Peabody, though, and their names appear frequently in the logbook at Sunshine and in Eliot's diaries.

Charles William Eliot left an enduring legacy on Mount Desert, as he did at Harvard University. He was a vocal advocate that the "whole island ought to be treated . . . as if it were a public park." His efforts, along with those of his neighbors in Seal Harbor and Northeast Harbor, resulted in the incorporation of the Hancock County Trustees of Public Reservations in 1903 and the ultimate creation of Acadia National Park.[143] Although Eliot had named his cottage Sunshine, in later years family members called it the Ancestral, in deference to him. More recently, the property was known as Blueberry Ledge.

The cottage was demolished in 2007.

1.177. Union Church,
Northeast Harbor, Maine.
Courtesy of Maine Historic
Preservation Commission.

Union Church

Northeast Harbor, Maine, 1887

...at North-east Harbor ... there is a handsome stone Union church, seating some three hundred people, wherein union services are maintained throughout the summer.

— *The Unitarian* [144]

In 1883 a number of the summer residents in Northeast Harbor began to use a one-room schoolhouse for their nonsectarian worship services. The Union Church Association was subsequently organized in 1886 with one hundred subscribers—thirty-five permanent residents of the town and sixty-five summer residents. Samuel N. Gilpatrick donated the land on which the church was to be built, and a building committee consisting of Charles William Eliot, Danforth J. Manchester, and Ansel L. Manchester was formed. In 1887, on behalf of the building committee, Peabody & Stearns was engaged to design Union Church for the non-Episcopalian population in Northeast Harbor. The church was dedicated on July 17, 1889.

The fieldstone structure sits on Schoolhouse Ledge overlooking the main street of town, a small, cross-shaped stone and wood building with a wood-shingled roof topped by a short belfry. The main entrance of the church faces west, while a secondary entrance porch to the south is reached by natural granite steps that lead up the steep slope from the street. The walls are constructed of glacial stone with quarry-faced granite quoins, and a board-and-batten transept wall. Stone buttresses in the southwest corner of the porch and the northwest corner of the transept anchor this "diamond-in-the-rough" jewel to its rugged landscape setting.

The interior walls of Union Church are plaster over lath, with a ceiling of boxed rafters over tongue-and-groove sheathing. A low vault is formed at the crossing of the nave and transepts, and a semicircular apse provides the backdrop for the pulpit, choir stalls, and organ. The church has been described as exhibiting a Scandinavian influence. [145]

Northeast Harbor was the hometown of Maine architect Fred Savage (1861–1924), who had apprenticed with Peabody & Stearns in Boston. Drawings in the Savage architectural archives in Northeast Harbor indicate that Savage may have been responsible for much of the design and construction of the Union Church building. The Peabody & Stearns project cards for the commission indicate that the firm was responsible for the original construction at $17,989.39 as well as alterations in 1913 totaling $2,314.82. It has been suggested that Savage, who had returned to Northeast Harbor in 1886 as an architect, may have done the work on behalf of the firm.

The Union Church was entered in the National Register of Historic Places in 1998. It is a year-round Church of Christ house of worship that describes itself as a "welcoming community church serving young and old from a variety of faith backgrounds."

1.178. Union Church,
Northeast Harbor, Maine.
Postcard, collection of the
author.

1.179. Union Church,
Northeast Harbor, Maine,
1887. Photograph of
watercolor by T. O.
Langerfelt. Courtesy of
Memorial Library, Boston
Architectural College.

Dupee-Sloane Cottage

Dark Harbor, Islesboro, Maine, 1897

William R. Dupee, 1842-1911
Henry T. Sloane, 1845-1937

1.180. Cottage, Dark Harbor, Maine. Postcard, courtesy of Maine Historic Preservation Commission.

If this Dark Harbor cottage originally had a name, it has not survived time or its several owners. Although it was designed and built for William Dupee of Boston in 1897, he sold it three years later to Henry T. Sloane, brother of William Sloane (Elm Court, Lenox) of the W. & J. Sloane furnishings company of New York City. This was Peabody & Stearns's first Islesboro cottage, but it was the firm's second commission for William Dupee. In 1880 he had commissioned a house at 400 Beacon Street in Chestnut Hill—which later gained renown as the Mary Baker Eddy home and the office for the world headquarters of the First Church of Christ, Scientist.

The Dupee-Sloane cottage is of wood construction, clad in shingles and clapboard. Two-and-a-half stories high, it stretches 140 feet along the shoreline of Ames Cove. Like a number of other cottages, it has a split personality—it presents a fairly controlled twin-gabled elevation on the water side of the cottage, while the land side is a riot of picturesque shingle details. A square entrance tower fronted by a skewed entry portico is similar to that used in the Dublin, New Hampshire, cottage Stonlea, built in 1891. Dormers and gables of many sizes and descriptions are decorated with diamond-shaped shingle decorations that echo the diamond-paned windows used throughout and move the surface of the building in and out. The western elevation, toward the water, was originally fronted along three-quarters of its length by a wide covered verandah. When this was enclosed at a later date, it provided additional interior space, but robbed the façade of much of its dramatic chiaroscuro. The southern end of the cot-

tage likewise was originally a grand two-story semicircular covered porch, which was later enclosed to provide an all-weather vantage point from which to view the water. In keeping with Peabody's interest in the shapes of New England houses, the northern cross gable on the water elevation was designed with a gambrel roof silhouette with a round top window in the upper floor. Although prominent in the sketched elevation, the gambrel detailing is visually lost in the shadows. After Henry Sloane purchased the cottage, he commissioned Peabody & Stearns to design alterations to the house in 1902, and further minor alterations were made in 1908; many of these changes are now evidenced in the façades of the cottage.

Early floor plans show the entrance to the cottage through a vestibule with a step down into a large living hall. To the left, a living room and parlor were located back-to-back, and both opened onto the two-story covered piazza. To the right of the hall, a dining room with bay window opened out onto the covered porch with views of the ocean. A butler's pantry led to the kitchen and back hall and stairs. Alternately, a separate hallway led to a chamber and private bath off of the main hall, providing a first-floor bedroom. On the second floor, six chambers and two baths provided accommodations for family and guests, along with four servant's rooms; the attic included a large bedroom and bath for the son of the family as well as two additional chambers, a spare room, and storage. Later plans indicate a bicycle room just off of the entry porch. The original cost of construction was $12,172.

William Richardson Dupee was born in Brighton, Massachusetts, in 1841. In 1863 he founded Nichols, Dupee & Co., Wool Brokers, a direct importer of "scoured and greased wool from South Africa, Australia, Europe, Canada, etc.," which was a major supplier to leading mills in "New England and Elsewhere."[146] The second owner of the cottage, Henry T. Sloane, was the son of the founder of W & J. Sloane in New York City. He attended Yale University and then joined his father's firm as a senior director and treasurer. A notation in the Peabody & Stearns archives suggests that he also commissioned farm buildings in Lenox in 1895. Sloane was a generous benefactor to Yale University; the Sloane Physics Lab there (1912) was one of two given to the university by brothers Henry T., Thomas C., and William D. Sloane.

The Dupee-Sloane cottage has remained in use as a summer cottage and is privately owned.

1.181. House for Wm R. Dupee, Esq., Dark Harbor, Maine, east elevation. Peabody and Stearns Collection, courtesy of the Boston Public Library Fine Arts Department.

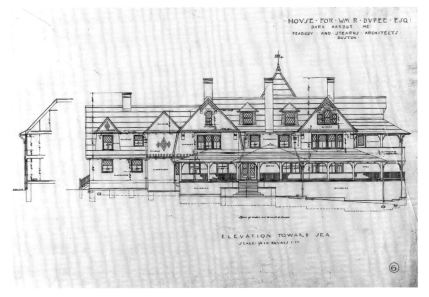

1.182. House for Wm. R. Dupee, Esq., Dark Harbor, Maine, elevation towards sea. Peabody and Stearns Collection, courtesy of the Boston Public Library Fine Arts Department.

1.183. Dupee-Sloane Cottage, waterfront façade. Courtesy of Maine Historic Preservation Commission.

Gilkey Farm

Islesboro, Maine, 1898

Henry Saltonstall Howe, 1848–1931

My home is still in Brookline, Mass., with such portion of
my time as I can spare in the summer, at Islesboro, Maine.
On Saturdays and Sundays I am a farmer and
do my share of a day's work in the woods or fields.
— HENRY S. HOWE,
Harvard University Class of 1869 [147]

1.184. Gilkey Farm,
waterfront façade.
Courtesy of Maine Historic
Preservation Commission.

Henry Saltonstall Howe of Brookline, Massachusetts, was an 1869 graduate of Harvard who achieved great success in cotton manufacturing. He hired Peabody & Stearns in 1898 to build an unusual cottage on Gilkey Harbor on Islesboro, known as the Gilkey farm.

The cottage bore considerable resemblance to the other Peabody & Stearns cottages in Maine. The land elevation presented a large, Shingle Style cottage with multiple gables juxtaposed with a quasi-gambrel and saltbox-style gable and roof; a more structured façade faced the ocean. Here an open piazza across the front was balanced at either end by one-story covered porches that projected perpendicularly from the house, a floor-plan element seen in the Blodgett cottage in Northeast Harbor, as well as in a number of the firm's Newport houses. Diamond-paned window sashes were used throughout the exterior. Inside, a large fireplace with built-in Colonial style settle welcomed the visitor to the two-story entry hall, which served as the living hall. The hall was framed on either side by a dining room and a library of equal size. A corridor on axis with the length of the cottage separated the entry vestibule and all of the secondary spaces from the main living areas; service areas and the kitchen were clustered off of the dining room, along with a storage area labeled "Golf." To the right of the vestibule the main staircase

with a large landing and a window seat preceded a first-floor chamber and bath. On the second floor the upper story of the living hall bisected the floor plan. Mrs. Howe's chamber was flanked by bedrooms for two of the Howe children, Miss Susie (Susan) and Parkman, while rooms for Dudley and Carlton along with a guest chamber were on the other side. The guest chamber included a unique interior feature: a bay window protruding into the upper space of the living hall—"a curious play on the hall as interior and exterior" [148] The third floor consisted of a guest room with separate maid's room and three servant's chambers—these areas were accessed by separate staircases because of the central roof area above the living hall. Peabody & Stearns's property record cards for the farmhouse indicate a total cost of $11,089.64, with a line item of $81.75 for travel expense. The Gilkey farm appeared in an advertisement for Cabot's Shingle Stains in the February 1901 edition of *Architecture* magazine, as well as on several Islesboro-area postcards.

A quite wonderful part of this cottage, however, was the landscaping, with an open expanse of lawn and a rectangular formal garden. Earle Shettleworth, Maine State Historic Preservation Officer, calls it the "most highly developed landscaping scheme of any Islesboro estate." [149] A walkway from the steps of the oceanfront piazza led down to a wide lawn and further down to the walled formal garden. The *Belfast Republican* extolled "the extensive gardens about the Henry S. Howe cottage"; in 1900 it reported that five acres had been added to the ornamental grounds: "Upon parts of these have been planted many hundreds of pieces of choice shrubbery brought from California." [150]

Henry Saltonstall Howe was born in Haverhill, Massachusetts; following graduation from Harvard College, he studied the business of cotton manufacturing and became the head of several New England cotton-manufacturing firms, including the Pepperell Manufacturing Company of Biddeford, Maine. He was a member of the Eastern Yacht Club as well as the Harvard, Country, and University clubs. In addition to his farm on Islesboro, Howe commissioned Peabody & Stearns to design his home on Ivy Street in Brookline in 1902. He also owned a large farm in Holliston, Massachusetts, for which Peabody & Stearns provided plans for the stable, dated 1907.

Howe's Gilkey Farm property was purchased by his son Dudley, who built a smaller cottage designed by local architect William E. Hatch in 1911. The larger acreage was divided and resold, and the Peabody & Stearns-designed Gilkey Farm cottage was demolished.

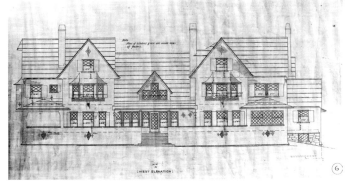

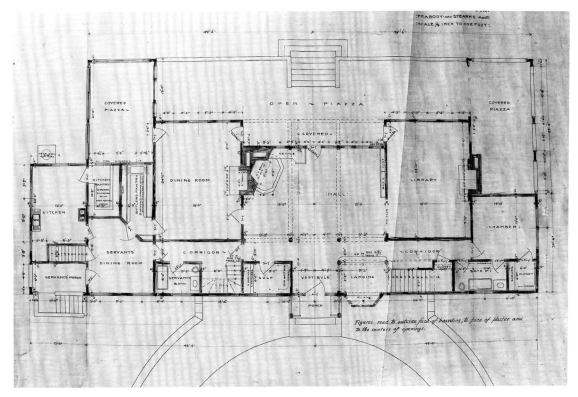

1.185. Gilkey Farm, front elevation, east. Courtesy of Dudley Howe Ladd, Islesboro, Maine.

1.186. Gilkey Farm, west elevation. Courtesy of Dudley Howe Ladd, Islesboro, Maine.

1.187. Gilkey Farm, first floor plan. Courtesy of Dudley Howe Ladd, Islesboro, Maine.

1.188. Gilkey Farm, transverse sections. Courtesy of Dudley Howe Ladd, Islesboro, Maine.

1.189. Gilkey Farm, advertisement (and detail, right) for Cabot's Shingle Stains. *Architecture*, February 1901, p. ix. Courtesy of Francis Loeb Library, Graduate School of Design, Harvard University.

The Hornbeam

Dark Harbor, Islesboro, Maine, 1899–1900

James Lawrence, 1853–1914

American Hornbeam *Carpinus caroliniana*. Common Names: Musclewood, Ironwood, Blue-beech, Water-beech. The word "hornbeam" comes from the words "horn" for "toughness" and "beam" an old English word for "tree" and refers to this tree's very hard, tough, wood.

— Leslie Day, "The City Naturalist— American Hornbeam Tree" [151]

The Lawrence family used to spend summers in the Bostonian-dominated town of Nahant, Massachusetts. However, in the mid-1890s, James Lawrence rented a cottage on Islesboro. After several years of being a tenant, Lawrence commissioned Peabody & Stearns to design a summer cottage on property he purchased in Dark Harbor. The Hornbeam was completed in 1900. His son once reported that he remembered his father sitting with Robert Peabody on the porch of the cottage, and James Lawrence congratulated the architect for coming in exactly on budget.[152]

The two-and-a-half story Lawrence cottage stretches 150 feet along a ridge on Warren Mountain that provides an unparalleled view of the water. The large gambrel roof is interrupted by a prominent full-height cross gable, as well as multiple dormers across the front and rear elevations, and creates the picturesque elevation for which the architectural firm was so well known. An informal hip-roofed entrance porch projects from the land side of the building, while on the sea elevation the entrance is topped by a large second-story piazza. The house was named the Hornbeam for the American hornbeam, or musclewood, trees that surround it.

The Lawrences were a prominent Boston family. James's father (also named James) was the son of the Honorable Abbott and Katherine Bigelow Lawrence; his mother, Elizabeth Prescott, died when James was only 9 years old. The following year his father married Anna Lothrop Motley, the daughter of Professor Thomas and Maria Bussey Motley. Young James Lawrence graduated from Harvard College, Class of 1874. After two terms at Harvard Law School, he moved to the Lawrence homestead on Farmers Row in Groton to become a farmer and livestock breeder. The *Harvard Register* reported in 1880 that "James Lawrence is living in Groton where he owns one of the largest farms in Middlesex County."[153] Lawrence was an active farmer—he served as vice president of the American Shropshire Sheep Association, was a trustee of the Middlesex Agricultural Society, and belonged to the Massachusetts Horticultural Society, the Guernsey Society, and the English Shropshire Association. He was not simply a farmer, however;

he served on the boards of several manufacturing companies, as well as the educational institutions of Lawrence Academy, the Groton School, and the Lawrence Scientific School at Harvard. He was a member of the Massachusetts House of Representatives in 1897, where he served on the Committee of Ways and Means. Lawrence donated the land for the site of the Groton School, which was one of many collaborative efforts between Peabody & Stearns and Frederick Law Olmsted.

James Lawrence used the Hornbeam for fourteen years, from the time it was completed until his death in 1914. After that time, the cottage was used only sporadically until the 1950s. The Hornbeam remains in private ownership by descendants of the original owner.

FACING PAGE
1.190. House for James Lawrence, The Hornbeam, elevation facing land. Peabody and Stearns Collection, courtesy of the Boston Public Library Fine Arts Department.

1.191. The Hornbeam, elevation facing the sea. Peabody and Stearns Collection, courtesy of the Boston Public Library Fine Arts Department.

HOUSE FOR JAMES LAWRENCE ESQ.
DARK HARBOR MAINE.
PEABODY AND STEARNS ARCHITECTS.

ELEVATION FACING LAND

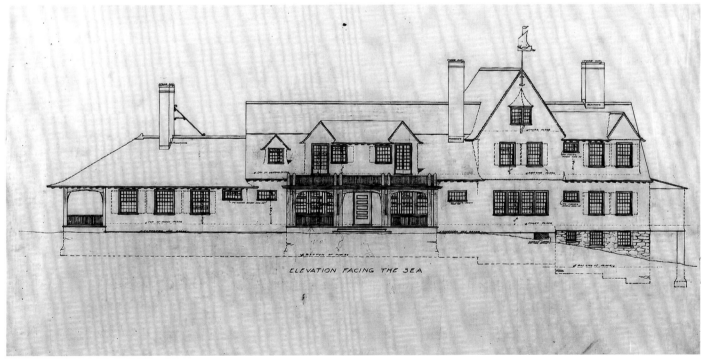

ELEVATION FACING THE SEA

1.192. Cow Cove, winter.
Courtesy of Mia Thompson Brown.

Cow Cove

Northeast Harbor, Maine, 1902

Francis Greenwood Peabody, 1847–1936

In 1902, Robert Peabody designed the Shingle Style–Tudor Revival cottage that overlooks the Northeast Harbor town landing for his brother, the Reverend Francis Greenwood Peabody. Robert Peabody's watercolor sketch of the house emphasizes the cottage's relationship to its natural site and the importance of its waterfront aspect as well, perhaps, as his and his brother's love of sailing. The massive stone foundation that supports the house above the overgrown bluff highlights the use of natural materials in construction, while its picturesque aspect provides a charming silhouette against the backdrop of the harbor.

The cottage is distinguished by the half-timbered gable motif that became integral to all of the Down East homes to follow. Although the cottage is relatively small in size, it is given stature by the bargeboarded gables, a multiplicity of pedimented and turreted dormers, and high chimneys reminiscent of the picturesque roofscapes of English country houses. The octagonal tower, a feature seen in many such homes, houses the staircase; three arched and leaded-glass windows illuminate the traditional window-seated landing.

Francis Greenwood Peabody was born in Boston, the namesake of Francis W. P. Greenwood, the King's Chapel minister who preceded his father's ministry. Like his older brother, Francis studied at the Dixwell School along with many children of wealthy parishioners of King's Chapel. Those same parishioners provided Francis with the financial means to attend Harvard University: he graduated from the College in 1869, and from the Divinity School in 1872. Following graduation, he married Cora Weld of West Roxbury, Massachusetts, who was the sister of Gertrude Weld Parkinson and a cousin of Stephen Minot Weld, both Peabody & Stearns clients. Francis Peabody taught at Harvard and is credited with the introduction of the subject of social ethics at the Divinity School where he served as dean from 1901 to 1906. He founded the university's Department of Social Ethics (teaching a course known familiarly to his students as "Peabo's drainage, drunkenness, and divorce")[154] as well as the Social Museum at Harvard.

Francis Peabody maintained a close relationship with his brother throughout their adult lives, the two of them frequently camping and sailing together, along with brother-in-law Charles William Eliot and other mutual friends.

Comparisons of early photographs of Cow Cove with its current condition suggest that few changes have been made to the cottage. It is privately owned.

1.193. Cow Cove,
watercolor sketch.
Courtesy of Memorial Library,
Boston Architectural College.

1.194. Cow Cove,
entrance façade. Courtesy
of Maine Historic Preservation
Commission

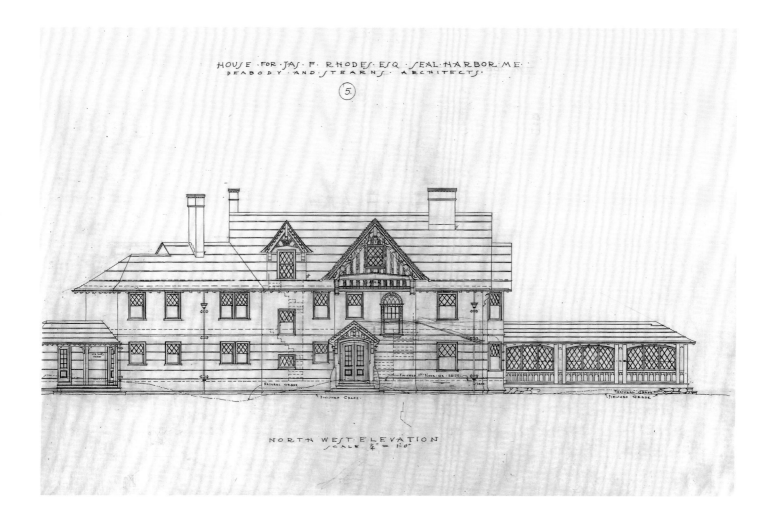

NORTH WEST ELEVATION
SCALE ¼" = 1'-0"

1.195. Ravenscleft, northwest elevation. Peabody and Stearns Collection, courtesy of the Boston Public Library Fine Arts Department.

Ravenscleft

Seal Harbor, Maine, 1899–1903

James Ford Rhodes, 1848–1927

> Hail to thee, Ravenscleft!
> Granite and waters blue,
> Trees of the emerald hue
> You do we greet!
> Fair may the home arise!
> And may the genial skies
> On our expectant eyes
> Shed influence sweet!
> — C. H. Toy, "Ravenscleft" [155]

Ravenscleft is situated on the most dramatic Mount Desert Island site on which the firm worked. It combined elements of Charles William Eliot's elevated and rustic landscape, and the simplicity of the basic Eliot floor plan, with the Tudor decorative elements of the Reverend Francis Greenwood Peabody's cottage. Peabody created a compelling summer cottage for historian James Ford Rhodes, one which was well used by Rhodes throughout the spring and summer months for many years.

Rhodes's unique site overlooks the gorge at Raven's Nest, on what is now Cooksey Drive in Seal Harbor. A note from Charles Eliot in August 1901 wel-

comed the Rhodeses to the community: "I hope Mrs. Rhodes will secure the piece of rock she has become attached to. . . . We should have been glad to have you as a near neighbor; we shall be highly content if you become a summer resident of Mount Desert on any part of the shore." [156] Ravenscleft is perched above the chasm and a steep vegetated slope that plunges down to the rocky shore, with a view of the powerful surf on the rocks below. It is best appreciated from the water, though. The main block of the house rises three stories, and its signature half-timbered gray and yellow gable juts forward on the water side. This gable is balanced by the turreted dormer to its east as well as the covered piazza that squares off the first and second floors of the main block. The structure is visually secured to its precarious site by the three-bayed covered piazza, which extends from the living room toward the chasm, and by the two-story service wing at the opposite end of the cottage, which appears to hug the ground.

To passersby, the northwest streetscape offers a more subdued but equally coherent elevation. The prominent gray and yellow half-timbered and barge-boarded gable repeats the motif from the waterfront façade; it is balanced by a Palladian leaded-glass window that lights the stairway landing. Two tiers of latticework windows add to the historical tone of the cottage façade.

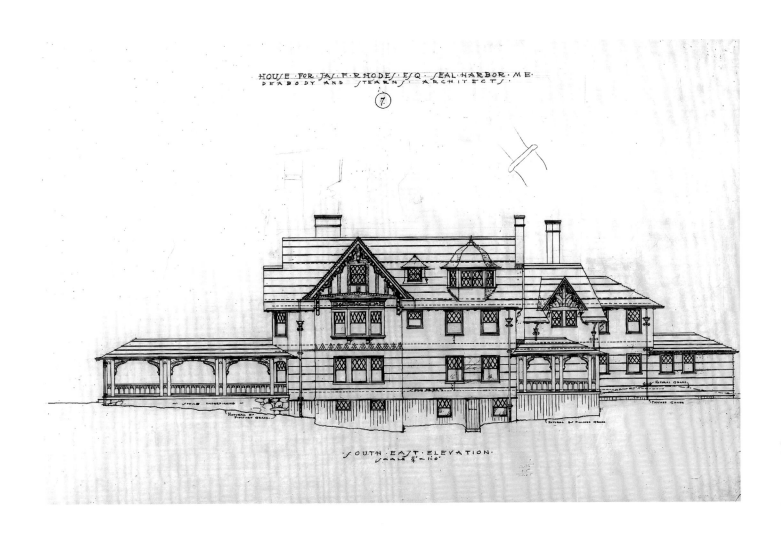

HOUSE FOR JAS F RHODES ESQ SEAL HARBOR ME
PEABODY AND STEARNS ARCHITECTS

SOUTH EAST ELEVATION
SCALE ¼"=1'0"

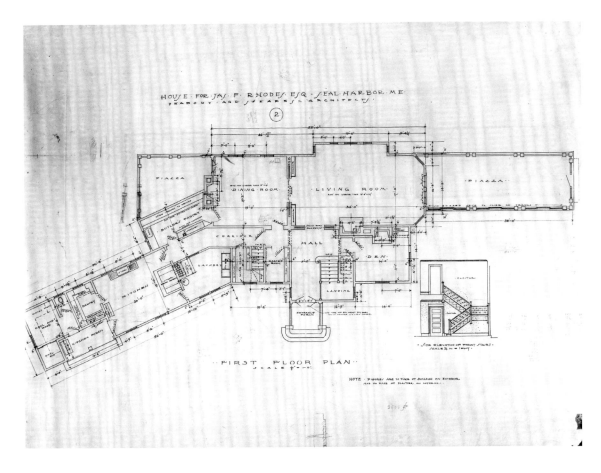

HOUSE FOR JAS F RHODES ESQ SEAL HARBOR ME
PEABODY AND STEARNS ARCHITECTS

FIRST FLOOR PLAN
SCALE ¼"=1'0"

1.196. House for
James F. Rhodes, Esq.,
Seal Harbor, Maine,
Ravenscleft, southeast
elevation. Peabody and
Stearns Collection, courtesy
of the Boston Public Library
Fine Arts Department.

1.197. Ravenscleft, first
floor plan. Peabody and
Stearns Collection, courtesy
of the Boston Public Library
Fine Arts Department.

1.198. Cottage at Seal Harbor, Maine, Ravenscleft, from the bridge. Courtesy of the Maine Historic Preservation Commission.

1.199. Ravenscleft. Postcard, collection of the author.

As in Eliot's Northeast Harbor cottage from twenty years earlier, the main living floor of Ravenscleft was simplified—it consisted of only three main rooms plus the stairhall. The main room was an American living room, which, along with the dining room, offered an ocean view. All family and formal activities took place in these rooms, which were separated by large sliding doors that could be opened on bright summer days and closed against cool evening breezes. Tucked behind the stairs, a small den with fireplace presumably served as Rhodes's study when he was in residence. Since the socially prominent Rhodes entertained many of the important leaders of the time (including, it is said, Winston Churchill in 1909), a service wing jutted off from the main house at an angle. The butler's pantry and passage separated the kitchen from the formal

dining room, and a back staircase allowed servants to circulate throughout the house as needed.

Rhodes was first a successful businessman and then a distinguished and influential American historian. As a young man, he spent several years in travel and study before he joined the family business of Rhodes & Card, producers and dealers in coal, iron ore, and pig iron in Cleveland, Ohio. He never lost his interest in learning, though, and resumed his travels and studies in the mid-1880s. A few years later he left for Cambridge, Massachusetts. Rhodes authored at least a dozen volumes on historical and contemporary subjects, including *History of the Civil War, 1861-1865*, and *History of the United States from the Compromise of 1850*. In 1912 he was selected to inaugurate a course of lectures at Oxford University on the history and institutions of the United States; he became well known among important international public figures and maintained an extensive correspondence on historical and policy-related issues.

Ravenscleft is a fine example of Peabody's ability to successfully interpret the Shingle Style. A modern commentary on the success of the cottage may be that it was featured in *Martha Stewart Living* magazine in May 2000. A recent three-year renovation of Ravenscleft has included foundation repairs, reshingling, a new roof, and restoration of the covered piazza as well as an extensive refurbishment of the interior. Replacement interior moldings have been custom-milled, and many rooms wallpapered with reproduction Voysey wallpapers, appropriate to the period of the cottage.

Ravenscleft remains in private ownership.

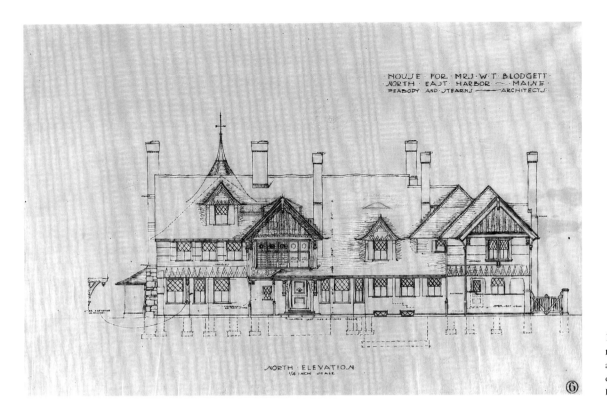

1.200. Westward Way, north elevation. Peabody and Stearns Collection, courtesy of the Boston Public Library Fine Arts Department.

Westward Way

Northeast Harbor, Maine, 1903

Abby Blake, (Mrs. William T.) Blodgett,

d. 1904

Westward Way utilized the Tudor half-timbered gables, elaborate bargeboards, and other familiar elements of the Peabody & Stearns' Shingle vocabulary, but in a plan and setting unlike Peabody's other Maine island cottages. In both its interior space and its exterior landscaping, it exhibits a consciously controlled structure not evident in Peabody's other Northeast Harbor commissions. Mrs. Blodgett's house featured a carefully planned and controlled landscape setting: a broad expanse of grassy lawn extended the vista from house to shore. The site was designed by landscape gardener Beatrix Farrand, who had a cottage in Bar Harbor (and who was later hired by John D. Rockefeller, Jr., to landscape many of the carriage roads in Acadia National Park).

Abby Blake Blodgett was the society widow of William Tilden Blodgett. Blodgett had made his fortune in New York City in his uncle's varnish-manufacturing company, building the business into "one of the wealthiest and most extensive in the country."[157] His personal accomplishments were many: he was one of the organizers of the Union League Club, one of the founders of *The Nation*, and one of the original incorporators of the Metropolitan Museum of Art—his extensive collection of artworks included Frederick Church's *Heart of*

the Andes, and Gérôme's *Pride of the Harem*. Twenty-six years after his death Mrs. Blodgett and her daughter Eleanor planned and built the cottage in Northeast Harbor.

The exterior detailing of Westward Way was perhaps the most diverse of any of Peabody's Northeast Harbor cottages. All of the gables are half-timbered, with decorative bargeboarding. Heavy saw-toothed and pendanted brackets support the second-story overhang on the street façade. A subtle diamond pattern in the shingles along the base of the second story continues around the cottage, effectively activating the large expanse of shingle and reducing the visual height of the structure. The foundation of the cottage was constructed of large boulders with graceful Romanesque arches. The use of natural boulders tied the structure to its natural setting and was Peabody's most successful use of this effect, which H. H. Richardson had realized at the Ames Gate Lodge in North Easton, Massachusetts, in 1880.

On the waterfront side, covered verandahs frame and control the façade. Between them, a massive turreted tower heavily decorated with yellow and gray half-timbering and circular motifs is balanced by the overhanging gable above the dining room. Two bell-roofed dormers treat the space between, above the open balcony and the enclosed loggia of the first and second floors. On the street side a large half-timbered gable and an equally large dormer dominate the façade. Five large leaded stained-glass windows provided lighting for the stairway and main hall area inside.

Consistent with Mrs. Blodgett's New York background, her house contained more specialized rooms

1.201. Westward Way,
entrance façade. Courtesy
of Maine Historic Preservation
Commission.

1.202. Westward Way,
sketch. Courtesy of
Memorial Library, Boston
Architectural College.

1.203. Westward Way,
waterfront façade.
Courtesy of Maine Historic
Preservation Commission.

and more elaborate spaces than the other Peabody & Stearns Northeast Harbor cottages. The floor plan of the house is organized by two intersecting axes; the first runs from the front door and entry hall through the house to the waterfront loggia area; the second axis runs perpendicular to the first, connecting the living rooms and dining rooms and dividing the main block of the house in two along its length. Centrally located in the floor plan is an oval reception room, perhaps unique in all of Peabody & Stearns's Shingle Style designs.[158]

The interior paneling and wood trim of Westward Way was reportedly originally painted dark green,[159] in keeping with the popular rustic aesthetic of the area. Large stone fireplaces dominated the principal

rooms; while these have been replaced with plainer wooden mantel pieces, the rooms have retained their heavy beamed ceilings. Upstairs, there were seven large bedchambers for family and guests, and five for staff. The Peabody & Stearns property record card indicates that the original cost of the cottage was $33,365.25.

Abby Blake Blodgett died in 1904, just a year after Westward Way was completed. Her daughter Eleanor commissioned Peabody & Stearns to design alterations for the Northeast Harbor cottage in 1912 and 1916, as well as alterations to her summer home in Bedford Hills, New York, in 1917.

Westward Way survives in remarkably original condition and is privately owned.

FACING PAGE
1.205. Gripsholm Manor,
north elevation. Peabody
and Stearns Collection,
courtesy of the Boston Public
Library Fine Arts Department.

1.206. Gripsholm Manor,
south elevation. Peabody
and Stearns Collection,
courtesy of the Boston Public
Library Fine Arts Department.

Gripsholm Manor

Islesboro, Maine, 1904

George W. C. Drexel, 1868–1944

Peabody & Stearns received numerous commissions from George W. Childs Drexel: the firm designed the Drexel home in Philadelphia on Locust Street in 1896 as well as numerous additions and alterations for the Wootton estate in Bryn Mawr (1896 through 1916).The designs for Gripshom Manor, an accompanying stable, and icehouse on Islesboro were done in 1903. Drexel's large cottage was located on a 160-acre parcel on the east side of Ryder Cove. Many of his Philadelphia neighbors had built in nearby Dark Harbor; however, according to the *Camden Herald*,[160] when Drexel came in to Dark Harbor on his steam-powered yacht, the residents complained of the smoke. So he sailed out and found property in Ryders Cove. It is hard to imagine a more beautiful site than that of Gripsholm Manor.

Gripsholm Manor was another of Peabody & Stearns's cottages with a split personality. It is of wood-frame construction with shingle siding and gable roofs, two-and-a-half stories high. On the land side the elevation is distinctly Tudor Revival: it is asymmetrically arranged, with a rectangular tower at the south end and a half-timbered portico and a projecting second-story gable in the center. The original double-hung sash windows have diamond pane lights. However, on the ocean side of the cottage, the façade presents an almost symmetrical Shingle Style. One-story hip-roofed

porches extend perpendicularly from either side with an open porch between—a familiar motif. The wide first-story doorway is sheltered by a second-story projecting bay, topped by an eyebrow window flanked by two small dormers. The interior woodwork was reported to be quite plain, not unlike that of many of the Peabody & Stearns–designed cottages of the era. In keeping with that theme, the fireplace in the large north parlor was built of rustic fieldstone. Property record cards from the Peabody & Stearns archive indicate that the cottage was constructed in 1903 for a cost of about $24,000.

George W. Childs Drexel was named for his godfather, George W. Childs, of Philadelphia, the publisher of the newspaper *The Philadelphia Public Ledger* and a good friend of Drexel's father,Anthony J. Drexel. George W. C. Drexel worked in his family's banking house for a time, but in 1893 he quit to become the publisher of *The Ledger*.When Drexel married the beautiful equestrienne Mary Irick of Vincentown, New Jersey, he and his bride received a home at 39th and Locust Street as a wedding gift from his father.

George W. C. Drexel was well known in his time for his interest in high-speed power boats. He handled his own power launches and was an expert machinist—decidedly not a common attribute for most of the members of his class.Among his fleet was the *Akbar,* a 60-foot wooden motor patrol boat that was later purchased by the Navy—in 1917—for harbor patrol duty in the Rockland, Maine, area through the end of World War I.

Gripsholm Manor was added into the National Register of Historic Places in 1985. It is privately owned.

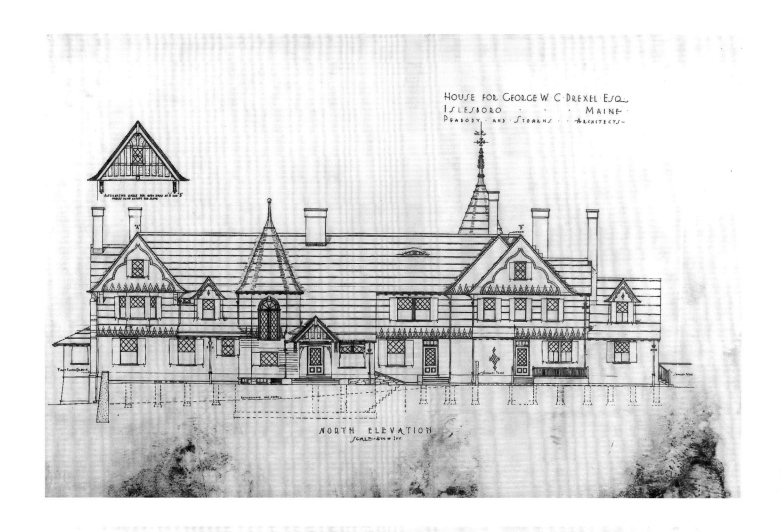

HOUSE FOR GEORGE W C DREXEL ESQ
ISLESBORO · · · · MAINE
PEABODY · AND · STEARNS · ARCHITECTS·

NORTH ELEVATION
SCALE ⅛ IN = 1 FT

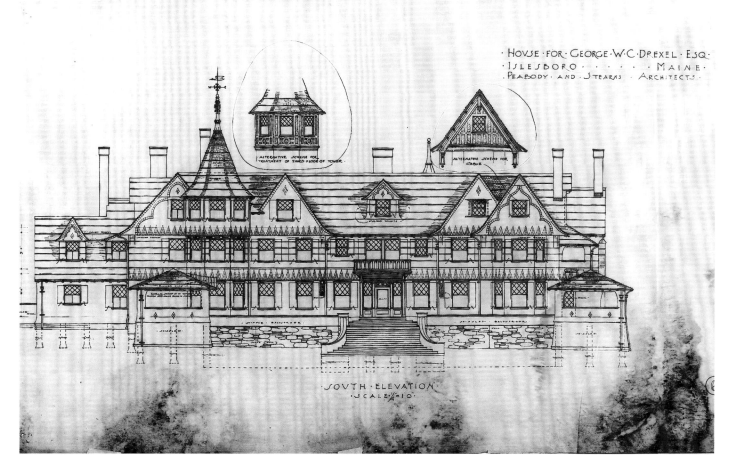

HOUSE · FOR · GEORGE · W·C · DREXEL · ESQ·
ISLESBORO · · · · MAINE·
PEABODY · AND · STEARNS · ARCHITECTS·

ALTERNATIVE SCHEME FOR
TREATMENT OF THIRD FLOOR OF TOWER

ALTERNATIVE SCHEME FOR
GABLE

SOUTH · ELEVATION·
SCALE ⅛=1-0

1.207. House for Mrs. R.H. Harte, North-East Harbor, Maine, Highwoods, east elevation. Peabody and Stearns Collection, courtesy of the Boston Public Library Fine Arts Department.

Highwoods

Northeast Harbor, Maine, 1905-6

Richard Hickman Harte, 1855-1925

Peabody and Stearns's last Down East cottage was Highwoods, the summer house of Pennsylvania physician Dr. Richard Hickman Harte. Harte was a personal friend of Francis Peabody and was introduced to cottage life on Mount Desert Island in 1904 when he and his family rented Peabody's cottage, Cow Cove. The Hartes commissioned Peabody & Stearns to design a home for them the next year. Because Mrs. Harte (Maria H. Ames, the daughter of Oakes A. Ames of North Easton, Massachusetts) suffered from rheumatism, they decided that the house should not be located directly on the water—Harte purchased land from Joseph Curtis slightly up Asticou Hill northwest of Francis Peabody's cottage, and Highwoods was constructed in time for the 1906 summer season.

Richard Harte was born near Rock Island, Illinois. He graduated from the University of Pennsylvania and studied abroad for several years, but returned to Pennsylvania to begin his career in surgery. Two years after Highwoods was completed, Harte commissioned Peabody & Stearns to design his permanent home in Abington, Pennsylvania.

A long driveway through the Harte property culminated in a circular drive in front of the house. A watercolor sketch of Highwoods done by Robert Peabody and a photograph from a later real estate brochure suggest that the cottage incorporated many of the elements that Peabody & Stearns had used in previous designs. The east elevation presented a long, compact structure that hugged its hillside site. The three-story main block of the house was dominated by a large intersecting gable with a massive stone chimney, and a smaller echoing gable projected out over the entry. Both gables included the Tudor Revival half-timbering of Peabody's previous Northeast Harbor designs. The west elevation drawings reveal an excavated, battered masonry lower level punctuated with lancet-type windows and underlaid with a rough stone foundation. This stonework was repeated in the structure of the large covered piazza that extended from the southern end of the main block of the house, to balance the service wing and to visually anchor the cottage to its site. In typical cottage fashion the main block of the house was nearly surrounded by piazzas and porches to maximize views of the harbor—the covered piazza that opened off the parlor and the living room was connected to the uncovered piazza "overlooking N. E. Harbor & Western Way."

The Harte cottage incorporated a more formal floor plan than most of its Peabody & Stearns–designed Northeast Harbor neighbors. It included both a formal parlor and a living room on the southern side of a wide main hall, with a den and a dining room separated by the wide staircase on the northern side. The parlor was evidently intended to serve principally as a reception room—it was the living room and the den that enjoyed the waterfront views afforded by the hilltop site of Highwoods.

Six bedrooms, three with fireplaces, were located on the second floor. The owner's bedroom included a balcony overlooking the water and an en suite bathroom. Another of the bedrooms shared the water view and had both an en suite bathroom and access to a sleeping porch. Two additional guest baths were located in the main block of the second floor. The service wing included several specialized rooms—including a sewing room and a linen closet—five servant's bedrooms, and a servants' bathroom. Highwoods was constructed for a total of $23,757.34.

Harte was influential in the decision in 1913 to allow automobile traffic in Northeast Harbor, a decision opposed by nearby neighbor Charles William Eliot. An article posted on August 30 indicates that the summer had passed with few if any incidents between auto and animal. In fact, the reporter suggested that the summer of 1913 "would have been a disastrous season, from the prevailing dullness all over the country" had it not been for the additional recreational opportunities provided by the automobile.[161]

Highwoods was destroyed by fire in the 1970s.

1.208. Highwoods, gable, east elevation. Courtesy of Mia Thompson Brown.

1.209. Highwoods, watercolor sketch. Courtesy of Memorial Library, Boston Architectural College.

New Hampshire

The beginnings of Dublin as a summer resort have an earlier date than
is generally supposed. There is evidence in the published history of
the town that the inhabitants were well aware that they lived amid
scenes of unusual natural beauty . . .

— H. H. PIPER, "A Sketch of Dublin" [162]

Redtop/Monadnock Farms

Dublin, New Hampshire, 1888

Colonel George Eliot Leighton, 1835–1901

. . . he has found Dublin the most desireable place for summer residence known to him. He has drawn others to the
town from St. Louis . . . a considerable western colony has
been attracted to the place. . . .

— GEORGE WILLIS COOKE, "Old Times and
New in Dublin, New Hampshire" [163]

Redtop is a handsome Shingle Style cottage with
outstanding views of Dublin Lake and Mount
Monadnock. Originally named Monadnock
Farms, the property was later the centerpiece of the
Arthur Shurcliff horticultural landmark, Morelands,
owned by Frederick and Margaret Brewster during the
mid-1920s through the 1950s.

Peabody & Stearns designed this rambling summer
cottage for George Eliot Leighton of St. Louis, on farm
property that Leighton purchased for $10,000 in 1887.
The structure has been the object of numerous additions
and remodels—Peabody & Stearns designed library and
porte-cochere additions to the original home in 1903;
in 1916 the structure was "Colonial Revivalized" for
Leighton's son, George Bridge Leighton, perhaps by St.
Louis architect John Lawrence Mauran; and Norton &
Townsend of New Haven did interior remodeling and
added a large servants' wing to the house in 1926 for
the Frederick Brewsters. Architect Robert A. M. Stern
describes Redtop as having been "a Chinese puzzle of
a house" when he was retained in 1979 by the current
owners to remove the servants' wing and to reconfig-
ure and restore the badly maintained property to its

original distinction. [164] Now the upper shingle surfaces
are stained red to match the steep shingled roof, making the obvious connection to its name.

Redtop is located on the northwestern shore of
Dublin Lake and oriented to the view down the full
length of the lake. A turn-of-the-century photograph
emphasizes its hilltop location, as well as an early golf
enthusiast captured by the camera. The use of clapboard
siding on the first floor with shingles on the upper
floors is reminiscent of many Queen Anne–styled cottages and helps to break up the mass of the house. Like
so many Peabody & Stearns cottages of the period, the
Leighton cottage appeared to have been an architectural accumulation over time. Angled tower rooms on
both front and rear elevations originally housed sleeping porches on the upper floor. Large covered porches
and eyebrow windows were stock design attributes of
the Shingle Style.

The first-story plan suggests a cottage planned
to take advantage of the views of the lake as well as
breezes off of the lake—most of the residence was only
one room deep. From the entry the guest could take a
right into the Sport Room, or a left in to the hall—certainly an important living space in the cottage—it measured approximately 15 feet by 28 feet, and included
a wide two-stage staircase and a large brick fireplace.
An arched opening led to the living room on the left or
to the dining room on the right. The square footage of
the service areas nearly equaled that of the living areas
and encompassed a china closet, a pantry, a kitchen, a
laundry, a storage area, and the shed.

Colonel George Eliot Leighton was a New Englander
by birth—he lived in Cambridge, Massachusetts, until
he was nine years old—but the mark of the west was
on him. He was raised and educated in Cincinnati but
moved to St. Louis to practice law. His title of colonel

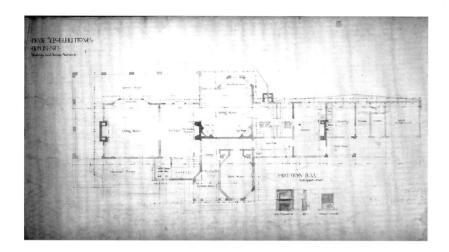

was a reference to his position in the Union Army as a leader of the Seventh Regiment, Enrolled Missouri Militia. Although he returned to legal practice after the war as general counsel of the Missouri Pacific Railroad, it was his marriage in 1862 to Isabella Bridge of Walpole, New Hampshire, that determined Leighton's financial success as well as the location of his summer home.[165] Isabella's father was the president of the Bridge & Beach Manufacturing Company, a cast-iron-stove manufacturer and the largest iron foundry in the West. When Bridge died in 1874, Leighton took over his role in the company. Meanwhile, Isabella had developed tuberculosis, and Leighton's choice of the cool country air of Dublin was an obvious attempt to find respite for her illness; poor Isabella died in 1888, and it is doubtful if she was ever able to stay in the sprawling cottage overlooking Dublin Lake. However, Colonel Leighton and his son George lived in the cottage every summer. The colonel was active and influential in St. Louis, serving as president of the Board of Trustees of Washington University, president of the Missouri Historical Society, and president of the board of trustees of the Church of the Messiah. He was an equally enthusiastic participant in his summer community, where he was one of the founders of the Dublin Lake Club, and he was instrumental in bringing a number of St. Louisans to the Dublin area.

The colonel died at his Monadnock Farms cottage on July 4, 1901, and the property was left to his son George Bridge Leighton (1864–1929). He and his wife Charlotte Kayser Leighton (the younger sister of neighbor Justina Kayser Catlin—see Stonlea) made the property their full-time residence in 1903. Property holdings were increased to 850 acres of farmland prior to the purchase of the parcel by the Frederick Brewsters of New Haven in 1929.

Although there have been many changes to the cottage over the years—porches have been enclosed, dormers have been added or enlarged, rooms have been added and deleted, and the trees have grown up around the property—Redtop still sweeps the lake with her presence and remains a private residence.

1.212. Redtop, first floor plan, presentation drawing. Peabody and Stearns Collection, courtesy of the Boston Public Library Fine Arts Department.

1.213. Redtop, northwest elevation, presentation drawing. Peabody and Stearns Collection, courtesy of the Boston Public Library Fine Arts Department.

1.214. Redtop, southeast elevation, presentation drawing. Peabody and Stearns Collection, courtesy of the Boston Public Library Fine Arts Department.

Stonlea

Dublin, New Hampshire, 1891

Daniel Catlin, 1837–1916

Work is going on upon the Catlin mansion, which,
it is estimated, will cost, including land, farm house, lawn,
etc., not far from $50,000.

— *Peterborough Transcript*, July 23, 1890

Three years after Peabody & Stearns created Monadnock Farms (Redtop) for George and Isabella Leighton, the firm was asked to design a cottage for Leighton's good friend and fellow St. Louisan, Daniel Catlin, just a stone's throw from the Leighton cottage. Although constructed of similar materials—clapboard and shingle—and sharing a view of Dublin Lake and Mount Monadnock, the Catlin's summer house, Stonlea, was totally different from its neighbor. Where Monadnock Farms was blocky and organic in format, with picturesque rooflines and towers tying the landscape to the sky, Stonlea was an elongated fan, stretched and curved along the ridge of a hill that looks directly across the northwestern end of the lake to Mount Monadnock. Colonial Revival details were original to the Catlin cottage, and the grand two-story portico that once graced its southwestern elevation gave it an elegance and grace that was of another time and place.

Leighton family history tells the story of the Catlins coming to visit George Leighton in 1889 and falling in love with the Dublin atmosphere. Catlin purchased acreage almost adjoining the Leighton farmland for $11,000 in 1889 and contracted with Peabody & Stea-

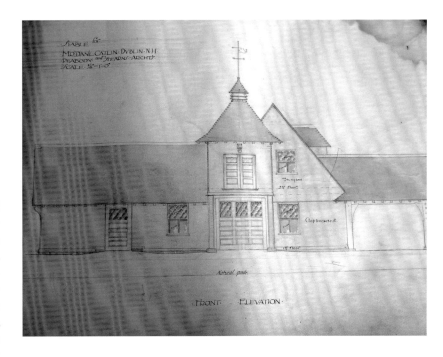

1.215. Stonlea, front façade, c. 1896. Dublin Public Library, Henry D. Allison Glass Negative Collection.

1.216. Stonlea, stable, front elevation. Peabody and Stearns Collection, courtesy of the Boston Public Library Fine Arts Department.

rns to build what would become one of Dublin's largest summer houses—"a monumental landmark" in the words of the Dublin Historic Resources Inventory of 1979. Project cards from Peabody & Stearns indicate an initial cost of about $35,000 for the construction of the house, with $6,500 of alterations in 1898. Five years later, Catlin was reported to be constructing additions, also designed by Peabody & Stearns, consisting of an ell, an office, and a smoking room. When complete, the house comprised 9,000 square feet of living space, with 17 gables, 15 principal rooms, including 8 bedrooms, 5 1/2 baths, as well as the service ell containing the kitchen, the servants' dining room, 4 bedrooms, and 1 bath.

Entrance was made from the land-view side of the cottage, through an angled vestibule that foreshadows the entrance to the Dupee-Sloane cottage built on Islesboro in 1897. The first floor was bisected by the main hall, separating the living room from the dining room. The dining room–kitchen ell swung back away from the lake. This provided the rooms with breathtaking views, but required unusual pie-shaped insertions into the plan. These were gracefully accommodated by the architects, noticeable only if one is measuring for the construction of doorways and cabinets, or the installation of carpeting. A gracious staircase led to the second floor, with large landings and a large window lighting the stairs.

Like Leighton, Daniel Catlin was another New Englander transplanted to St. Louis—born in Litchfield, Connecticut in 1837—his family moved to St. Louis in 1850 in order to begin the manufacture of tobacco, which was a new industry to the state. Young Daniel took over the control of the business in 1859, and by 1876 had enough success to warrant the incorporation of the company as the Catlin Tobacco Company, manufacturer of fine-cut chewing and smoking tobaccos and one of the leading industries of St. Louis. In 1895 the company was purchased by the American Tobacco Company, and Catlin retired to other interests. Despite the fact that he was not college-educated, Daniel Catlin became one of the business and cultural leaders in St. Louis. He was a director for a number of local financial concerns including the State National Bank, was one of the founders of the St. Louis Trust Company and was on the board of the Church of the Messiah (an 1879 Peabody & Stearns design), plus being a liberal patron of the fine arts and a former director of the St. Louis Museum of Fine Arts (another Peabody & Stearns design, 1881). Catlin lived in a Peabody & Stearns–designed home at 21 Vandeventer Place in St. Louis (designed and built for Henry Newman in 1882), while his brother Ephron had Peabody & Stearns (presumably represented by Pierce Furber) design his home at 15 Vandeventer Place. Daniel Catlin was well known for his personal gallery of paintings, and shortly after his death, his wife Justina Kayser Catlin donated a collection of thirty paintings to the St. Louis museum.

The appearance of Stonlea has changed considerably in the intervening years. The commanding two-story portico with its curved balustrade has been removed, although the roofscape and dormers remain very much as originally built. In addition, the deep covered porch that stretched around the living room was removed, presumably when the office and smoking room were added.

The cottage is privately owned.

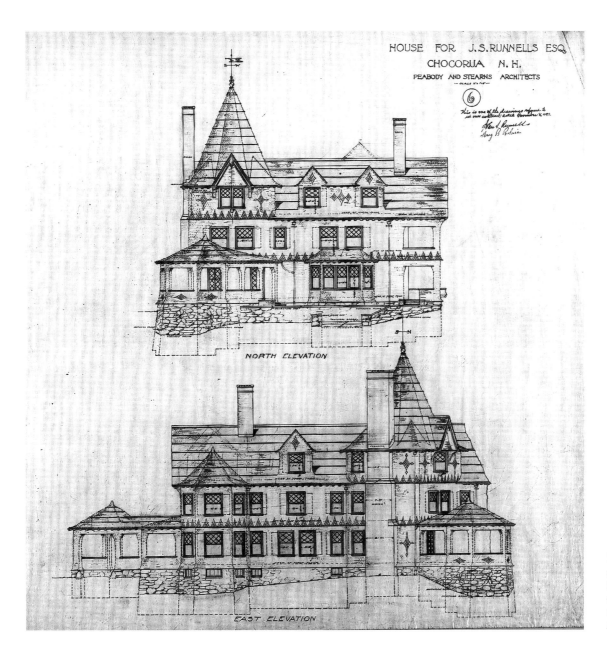

1.218. Willowgate, north and east elevations. Peabody and Stearns Collection, courtesy of the Boston Public Library Fine Arts Department.

Willowgate

Chocorua, New Hampshire, 1900

John Sumner Runnells, 1844-1928

John S. Runnells, general counsel of the Pullman Palace Car Company, has a lovely home on the banks of Lake Chocorua, near the site of his birthplace....
— Nahum J. Bachelder, *New Hampshire Agriculture*[166]

Willowgate was a cottage determined to be built. Local lore relates that John Runnells purchased property on the Fowler's Mill Road once owned by Mary J. Gilman. His cottage, which may have been constructed around the origi-

nal Gilman farmhouse, was destroyed by fire shortly before its completion; Peabody & Stearns was retained to build Willowgate at a higher elevation on the same property.[167]

The resulting Willowgate had commanding views of Chocorua Lake and Mount Chocorua. Similar in many details to the James Lawrence cottage on Islesboro, built at about the same time, Willowgate's "witches cap" tower was a dramatic addition to the design, but the triangular plan and interior courtyard may well have been unique in Peabody & Stearns's work. Willowgate was a classic example of a Shingle Style cottage, with all manner of terraces, covered piazzas, dormers, and bow windows incorporated into the design. Entry was made from the porte-cochere, up granite steps and across one of the many piazzas into a spacious vestibule with coa-

1.219. Willowgate, first floor plan. Peabody and Stearns Collection, courtesy of the Boston Public Library Fine Arts Department.

1.220. Willowgate, c. 1905. Tamworth Historical Society.

1.221. Willowgate,
c. 1905. Tamworth Historical
Society.

troom and half-bath. Visitors might be shown into the adjoining den, or into the large hall, whose gracious stairway was interrupted by a large landing overlooking the enclosed courtyard. A library and dining room, each with adjacent outdoor space, completed the group of formal rooms on the first floor. Service areas included an enormous kitchen, pantry, and butler's pantry, as well as servants' dining room and flagstone piazza. The Runnells cottage was modest in size (3,480 square feet) and was completed at a cost of $17,588.14.

John Sumner Runnells was a summer resident who was intimately familiar with the Chocorua landscape—he was raised in nearby Tamworth, where his father, Elder John Runnells, was pastor of the Free Will Baptist Church. He graduated from Amherst College, Class of 1865, and studied law in Dover, New Hampshire. Runnells found opportunity in Des Moines, Iowa; he moved there in 1868 to be a private secre-

tary to Governor Samuel Merrill. Years later, in 1887, Runnells and his wife (the former Helen R. Baker, daughter of the former governor of New Hampshire) moved to Chicago, where he became general counsel for the Pullman Palace Car Company and the senior member of the firm Runnells, Burry & Johnstone. Runnells advanced to the position of president of the Pullman company, which position he held until 1922. The Runnells had four children, three daughters, and one son; their daughter Alice Rutherford Runnells married William James, Jr., son of the noted American psychologist, whose summer home, Stonewall, was also in Chocorua.

In addition to Willowgate, John Runnells commissioned Peabody & Stearns in 1917 to design an addition to the Runnells Electric Power Plant located in Chocorua.

Willowgate was torn down in the 1930s.

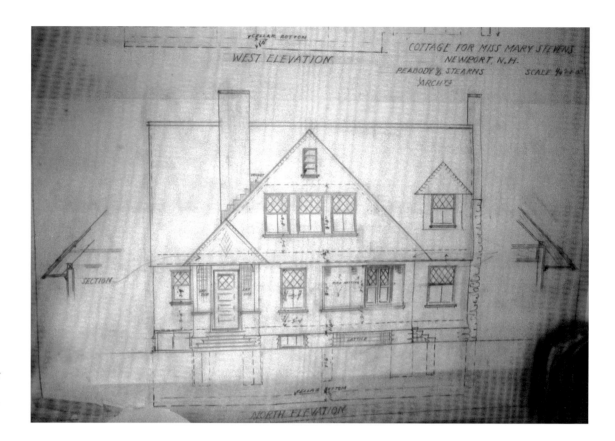

1.222. Cottage for Mary Stevens, front façade, c. 2006. Courtesy of Kathy Walsh and Dan Lloyd.

Cottage

North Newport, New Hampshire, 1906-7

Mary Haven Stevens, 1859-1953

The Mary H. Stevens cottage is one of a few small country cottages designed and built by Peabody & Stearns. It is privately owned and lived in all year—no longer just a summer cottage. It is in wonderful condition, from the original diamond-paned windows to the myriad of original built-ins. The question that arises in such instances of a cottage in a small town without a large resort population is, why here?

Newport, New Hampshire may seem an unlikely resort location. However, some nineteenth-century residents of the community felt otherwise. In 1879, Edmund Wheeler (a relative of Mary Stevens's mother) published a history of Newport. He was perhaps acting more as a promoter of the town than as a historian when he wrote "Newport as a Summer Resort," in which he extolled the attractions to the summer tourist. The town's proximity to Lake Sunapee was surely its major attraction, although "the lovely view from the dome of the court-house" as well as from surrounding hills and mountains, were gratifying to the "lover of charming scenery." Wheeler estimated that "more than a thousand persons spend more or less of their summers here, thus showing that its merits have been in some measure appreciated," although it is somewhat unclear as to whether those thousand persons were

in Newport alone, or in the general Newport–Unity Springs area.[168] Wheeler also related that in 1874 two mineral springs in Newport had been purchased by Hazen P. Hutton, a doctor of Boston, "with the view of providing suitable hotel accommodations for such as might wish to resort to them. . . ." Hutton's ultimate success is unrecorded.

Mary Haven Stevens was born in Minnesota, although both of her parents were from New Hampshire. Her mother, Lucy Phebe (Putnam) Wheeler, was born in Newport, New Hampshire, and her father, Frederick Johnson Stevens, was from Springfield, New Hampshire; they lived for a number of years in Minnesota, in a small town that her father named Meriden. When the family returned to the East, they settled in Southborough, Massachusetts. Mary graduated from Framingham Normal School in 1878, did graduate work, and was appointed to the position of teacher of French in 1891. She never married.

In September 1905, Mary purchased a four-acre parcel of farmland in North Newport from Esther Royes for the sum of $400—it appears that her intention was to move and renovate the existing house for use as a summer cottage. Two months later she received a letter from the Peabody & Stearns office informing her that the existing house was in disrepair and "it seems to us that there would be no economy in trying to use the present house as part of the new, especially as we believe the repairs would have to be very extensive after moving it to the new location, and Mr. Kendall says he fully agrees with you that the house ought to

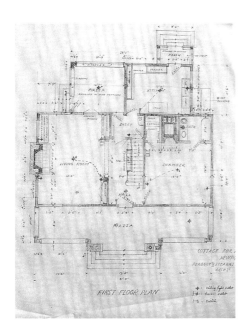

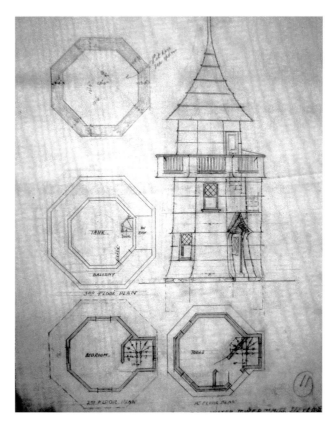

1.223. Cottage, first floor plan. Peabody and Stearns Collection, courtesy of the Boston Public Library Fine Arts Department.

1.224. Cottage, water tower. Courtesy of Kathy Walsh and Dan Lloyd.

be set back further from the road than the present house. We think you will be much better satisfied if you start new, and we hope you will decide to."[169]

Plans drawn by the firm indicate a quaint cottage almost identical to what exists today. The cottage is sited parallel to and back from the road on a gently sloping lot. The steeply pitched roof shelters a deep porch stretching across the front of the house, and the two-story intersection gable with bay window marks the wide entry way. All is shingled, including the half-columns at the front steps. Diamond-paned windows are used throughout. The wide center hall opens to a living room with a wall of built-ins on one side and a chamber with attached bath on the other. A kitchen and covered piazza make up the rear of the first floor. The second floor contains four bedrooms and a second full bath. Additional plans detail the various built-ins, with a sideboard and pass-through on one side of the living room archway and a bookcase on the other. Both include diamond-paned upper doors that match the windows of the house; these built-ins, like the majority of the woodwork throughout the house, were stained a dark, translucent green. Quarter-sawn pine floors were used throughout the house. The cottage was constructed for $8,891.07 with an additional $1,456.45 in alterations. The Peabody & Stearns archives also include plans for a water tower for Miss Stevens's property. The tower included floors for the water tank, tools, and a bedroom.

In 1942, Stevens deeded her cottage to her unmarried younger sister, Grace, who was a medical doctor. The property was sold out of the family in 1952.

1.225. Cottage for Mary Stevens, front façade, c. 2006. Courtesy of Kathy Walsh and Dan Lloyd.

Connecticut

On a noble hill, midway between Stamford and Greenwich, and which commands a view of Long Island Sound, dear to the soul of every yachtsman, and which permits the eye to sweep all the surrounding country, Mr. Havemeyer has a summer home dedicated to domestic comfort. The breeze finds you somewhere on the extensive piazzas on the hottest of days, and it kisses you into cheerfulness, albeit you may now and then think regretfully of the sweltering city.

— HAMILTON BUSBEY,
Recollections of Men and Horses [170]

Hilltop

Greenwich, Connecticut, 1890

Henry O. Havemeyer, 1847-1907

...he lived a great deal of the time at his country place, where he took great interest in the breeding of fancy cattle and sheep....

— *Boston Daily Globe*, December 5, 1907 [171]

Henry Havemeyer purchased eighty-five acres on Palmer Hill in Greenwich in 1888 when he was forty-one years old and already a wealthy man. The property was a perfect choice for his residence, with distant views of Long Island Sound. Peabody & Stearns was hired to prepare the designs for the Hilltop country house and farm; records show that the house and stable were completed by December 1890 for a total building cost of $97,296.54 and that farm buildings—hay barn, stable, and cottage—were added by May 1893 for an additional $17,954.53.

Hilltop had many familiar Shingle Style features. It had the strong yet picturesque lines that are identified with the Peabody & Stearns "look." Two intersecting gables projected out from the three-story main house on the south side overlooking acres of lawn and garden. The foundation and first story were of stone, the upper stories of shingle. Large windows provided light and air; eyebrow windows and multiple chimneys interrupted the broad expanse of roof. To the west a long covered porch dependency stretched out, ending in a round conservatory building, similar to details included in Bleak House in Newport and East House at Indian Neck, Wareham. This feature, combined with the simple lines of the bands of windows, contributed to the horizontal aspect and rootedness of the estate.

In 1883, Henry Havemeyer married Louisine Waldron Elder; together they became important patrons of the arts in the United States. Through Louisine's influence and her friendship with Mary Cassatt, the Havemeyers became serious art collectors, assembling the impressive selection of European Impressionist paintings that later formed the foundation of the Metropolitan Museum of Art's collection of works of that period. They were passionate about their homes as well. The interiors of Hilltop were decorated by Samuel Colman in a simple style—in contrast to the lavish interior of the Havemeyers' New York residence at 1 East 66th Street, which Colman and Louis Tiffany were completing at about the same time. Art historian Frances Weitzenhoffer describes Hilltop: "large, well-lit rooms," "the library was the principal room, with bookshelves, paintings and musical instruments," and "numerous fireplaces of tile and brick, walls covered with Japanese papers of subdued tones, and delicately constructed furnishings designed by Colman." Only the dining room had dark paneling, fashioned after a seventeenth-century Dutch painting. [172] A grandson recalls that it was Louisine who loved Palmer Hill the most. [173] While at Hilltop she enjoyed the country life, frequently cooking for the family and becoming very involved in gardening. She spent summers there until a stroke in 1927 prevented her from continuing her schedule.

In addition to the main house and extensive grounds, the estate included a Shingle Style cottage for the estate manager, a stable, livestock barns, and three greenhouses. Hilltop was described in the *Greenwich Graphic* as including "all the elaborate features of a gentleman's extensive country estate." [174]

·NORTH·ELEVATION·

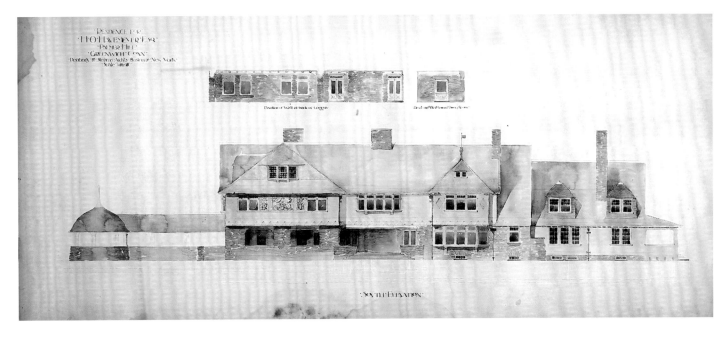

·SOUTH·ELEVATION·

1.229. Hilltop, sketch, Greenwich, Connecticut. Courtesy of Memorial Library, Boston Architectural College.

1.230. Havemeyer farm building. *Architectural Record*, July 1896, p. 96. Courtesy of the Frances Loeb Library, Graduate School of Design, Harvard University.

Henry O. Havemeyer's grandfather and father had been pioneers in the sugar-refining industry in America, and Henry and his brother, Theodore, continued the family legacy, resulting in the creation of the controversial American Sugar Refining Company. Louisine's father was also a leader in the industry—Sugar King George W. Elder. Although their permanent home was in New York City, the Havemeyers were good citizens of Greenwich—they donated the money to build the Greenwich School (now the Havemeyer Building)

and were patrons of other worthy causes in the town. An article in 1908 in the *Connecticut Magazine* stated that "Mr. Havemeyer has been so large a part of Greenwich for so long a time that to-day he is considered one of her own sons."[175]

In the 1940s, Hilltop had fallen into disrepair. The house and nearly two hundred acres of land was sold, and Hilltop was torn down to make way for a development of single-family homes for World War II veterans.

Adee Memorial Boathouse

New Haven, Connecticut, 1911

Yale University

George Adee Memorial Opened Without Ceremony—
Football Men for Crew
— Special to the *New York Times*, January 10, 1911

The Adee Memorial Boathouse was demolished in 2007 to make way for the new Pearl Harbor Memorial Bridge that will span New Haven Harbor as part of the Interstate-95 highway expansion. But it stood for nearly one hundred years at the shore of the harbor, at the mouth of the Quinnipiac River.

Robert Peabody was on the Harvard University crew team when he was a student, so we must assume that designing boathouses was near and dear to his heart. And the fact that Yale University is Harvard's ultimate rival must have made this commission all the more fun. George Augustus Adee (d. 1908), for whom the Yale boathouse was named, was Class of 1867 at Yale—and may even have rowed against Peabody when they were students.

The Tudor-influenced boathouse was completed in 1911, at a time when New Haven Harbor was less crowded and less polluted. There was room for fifty rowing shells in its storage area, and the Adee was a popular hangout for the members of the rowing teams. It was constructed on five hundred pilings on flooded land and was originally surrounded by water on all sides, with a small bridge connecting the building to the shoreline. Its plum-colored and blackened-brick façade, with terra-cotta trim, was a bold contrast to the other buildings on the New Haven waterfront. Exterior detailing included gargoyles fashioned to look like bulldogs (the Yale mascot) on the west façade and the Yale coat of arms over the door

The second floor of the boathouse contained 346 lockers for members of the crew. In addition, twenty-four rowing machines were installed on the second floor for crew conditioning and training. The *New York Times* noted that "a new feature is that of having large mirrors which can be placed beside the rowing machines" to enable the oarsmen to observe better "rowing form."[176] Two photographs and plans for the boathouse were published in *The Brickbuilder* magazine in 1911.

Rowing became an extremely popular sport in the 19th century—Yale students began rowing in 1843 and were organized into the Yale Navy in 1853. In 1852, Yale rowers invited their counterparts at Harvard to a contest of skill, which led to the first formal intercollegiate athletic competition in America, the race taking place on Lake Winnipesaukee, New Hampshire; Harvard was the victor. Yale built its first boathouse, a simple barnlike structure, in the 1860s at the mouth of the Quinnipiac River. In 1875 this was replaced by a square Stick Style boathouse off of Chapel Street. This charming structure deteriorated rapidly, however, and was found to be unsafe in the spring of 1909—luckily, fund-raising for the newer Peabody & Stearns design had already begun. It opened on January 10, 1911,

1.231. Yale boat club house, New Haven, Connecticut. *The Brickbuilder*, vol. 20, no. 5, pl. 60, 1911. Courtesy of the Rotch Library, Massachusetts Institute of Technology.

"without formal exercises of a dedicatory nature" and reportedly cost $100,000 to build—the Peabody & Stearns records indicate a cost of $88,936.63 for a two-story building covering 12,399 square feet.

The reason for the football men on the crew? The captain of the rowing team determined that "more rugged oarsmen" were required for the bow and decided that the football team members would serve the purpose—even though many had never rowed before. He reported that "the football men will be kept at work till they are distanced in the competition."[177]

The Adee Boathouse served its purpose well, but for less than twelve years. By 1916, Yale University determined that the increasingly crowded conditions in the New Haven Harbor were not conducive to the sport, and decided to move to a site at Derby on the Housatonic River. A plan was devised to move the Adee upriver by barge, but ultimately a new Derby boathouse was designed by James Gamble Rogers, (Class of 1889), and opened in 1923.

The Adee was recognized as a significant structure in the 1930s, when it was recorded by the Historic American Buildings Survey. The Connecticut Trust for Historic Preservation included the boathouse in its list of threatened historic places in 1997, in response to the demolition order for the highway construction. Although the state's Department of Transportation and the City of New Haven reportedly considered moving the boathouse to the Long Wharf tourist area, that plan proved to be too expensive. The State of Connecticut had reportedly agreed to pay for a replica of the building, reusing as many decorative elements of the original as possible.[178]

1.232. Adee boathouse, undated photograph.
From pictures of Yale University's buildings and grounds, 1716–1980.
Manuscripts & Archives, Yale University.

Chapter 2

The Middle Atlantic States

New Jersey, New York, and Pennsylvania

Long Branch, with which we may include Elberon, Hollywood, and West End,
is one of the most popular watering-places on the continent, and one of the
most expensive.

— S. Edwin Solly, *A Handbook of Medical Climatology* [1]

Beyond Bryn Mawr, there follows a succession of small villages with country
places interspersed and spreading out for two or three miles on each side of
the railroad. Rosemont, Villa Nova, Radnor, Wayne, Devon. . . . out from the city,
covering a beautiful rolling country with high hills and deeps valleys, of which
city wealth has made a vast garden. Millionaires find that "gentleman farming"
is the easiest way of spending money, even easier than a yacht. They enjoy
the expensive luxury and incidentally they beautify the country, improve the
strain of livestock, and subjectively improve themselves by the exercise and
the fresh air they obtain. . . .

— J. W. Townsend, *The Old "Main Line"* [2]

New Jersey, New York, and Pennsylvania all
have venerable histories; each was one of the
original thirteen colonies, and as such was
an important historical and cultural center. During the
nineteenth century these states also developed as centers of heavy industry, especially in the fields of glass,
iron, and steel production. Industrial products require
transporting, and many of the nation's railroads had
their creative and physical beginnings in the region
as well. These industries and the railroads became the
source of wealth for many of the men who bestowed
architectural commissions on the leading national and
regional architectural firms. In addition to these growing industrial interests, there was room in all of the
states for recreational activities, and beautiful woodland
and waterfront areas were discovered and transformed
into resort or seasonal second-home communities.

The coast of New Jersey provided the principle
Middle Atlantic beach resort communities of the late
nineteenth century: Long Branch, Elberon, Monmouth
Beach, and the boardwalk town of Asbury Park on the
northern New Jersey Shore; Atlantic City and Ocean

City farther to the south; and Cape May at the south-
ernmost tip. Peabody & Stearns's resort commissions
were clustered in the mid-state shore area of Monmouth County—in Elberon and Monmouth Beach.
Early in the 1800s this area had been a haven for popular theatrical performers as well as for many presidents
later in the century and into the twentieth: Chester A.
Arthur, James Garfield, Ulysses S. Grant, Benjamin Harrison, Rutherford Hayes, William McKinley, and Wood-
row Wilson all reportedly visited and vacationed in the
area. It was here that President Garfield was brought to
recuperate following the attempt on his life in Washington, D.C.; he died of his gunshot wounds in Elberon
on September 19, 1881.

Long Branch is familiar through the paintings of
Winslow Homer from the late 1860s, although its
history as a destination dates back to the late 1700s.
The town boasted beaches, a few hotels, and summer estates. To its south, is Elberon, which was first
developed by Lewis B. Brown, whose initials and last
name gave the area its name. He purchased a mile and
a quarter of oceanfront property in 1866, and during

2.1. Cottage where President James A. Garfield was sent when wounded, Elberon, New Jersey. Postcard, collection of the author.

the next year he and two other investors laid out and constructed Ocean Avenue. Lots sold at an opening price of $1,250 per acre. Land values continued to rise, peaking in the boom of 1902. South Elberon attracted Solomon R. Guggenheim, Hamilton F. Kean, and Lewis Kahn, for their "country seats."[3] Elberon was the location of the H. Victor Newcomb residence, designed by McKim, Mead & White in 1880, which attained nearly iconic status in studies of the emerging Shingle Style in American architecture. North of Long Branch, Monmouth Beach was incorporated as a borough in Monmouth County in 1906.

In addition to the New Jersey commissions included in this chapter, Peabody & Stearns may have also worked on the summer cottage for William J. Hutchinson located in Sea Bright, and for George F. Baker, the prominent New York banker and railroad president. Bruce Price designed Baker's cottage in Galilee featured in the *American Architect and Building News* (April 5, 1886); however, financial records in the Peabody & Stearns archives indicate that they designed a "Monmouth Beach Stable" as well as a barn, a bathhouse, and windmill, all at Silver Lake in 1886. Baker was also involved in both the Elberon Casino and St. Peter's Church in Galilee .

Without question, Peabody & Stearns's most significant commission in the state of New Jersey was for the Lawrenceville School campus in Lawrenceville, created during the years 1885–1902 (fig. 2.2). Working with Frederick Law Olmsted as landscape architect, the firm was responsible for all of the original buildings of the school and for creating a new typology for school residential architecture. Other commissions in New Jersey included several railroad stations for the Central Railroad of New Jersey, including the Little Silver station.

New York State's resort opportunities ran the gamut from the venerable hotels and racetrack in Saratoga Springs to the commuter country estates on Long Island. The lakes and woods of the Adirondack Mountains drew wealthy patrons from the cities for seasonal residence and sporting activities, while the West Point–Hudson Highlands area was a popular stop on the "American tour," due to the accessibility of the Hudson Valley area and its historical interest. Peabody & Stearns received many residential and commercial commissions in New York City, but the firm's involvement in the leisure architecture market in the state was limited to Highland Falls, with the several commissions for J. Pierpont Morgan in the late 1880s. The Morgan commissions may have encouraged the firm to enter an architectural competition for a building at the Military Academy at West Point, for which they were not successful. Peabody & Stearns's involvement on Long Island was minimal and undocumented. Regarding the Adirondacks, notations in the Peabody & Stearns property record cards and an unexamined plan for the Saranac Inn near the town of Saranac Lake suggest the firm's possible involvement in that community; a visit by Robert Peabody is documented by his signature in the hotel's register on September 13, 1892.

In the state of Pennsylvania, the Pocono Mountains and Lake Erie districts were naturals for resort development. However, it was in the verdant farmland outside of Philadelphia that the country houses of Peabody & Stearns's clients were clustered and that became a legend in their own time. The area called the Main Line was popularized (and in many cases populated) by the owners and directors of the Pennsylvania Railroad Company. In concert with the impulses of the times, those who could afford to escape the heat of the city did so, at first to hotels and turnpike inns outside of

2.2. Lawrenceville School, Memorial Hall, Lawrenceville, New Jersey. Postcard, collection of the author.

Philadelphia, and later to their own country houses and estates. Peabody & Stearns had commissions for at least seven country houses on the Main Line and in Chestnut Hill—of these all but one were intended as part-time residences. The firm designed some of these clients' Philadelphia town houses as well. The architectural archives at the Boston Public Library include drawings and financial records for a house for Mrs. Chandler in Wissahickon Heights, Pennsylvania. This is a Federal-style house of stone, with a gambrel roof, a formal balustrade on the roof, and elaborately trimmed window surrounds. Whether this house was ever built, or if perhaps it was an alternate design to the Walter Lewis Ross house (whose wife was Julia Peabody

Chandler), is unknown at this time. There is also a suggestion that Peabody & Stearns worked on the Radnor, Pennsylvania, house of Paul Mills, cousin of George W. C. Drexel.

In other areas of the state it had commissions for a year-round residence for Dr. Richard Harte in Abington (Harte's summer home in Northeast Harbor was built by Peabody & Stearns in 1905), and at least a dozen commissions for residences and several commercial buildings in Pittsburgh. Robert Peabody's association with the Carnegie family on Cumberland Island, Georgia, led to the firm's inclusion in several competitions in Pennsylvania, including one for the Capitol in Harrisburg.

2.3. Roof of terminal building, Central Railroad of New Jersey. From the Collections of the Library of Congress.

New Jersey

St. Peter's Church in Galilee

Monmouth Beach, New Jersey, 1880–81

> The church of St. Peter of Galilee (Protestant Episcopal), one of the prettiest, most noted and most happily named churches on the coast, has no settled pastor, but prominent divines of the denomination officiate there during the summer.
> — GUSTAV KOBBE, *The New Jersey Coast and Pines*[4]

The St. Peter's Church in Galilee was organized in 1873 as a mission of St. James's Church of Long Branch. A chapel was built at that time at a cost of $8,000 and dedicated on August 26, 1873. It was reorganized as a parish several years later, and finally incorporated as St. Peter's Church in Galilee at Monmouth Beach in 1882.[5] A building lot was purchased in 1877 and the second St. Peter's in Galilee was built, designed by Peabody & Stearns. References in Peabody's datebook indicate several visits or conferences in the first quarter of 1881.

Wolverton's Atlas of Monmouth County, New Jersey (1889) located the property on Ocean Avenue in Monmouth Beach, several lots north of the Life-Saving Station and next door to the property of J. L. Riker. Almost all of the properties in the neighborhood ran from the shore of the Atlantic Ocean across Ocean Avenue and through to the Shrewsbury River; the church building was originally constructed on the shoreline of the Atlantic, but it was later moved to the west side of Ocean Avenue to protect it from storm surge and erosion.

The church was small, as befitted a summer chapel; it was constructed in a meeting-house design with a wood frame for a cost of $14,182.73. A corner tower rose above the small church, while the stained-glass and trefoil-headed lancet windows in the gable ends were prominent features of the building. Local legend has it that the area was called Galilee because of the number of fishermen in the area and the biblical verses that connect fishers of men with the Sea of Galilee. The Galilee Fishing Association was organized in 1884 and was a major supplier of fish to New York City until about the 1940s.

St. Peter's in Galilee was used as a church only until the early 1940s, after which it stood vacant. A later owner of the property, Clinton Cook, reportedly petitioned the local zoning board for approval to use the building as a theater in 1949, but his application was denied.[6]

St. Peter's in Galilee was destroyed by fire on Sunday, May 1, 1955.

2.4. St. Peter's Church in Galilee, Monmouth Beach, New Jersey. William J. Leonard. *Seaside Souvenir*, 1903. Courtesy of Randall Gabrielan.

Elberon Casino

Elberon, New Jersey, 1883

> . . . an example of what may be called the new
> American school of domestic architecture, which
> is striking out a form and feeling of its own.
> — *The Builder*, December 1886

When the Elberon Casino was constructed in 1883, it represented a comparatively new building type in the United States. George Sheldon included four casinos in *Artistic Country-Seats*—three by McKim, Mead & White and this one by Peabody & Stearns. Sheldon considered the McKim, Mead & White casino in Newport, Rhode Island (1880), to be the prototype of the genre, followed closely by that firm's design for the Short Hills Casino in Short Hills, New Jersey. Their fine design for the casino on Narragansett Pier in Rhode Island appeared in 1886. The Peabody & Stearns Elberon Casino caused Sheldon unexpectedly to digress into a soliloquy on the hardship of being an architect. Unlike a painter or sculptor, who can retire to his studio and create his art at the slightest whim, an architect must wait for a patron who wishes to build his building before the work stands as a completed artwork. And, unlike the painter or sculptor who maintains full artistic control of his creation, the architect's completed form has been subjected to the pokes and prods of his patron, the patron's spouse and decorator, perhaps the landscape architect and, if it's a public building or club building, the considered

opinions of all of the members of the building committee. It may sometimes be hard to see the genius of the architect amid the meddling of all of the involved parties. It was in this regard that Sheldon reported that "the erection of so artistic and convenient headquarters as the Elberon Casino speaks favorably not only of the architects, but of the conditions that gave them their opportunity."[7]

The Elberon Casino was commissioned by a group of eight summer residents who intended it as a social club for their peers. Elberon is located directly adjacent to the town of Long Branch, whose beach and resort amenities attracted an unpredictably mixed crowd from nearby New York and Philadelphia area neighborhoods. The incorporators of the casino—H. Victor Newcomb, George R. Blanchard, John Sloane, James A. Garland, Horace Porter, Amos Cotting, Granville T. Hawes, and Richard Talbot—created a controlled environment with the amenities that they required—a general lounging room, a reading room and a "*bijou* theater, with stage, two dressing-rooms, and auditorium." Thus, in addition to the expected activities of a men's club—reading, a game of cards, perhaps a drink at the bar—theatrical programs, a series of piano recitals by German-born Miss Adele Lewing in August 1889, and a flower show by the Elberon Horticultural Society in 1904, were hosted in the casino. A period photograph reveals badminton nets stretched across the lawn in front of the club's porte-cochere, suggesting the possibility of outdoor activities as well. Dues were set at $150 per year, and this along with the rigorous social qualifications for admission kept the membership small. The stated mission of the Elberon company was "to improve, beautify and develop the lands, . . . to erect buildings for public gatherings and club purposes."[8] In addition to the casino, the group constructed the Elberon Hotel, described as "one of the most elegant and perfectly furnished and appointed hotels on the seashore."[9]

The Elberon Casino structure was modestly sized and finished. The interior finish of the rooms was described as being of natural light wood. The exterior was almost stylized in its simplicity—plain shingles sheathed most of the exterior surface, with untrimmed door and window openings. A Palladian-style window with scrollwork surround was the only decorative feature on the streetsized façade. Multiple decks provided ample access to the outside air and views. A covered walkway to a domed pavilion—a familiar Peabody & Stearns design feature—complemented the horizontality of the overall structure. Built for a mere $17,725, it was intended to be a modest, although exclusive, meeting place.

The casino was located at the corner of Lincoln and Elberon avenues, in a residential area of the town, approximately one block back from the iconic Shingle Style Ocean Avenue residence of H. Victor Newcomb. Other neighbors included John Sloane, George W. Childs, Henry A. C. Taylor, and the cottage of General Grant. Beautifully manicured lawns surrounded the Casino, helping it to blend with the residential nature of the neighborhood. A circa 1940 postcard view of the property documents that it had been purchased by F. Housman and remodeled as a private home, Thorne Hedge.

The Elberon Casino building was demolished in 1959.

2.6. Elberon Casino, repurposed as Thorne Hedge, home of F. Housman. Postcard from the Robert W. Speck Collection, Deal, New Jersey.

2.7. Elberon Casino. Messrs. Mead and White" mistakenly listed as architects. From *The Builder,* December 25, 1886, vol. 51. Courtesy of the Boston Public Library Fine Arts Department.

2.8. Elberon Casino, Elberon Avenue, Long Branch, New Jersey. Postcard, from the Edward F. Thomas Collection, HistoricLongBranch.org.

New York

Cragston

(additions and alterations)

Highland Falls, New York, 1886

J. Pierpont Morgan, 1837–1913

Sometimes the Morgan summer place, Cragston, at
Highland Falls, is filled with informal parties of young
people who have drifted over from neighbouring
houses; somewhere a little apart from the life and
movement may be seen Mr. Morgan, sitting in a wide-
armed chair, self-absorbed, and outwardly chiefly interested in his cigars, of which he lights one after another.
— Carl Hovey, *The Life Story of J. Pierpont Morgan* [10]

Cragston is an example of a Peabody & Stearns
commission to design additions and alterations
to an existing property and to provide additional designs for significant farm outbuildings. John
Pierpont Morgan recognized the beauty and tranquility
of Highland Falls, New York, early on, and it became the
site of his favorite summer retreat. According to his biog-
raphers, the Morgan family moved up to Cragston early
in the spring and remained all summer. Morgan himself
commuted to Manhattan every day by train or by boat.
Unlike many of his contemporaries, Morgan did not
desire the summer social scene of Newport, preferring
the old farmhouse surrounded by the fields and farm-
lands on the west bank of the Hudson River. [11]

In July 1871, J. P. Morgan's banking firm merged
with the Philadelphia banking house belonging to
Anthony Drexel, producing the firm of Drexel, Morgan & Company. Shortly after that, he purchased
the Cragston property for $60,000. In 1886, Morgan
commissioned Peabody & Stearns to expand and
modernize the existing farmhouse. The new design
added asymmetrical wings to the house, a full third
story, a widow's walk, and a conservatory. [12] New
landscaping included a terrace with views of the
Hudson. When complete, the farmhouse totaled
thirty rooms. The exterior was finished in clapboard, with white trim and dark shutters. Details
were eclectic: the covered entrance portico was
prescient of that on the Shingle Style Drexel cottage Gripsholm Manor on Islesboro (1903), and a
diamond-paned oriel window continued that Tudoresque feeling. On the garden side of the house,
the additions were more in keeping with the farmhouse heritage of the residence. While the interior
renovations were considerable, the house retained
its country feeling. Years later, L. Soulsby wrote
from "Cragston on the Hudson": "October 24, 1916.
. . . .I arrived at a most home-like, small-big country
house, which looks as if the chairs and tables and
rooms had found their place because somebody
had wanted them *just there*, and were so comfortable. . . ." [13] The property record card lists the original renovation expense in 1886 as $28,472, plus

cottages totaling another $23,028. Morgan later commissioned a dairy building, a "2nd house," and other alterations in 1888 and 1889.

The Cragston property ultimately totaled nearly 750 acres (although some reports expanded the estate to up to 2,000 acres), stretching for nearly half a mile along the Hudson River between the Bear Mountain Bridge and West Point. The house was situated on a bluff that provided a spectacular view of the river—some said as far south as Sing Sing. It was surrounded by groves of cedar and elm trees, and grounds accented by items collected by Morgan in his travels. Extensive greenhouses and gardens built on the property included a 2-acre rose garden. The farm raised horses, prizewinning cattle, and Morgan's champion collie dogs.

The dairy building looked like something out of the English countryside. The building was of brick construction with a steeply pitched roof and cupola. An ell original to the structure, with timber-frame detailing, completed the quaint appearance. Biographer Jean Strouse reports that "when the contractors turned in a bid for the new dairy, [Morgan] told Peabody & Stearns he had no intention of "going ahead on such a basis. I understand it is nearly double what Mr. Vanderbilt's dairy cost, which from all accounts is too high."[14]

Cragston was well used. For the annual Fourth of July picnics, crews of men fired torpedoes and rockets from the Hudson River shore.[15] A *New York Times* article on February 22, 1895, reported that Morgan opened Cragston for a Washington's Birthday celebration for many of the family's friends and associates. "Every train since noon brought from a dozen to twenty guests. All the sleighs in this village have been kept busy during the day conveying the arrivals to Mr. Morgan's home."

John Pierpont Morgan has been the subject of at least a dozen biographies and was unquestionably one of the larger-than-life figures of the Gilded Age. He was well known for his yachts, all named *Corsair,* and for his signature cigars. Morgan did not personally commission other buildings from Peabody & Stearns. However, in 1884 he donated $4,000 for the building of the Groton School in Groton, Massachusetts, and in that way was reconnected with Peabody & Stearns, the designer of the original buildings at the school. J. P. Morgan died in Rome on March 31, 1913. His wife, the former Frances Tracy, continued to reside at Cragston until her death in 1924.

In 1928, Morgan's son, J. P. Morgan, Jr., sold the Cragston property to a real estate syndicate. The Cragston Yacht and Country Club remodeled the main house into a clubhouse and enlarged the existing boathouse and dock. A nine-hole golf course was laid out on the property. The club opened on August 2, 1930, but closed the next year. Later developers planned to construct a "high-class residential colony" on the property.

Cragston burned in the 1940s and a new house was built on the old foundation.

The dairy building was converted to a residence and is in private ownership.

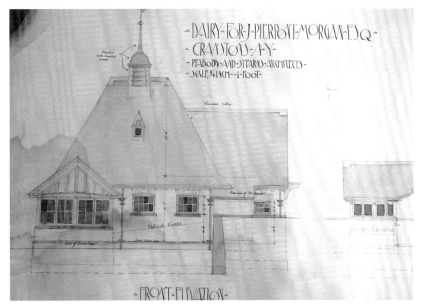

Pennsylvania

2.13. Oakley, façade.
Courtesy of the Chestnut Hill
Historical Society.

GARDEN FRONT.
SCALE ¼"=1'0'

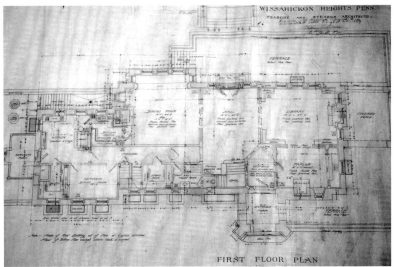

FIRST FLOOR PLAN

2.14. Oakley, garden
front elevation. Peabody
and Stearns Collection,
courtesy of the Boston Public
Library Fine Arts Department.

2.15. Oakley, first floor
plan. Peabody and Stearns
Collection, courtesy of the
Boston Public Library Fine
Arts Department.

Oakley
Wissahickon Heights, Pennsylvania, 1899–1902

Walter Lewis Ross, n.d.

In 1896, Walter Ross and his wife Julia Peabody Chandler Ross acquired the lot of land at 500 West Moreland Avenue from the estate of Henry Houston, father-in-law of soon-to-be neighbor George Woodward. A building permit for the house and carriage house was issued on September 6, 1899.[16]

Oakley was designed in a familiar late Queen Anne style with multiple dormers and gabling to create a lively if somewhat confused exterior. Like many of the country houses in the area, it was built of stone, with coordinating stone sills and flat arched stone lentils. Windows throughout were diamond-pane above single-pane. On the garden front, windows in the library and hall had stone arches above, while the deep bay window in the dining room was covered with a deep sloping roof, similar to that on the covered porch. A gable on the second floor of the service wing was finished with a shingled surface and detailing. Entrance to the two-and-a-half-story country house was from the covered entrance porch into the vestibule. In an unusual twist on the usual house plan, the entire front of the house with the exception of the parlor (which had no window on the front façade) was service area—the main staircase, a coat and toilet room, a storeroom, and the servants' dining room. From the vestibule the guest might enter the parlor to the right, which led into the spacious 18-by-24-foot library, or into the equally spacious hall. The dining room was accessed from the hall, with double sliding doors that closed to provide privacy from the activities of the house. The three main rooms (library, hall, and dining room) all looked out over the garden and the large terrace. The parlor and the dining room were finished with painted pine woodwork; the hall and library had quartered oak. Notations on the Peabody & Stearns plans indicate that both the dining room and the hall were to have wainscoting and that all of the floors were quartered oak.

Walter Lewis Ross was a member of the banking and brokerage firm of Ross, Morgan & Company. He was a member of the New York Stock Exchange and the Philadelphia Stock Exchange, and was of enough note to be included in Moses King's book *Philadelphia and Popular Philadelphians*, published in 1891. His wife, Julia, was well connected with the Peabody, Chandler, and Draper families in New England.

The Rosses owned Oakley until 1925, when the house was sold to Frederick Strawbridge. In 1961 the property was divided, and the one-and-a-half-story Tudor-style Peabody & Stearns–designed carriage house was converted to a separate dwelling.

Both Oakley and the carriage house are extant and are private residences.

Ashwood

Villanova, Pennsylvania, 1894

Jacob Da Costa, 1833–1900

Ashwood was recorded by the Historic American Buildings Survey in 1958. It is described as an eighteenth-century farmhouse with nineteenth-century additions; a watercolor done in 1888 by Eugene Castello and later photographs portray a frame house—a "large dignified, but plain suburban residence."[17] Further investigation reveals, however, that "upon purchase of the property by Dr. Da Costa in 1888, Ashwood became a tenant house on the land, and Da Costa built a large stone mansion further up the hill to which he gave the old name of Ashwood." The Ashwood that Peabody & Stearns designed, then, was the stone country house built in 1894.

Dr. Jacob Mendes Da Costa was born on the Island of St. Thomas, West Indies, in 1833. His parents were of a wealthy and respected Sephardic Jewish family in the community—a memoir of Da Costa indicates that his father, John Mendes Da Costa, "lived at leisure as a gentleman of wealth in the West Indies, where his ancestors had been bankers and planters."[18] The family moved to Europe when Jacob was a young child; when they later came to the United States in 1849, financial reversals in his family necessitated that Jacob turn to a practical education. He entered the Jefferson Medical College in Philadelphia and graduated in 1852. Da Costa furthered his medical studies in Paris and Vienna, and returned to Philadelphia, where he became well known as a teacher, a writer of medical texts and articles, and as a legendary diagnostician. Harvard University conferred the degree of LL.D. on him in 1897.

There was little notice of Ashwood made at the time of its construction. Photographs show that it was a large two-and-a-half story rough-stone country house. Entrance was made from the stone-arched porte-cochere, whose buttressed corners and rough-hewn arched windows gave it a definite Old World feeling. Windows in the main core of the residence were deep-set and untrimmed, with the exception of a bank of Jacobeanesque windows in what was perhaps the main hall of the house. A sheet of interior details shows that the hall and entrance areas were heavily paneled and that the staircase was hidden from the hall area behind a stylized archway. Plans for the gate lodge present a charming living space, featuring a living room with tower, a kitchen and a large storeroom on the first floor, and stairs to the sleeping chambers on the second floor.

Da Costa had his portrait painted by both Thomas Eakins and by Robert Vonnoh (1858–1933). The Vonnoh was exhibited at the Chicago World's Columbian Exhibition, and the Eakins now hangs at the Pennsylvania Hospital in Philadelphia, in which city Da Costa

2.16. Ashwood, entrance façade. Archives of the Radnor Historical Society.

2.17. Ashwood, gatehouse. Archives of the Radnor Historical Society.

2.18. Ashwood, stable. Archives of the Radnor Historical Society.

maintained his principal residence and his medical office at 1700 Walnut Street. Peabody & Stearns added a design for an addition and perhaps a spring house for this property to their list of commissions

Dr. Da Costa died unexpectedly at Ashwood in September 1900. His son, Charles Frederick, inherited the property; following his death in 1923, the sixty-one-acre Ashwood estate, including the main house, gate lodge, stable, barn, and farmhouse, was sold to a developer. The main house was destroyed by fire in the 1960s. The stone gate lodge still stands, readapted to its use as a banking institution.

2.19. Home of George Childs, original façade, c. 1881. From Print and Picture Collection, The Free Library of Philadelphia.

Wootton

(additions and alterations, 1896–c. 1910)

Bryn Mawr, Pennsylvania

George William Childs Drexel, 1868–1944

Many farms outside of the Bryn Mawr tract were early bought by Philadelphians for country houses. Among the first to purchase was George W. Childs, who took up a large property on the new road that had just been laid out.

— John W. Townsend. *The Old Main Line* [19]

Wootton may be the only house included in this book that was designed by another architect for another client. The original house is attributed to the office of Philadelphia architect John McArthur for George William Childs (1829–1894)—publisher of the *Philadelphia Public Ledger*. Childs was a good friend of Anthony Drexel, founder of Drexel University; they were business partners in many ventures, including the development of the residential communities of Wayne and St. Davids. Drex-

el's youngest son, George W. C. Drexel, was Childs's godson and he ultimately inherited the property. He became one of Peabody & Stearns's loyal clients: he commissioned both Gripsholm Manor, a summer cottage on Islesboro, Maine (1893), and his Rittenhouse Square city residence (1896), as well as substantial alterations and additions to Wootton beginning in 1896.

George W. C. Childs had purchased 110 acres in Bryn Mawr and named the property Wootton, after the ancestral home of the Duke of Buckingham, a personal friend of the family. According to an article in the *Bryn Mawr Home News*, " ...Wootton had its origin in the desire of Mrs. Childs to build a simple home which should be a retreat for the family, midway in season and elaborateness between the Philadelphia residence and the establishment at Long Branch." [20] While Childs originally commissioned an unpretentious red brick summer retreat, the estate was considerably enlarged and embellished over time by both the Childs family and by George W. C. Drexel.

Drexel worked at his father's banking house until he was twenty-five, at which time he joined George Childs

at the *Public Ledger;* he remained at the newspaper until its sale in 1904 to the *New York Times*. Drexel married Mary Irick in 1891, and two years later they commissioned Peabody & Stearns to design a mansion at 18th and Locust streets, where they lived until 1917. The Rittenhouse Square mansion was sold in 1924 to Edward Bok to become the new home of the Curtis Institute of Music.

When Drexel inherited Wootton, he made nearly $120,000 worth of additions and alterations in 1896–98 alone, expanding west and south with large wings for dining and reception rooms; later commissions included a series of double cottages for servants' quarters; a servants' ell in 1902, an aviary and greenhouses, stable and garage complex, ornamental bridges, and more. He continued making alterations through at least 1910. The country house once described as "an English manor of the relentless school"[21] ultimately contained fifty rooms on an estate variously described as between two hundred and four hundred acres.

Wootton was constructed of brick with a slate roof. The main façade featured much limestone, with limestone trim around the windows and timber detailing on the gable ends. The visitor who entered the vesti-

bule and the large entrance hall was greeted by Drexel's collection of medieval armor, lances, pikes, and shields. The first floor also included a drawing room to the right of the entrance, a library, billiards room (later known as the smoking room), dining room, and morning room. Large stained-glass windows and heavy dark furniture dominated the space. "The dining room could have held a meeting of the knights of King Arthur's court," Drexel's niece recalled.[22] On the second floor, in addition to the Empire and the Peacock rooms (so named for their furnishings), were chambers for the mother-in-law Mrs. Irick and for Mrs. Childs, when they visited, and an additional guest chamber. Chambers for Mr. and Mrs. Drexel included a porch where Mrs. Drexel used to eat breakfast. The room over the porte-cochere was enlarged to make an additional sitting room.

Wootton was sold to the Sisters of the Immaculate Heart of Mary in 1948, following the death of Mary Irick Drexel. All of the furnishings were sold at a six-day public auction in 1949. In 1950 the St. Aloysius Academy for Boys moved to the estate, where it now occupies the former stable complex. The main house serves as a convent and conference center.

2.20. Wootton, rear view. Courtesy of the Radnor Historical Society.

2.21. Wootton, south elevation. ©2009 W. F. Milliken.

Laurento

Radnor, Pennsylvania, 1901

Craig Biddle, 1879–1947

The mansion of "Laurento" looms majestically on its hilltop, rising high and stately above the surrounding trees and shrubbery, quite dominating the landscape for many miles around.

— *American Homes and Gardens*, February 1907

The Italian Renaissance–style Laurento was considered one of the "show places on the Main Line" during its eighty-year tenure. George W. C. Drexel, whose country estate Wootton was close by in Bryn Mawr, gave Laurento as a wedding present to his nephew Craig Biddle.

Barr Ferree described Laurento as a large light brown brick house with spacious fronts, whose length was emphasized by a strong string-course between the first and second stories and a low sloping broad roof. He reported the design to be "thoroughly distinguished."[23] The entrance façade was fronted by a terra-cotta porte-cochiere, constructed of four great piers, while the terrace front (the main elevation of the house) featured projecting terra-cotta loggias that framed a monumental "triumphal arch" and Roman Ionic column entrance. Steps led down to a large terrace and ultimately to the expansive slope below. Construction of the house and stable totaled $147,122.

Craig Biddle was the youngest son of Edward and Emily Drexel Biddle; like his older brother, Livingston (see Westview), he had been raised by his Uncle George and Aunt Mary Drexel following the death of his mother in 1883. Craig Biddle was a sportsman—he was a recognized tennis player, a prominent cricket player at the Merion Cricket Club, and such a noted horse-racing enthusiast that at the Rittenhouse Club dinner given by his wedding ushers in Philadelphia, the table was decorated with a miniature racetrack and stables made of papier-mâché. Small mechanical horses were raced around the track between courses of the meal. Biddle was described in the *New York Times* as one of the "dashing young men" of Eastern Society at the turn of the century.[24]

Laurento was ideally situated on 113 acres on a bluff overlooking Little Darby Creek. Olmsted Brothers were the landscape architects for the project, and their correspondence reveals much about the process of construction. Frederick Law Olmsted, Jr., visited the property on November 15, 1900, with Mr. Peabody and Mr. Gallagher of Peabody & Stearns, Craig Biddle and his fiancée, and Mrs. Drexel (presumably Aunt Mary Drexel, whom Olmsted credited with "a very good knowledge of the design and management of a country estate").[25] Two building sites were discussed in detail, the one favored by Biddle and his future wife being that which was higher and provided a longer-range view and more "commanding situation." While Olmsted favored a lower, less formal, and incidentally, less structurally ambitious site, he recognized that Biddle's chosen site would have a cooler situation more open to the breeze, a "distinct advantage" for a summer house. However, Mr. Biddle was sensitive to the prices of landscape services (perhaps because his uncle was paying for the work), indicating on November 22, 1900, that "I want it clearly understood that I want the work to be done on as moderate a scale as possible." Olmsted's reply included a carbon copy to G. W. C. Drexel, presumably appealing to his more defined sense of decorum (and more generous checkbook). He suggested that given a "building of the size and dignity of your new house we feel that some extension of the formal treatment of the building to the right and left [would be desirable]." The many letters capture the give-and-take between client and landscape architect as well as between building architect and landscape designer.

Inside Laurento, a small paneled vestibule painted in white admitted visitors to the French gray paneled reception room, described by Ferree as "cool and charming"—designed and furnished in Louis XVI style. In plan, the Great Hall was flanked with aisles and a main corridor decorated with a series of busts of Roman emperors leading to the various rooms of the main floor. White marble floors were spread with rich Oriental rugs. The library walls were covered with red-striped damask and paneled with mahogany. The billiards room was situated at the far end of the main corridor. Its paneling was of wood topped by a carved leather frieze depicting hunting scenes; the floor was covered with red bricks, with many small Oriental rugs. The yellow-painted breakfast room and the dining room, which was paneled in dark oak with an ancient tapestry frieze above, were across the great hall.

In 1911, Laurento was sold to banker-broker Archibald Barklie, who renamed the property Inver House and commissioned Wilson Eyre to do additions and alterations. After several more changes in ownership, Laurento was demolished in the 1980s and replaced by a town-house condominium development. The original entry gates—"high sandstone piers capped with standing lions and supporting a wrought-iron arch . . . a stately, handsome entrance"—survive.

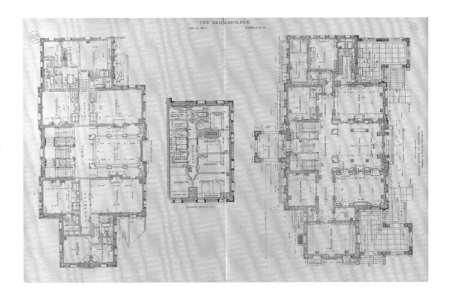

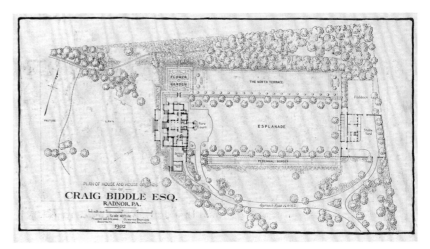

2.24. Laurento, floor plans. *The Brickbuilder*, vol. 12, no. 6, pl. 42 and 47. Courtesy of the Rotch Library, Massachusetts Institute of Technology.

2.25. Laurento, plan of house and grounds. Peabody & Stearns and Olmsted Brothers. *Architectural Review*, September 1905. Archives of the Radnor Historical Society.

2.26. Laurento, stable. Courtesy of Memorial Library, Boston Architectural College.

Penshurst, 1902

Narberth, Pennsylvania

Percival Roberts, Jr., 1857–1943

Percival Roberts, Jr., Narberth, Pa., is greatly improving
his country seat there.…They have a very fine range
of greenhouses, which they are filling up with the
newest and best of everything. An extensive Italian
garden is being made and lots of outdoor planting
is being done.…"
— "The Gardener's Club," *Gardening*, 1904 [26]

2.27. Penshurst, façade.
Courtesy of Memorial Library,
Boston Architectural College.

Penshurst was probably the largest and most extravagant of the houses designed by Peabody & Stearns and built as a single project (as opposed to Elm Court, which achieved its total of ninety-four rooms through years of additions). The Peabody & Stearns project record card for Penshurst indicates that the total actual cost of the construction was $574,519.16.

Penshurst was designed as a seventy-room, Elizabethan-style manor house in a traditional U-shaped plan and was constructed of red brick and limestone. A large entrance hall, with fireplace and staircase, led visitors through twin-arched doorways to the vaulted Great Hall. Period photographs show rooms that were paneled and decorated with architectural artifacts imported from Great Britain; fastidiously decorated by Irving & Casson of Boston, the first-floor plan included a drawing room, library and picture gallery, billiards room, office, dining room, and morning room.

Penshurst was sited on 571 acres of Pennsylvania farmland and countryside. The Olmsted brothers' landscaping included formal gardens and extensive and intricate terracing elements and was the crowning glory of the property. Outbuildings included an extensive greenhouse complex, dairy barns, stables, electrical plant, chapel, and water tower. Although Penshurst is often considered to have been a primary residence, the influential Boyd's Blue Book listed the Roberts residence as 1935 Chestnut Street in Philadelphia, with Penshurst as their "sum res"—summer residence. It was illustrated in the *Architectural Record* (1905), in *Indoors and Out* (1905) and in the *American Architect* (1926).

Percival Roberts, Jr., was the son of Percival and Eleanor Williamson Roberts; his father was the owner-proprietor of the Pencoyd Iron Works at Bala Cynwyd. After graduation from Haverford College, Class of 1876, young Roberts spent several months working for the Pennsylvania Geological Survey. He later took postgraduate work in metallurgy and chemistry at the University of Pennsylvania before joining one of his father's companies, where he worked his way up to president. When Pencoyd Iron Works merged into the newly formed American Bridge Company of New York, he was chosen to be president of that corporation. The year before Penshurst was constructed, he agreed to join in the creation of the United States Steel Corporation; he remained a member of the board of directors until his retirement in 1934. When he died in 1943, he was called the "Greatest Practical Steel Man in the World." [27]

Penshurst came to an untimely end at its owner's hand. In 1939, Lower Merion Township announced its plans to build a trash-incinerating plant adjacent to the Penshurst property. Roberts was outraged and, in retaliation, had the house demolished. All of the furnishings were sold at auction by Samuel T. Freeman & Company of Philadelphia in that year. The land lay vacant for thirty years. In 1970 it was purchased by a developer who subdivided it and sold lots for residences. The elaborate garden gate remains to speak of the elaborate country house that once dominated the landscape.

2.28. Penshurst, parlor.
Courtesy of Memorial Library,
Boston Architectural College.

·HOUSE·FOR·DR·GEORGE·WOODWARD·
·SAINT·MARTIN'S··PHILADELPHIA·PENN·
·Peabody·&·Stearns·Archts··Boston·Mass·

·NORTHEAST·ELEVATION·
·Scale·¼"=1'·0"·

Krisheim

Chestnut Hill, Pennsylvania, 1910

George Stanley Woodward, 1863–1952

Benedicite, omnia opera Domini, Domino
(O all you works of the Lord, bless you the Lord)
— Inscription on the Exterior of Krisheim [28]

Krisheim has an aura that makes it a very special house in this collection of special houses. The reason for this can only be that the spirit of its original owners live on in the stones and mortar of one of Peabody & Stearns's legendary country houses.

At 27,000 square feet Krisheim is one of the largest of the architectural firm's country house commissions. The size is not what makes it remarkable, however. George and Gertrude Woodward were clearly passionate about their lives and their creations. They fell in love with the designs of Peabody & Stearns in 1895 and hired James Frederick Dawson of Olmsted Brothers to plan the Krisheim landscape nearly ten years before the house was built. The house was thoughtfully constructed and decorated with the creations of consummate craftsmen of both national and local renown—including Tiffany glass and Rookwood pottery, Henry Mercer tiles, Samuel Yellin ironwork, and Violet Oakley murals. Perhaps God really *is* in the details.

George Stanley Woodward was not the typical country house client. He was a graduate of Yale University (Class of 1887) and the University of Pennsyl-

vania medical school. Life takes unpredictable turns, however, and following the death of his father-in-law, railroad entrepreneur and real estate developer Henry H. Houston, Woodward reinvented himself as a real estate developer and manager in the Philadelphia suburbs. His early housing projects were for single-family residences in the northwest sector of Philadelphia. By 1909 he had developed an interest in multiple-family rental properties and expanded to the construction of high-quality low-income housing in the Chestnut Hill area. These duplex units by the firm of Duhring, Okie & Ziegler were innovative and remarkable for the time. Woodward also built a number of larger single residences for sale rather than rental north of Pastorius Park in Chestnut Hill. His personal involvement in real estate development wound down during the Depression, but the companies that he created, the George Woodward Company and the Woodward House Corporation, continue to manage the rental of the double houses that he was instrumental in building.

Olmsted Brothers landscaped many of Woodward's projects. Their files list St. Martin's Development in Chestnut Hill, Fairmount Park Extension and Lincoln Drive, and Pastorius Park, in addition to Krisheim. Photographs in the collection of the Chestnut Hill Historical Society preserve images of formal gardens that surrounded the house, while references in contemporary gardening periodicals suggest that the outlying property was lush and natural, although not without judicious manipulation from the landscape architects:

Krisheim . . . overlooking the Wissahickon Creek . . . has one of the finest retaining walls . . . to be found in the country, winding for hundreds of feet in and out along the broad curved walk, following the line of the creek. . . . this wonderful wall is "beautiful for situation" as well as most wisely and cleverly managed; and when the estate is thrown open for public inspection it attracts visitors from all sections of the country.[29]

There was much tragedy in George and Gertrude Woodward's lives. Their oldest son, Houston, was killed in action in France in World War One, and their daughter Gertrude ("Quita") died of Hodgkins disease in 1934. But there was much joy as well. In their memoirs—George published *The Memoirs of a Mediocre Man* in 1935, and Gertrude published a memorial memoir for Quita at about the same time— the Woodwards come alive. The family summered at Falmouth Foreside near Portland, Maine, when their children were young. They spent the summer of 1916 in Jackson Hole, Wyoming, and thereafter returned to their camp on Leigh Lake for many years. There the Woodwards "lived out of doors day and night, our dining table was under a tent fly, and only when it rained were our sleeping cots pulled into the tents or leantos."[30] This was radically different from the vacations

of even the Bar Harbor rusticators. The Woodwards enjoyed the traditional pastimes of the era as well: the family took its first of many trips to Europe in the summer of 1914, and sailed to Africa in 1928 to motor through the old cities of North Africa.

Krisheim was designed as a two-and-a-half-story stone English Tudor country house, arranged with two wings flanking the center section to create a U shape around the entrance drive. Cut stone surrounded the leaded-glass windows, and multiple individual and gabled wall dormers trimmed with half-timbering continued the Tudor theme. A massive two-story stone frontispiece with arched door, oriole window, and gabled dormer welcomed guests to the house. The floor in the vestibule told the story of the historic development of the surrounding area in handcrafted Mercer tiles. A passage from the vestibule led to the office, where the plans specify: "Space for organ pipes"—this for the tremendous pipe organ that Woodward had installed in Krisheim. The living hall gave entrance to the library and adjacent study, or into the dining room, each with a large bay window with built-in window seat. At the top of the stairs to the second floor, carved figures on

2.30. Krisheim, first floor plan. Peabody and Stearns Collection, courtesy of the Boston Public Library Fine Arts Department.

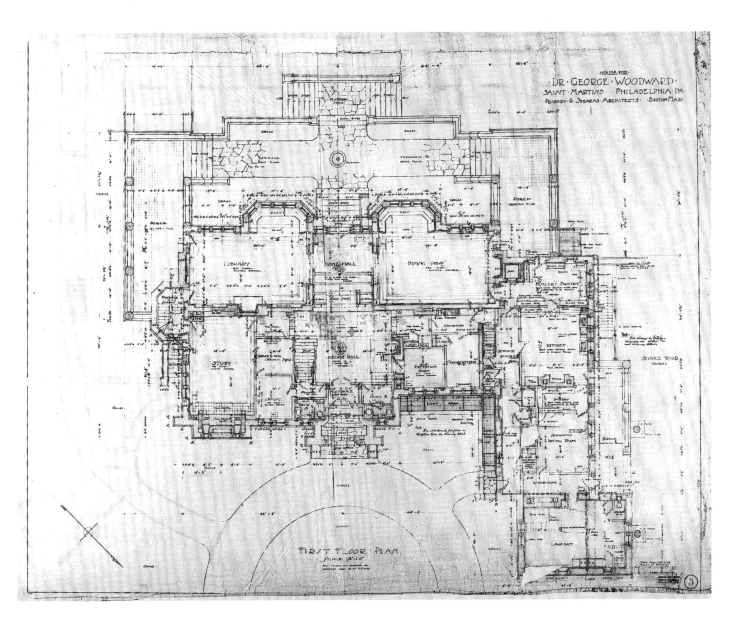

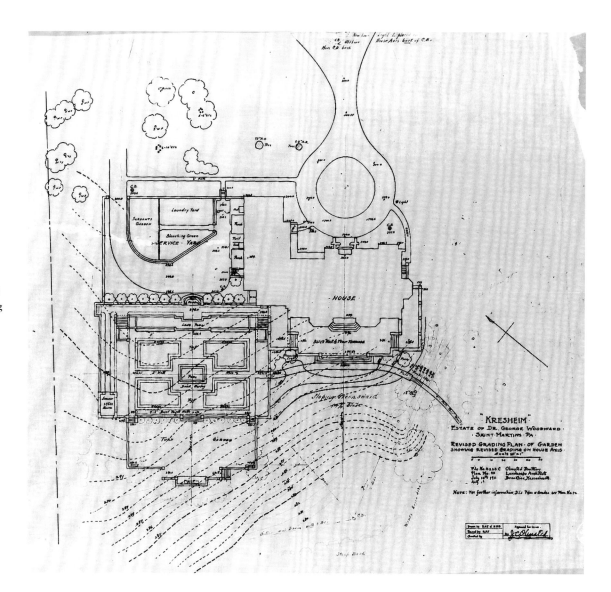

2.31. Krisheim, Olmsted brothers revised grading plan of garden, 1911. Peabody and Stearns Collection, courtesy of the Boston Public Library Fine Arts Department.

2.32. Design for Krisheim Gate. Note inscription, "We accept this sketch with pleasure. Go ahead. GW." Peabody and Stearns Collection, courtesy of the Boston Public Library Fine Arts Department.

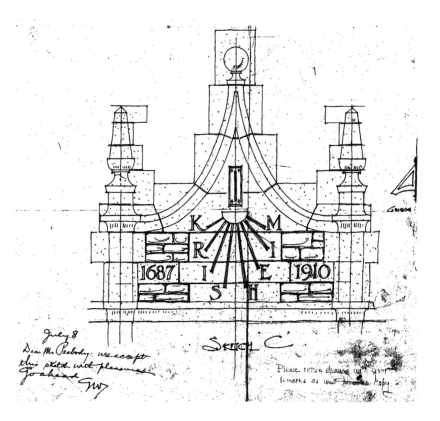

the posts of the banister represented the historic leaders of Pennsylvania.

Records indicate that the gate lodge was constructed in 1900, although the main house was not built until July of 1910—as the quotation that opens this book suggests, the Woodwards were not in a hurry to construct their country house, but knew exactly what they wanted. The original cost was $132,869.50, with additions over the next two or three years bringing the total expenditure to almost $220,000. During the same period, Woodward also commissioned Wilson Eyre, Jr., to design a gardener's cottage and cottage outbuildings.[31]

Krisheim was acquired in the 1960s by the United Presbyterian Church, U.S.A. for use as a retreat and conference center. In October 1983 the house and seven acres were reacquired by members of the Woodward family. The first floor of the interior was meticulously renovated with reference to the original Peabody & Stearns plans. The upper two floors are currently subdivided into several living units.

Krisheim is a private residence.

2.33. Westview, garden façade. Courtesy of Thomas A. O'Callaghan, Jr.

Westview

Bryn Mawr, Pennsylvania, 1919

Livingston L. Biddle, 1878-1959

"Westview," built where there had been a cornfield on the highest part of the estate, was undoubtedly named for its view across the fields of "Wooton" and the rolling country beyond.
— The Philadelphia Vassar Scholarship Benefit Designers' Show House program, 1976

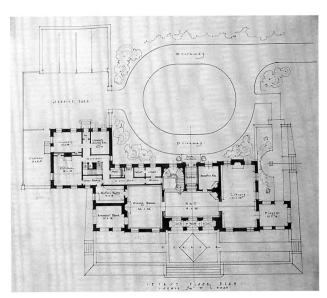

2.34. Westview, first floor plan. Peabody and Stearns Collection, courtesy of the Boston Public Library Fine Arts Department.

Westview was among the last of the Peabody & Stearns commissions. Records suggest that the planning was begun in 1916, and the house was completed in 1919, two years after the demise of both Robert Peabody and John Stearns; the design of the house was likely created by Appleton or young Stearns. Nonetheless, it is a credit to the name of the firm, and one of the few Peabody & Stearns Main Line country houses that survives intact.

2.35. Westview, front
façade. Courtesy of Thomas
A. O'Callaghan, Jr.

2.36. Westview, front
hall. Courtesy of Thomas A.
O'Callaghan, Jr.

Westview, constructed of sand-colored pebble-dash stucco above a granite foundation, might be described as a restrained version of Craig Biddle's earlier Laurento. High arched windows form a rhythmic pattern across the garden façade of the house. The marble string course accentuates the recessive second floor, partially hidden by the low-pitched hipped roof with extended eaves. Small one-story wings on either end of the large central block frame a central open loggia constructed of Roman arches and decorated with frescoed walls and groined vaults. Stone steps led down from the terrace to an immense lawn of grass, and a swimming pool and Italianate stucco poolhouse surrounded by formal boxwood once stood beside the house. The 14-foot-high front door under a massive oak canopy suspended from iron chains dominates the entrance façade of the house. The ironwork here and throughout the house was designed and created by Samuel Yellin, the well-known Philadelphia ironmaker and craftsman.

Livingston Ludlow Biddle was the middle son of Edward Biddle and Emily Drexel, daughter of Anthony J. Drexel. Emily Biddle died in 1883, leaving three young sons. The younger two, Livingston and Craig, were taken to be raised by her father—and ultimately went to live with their uncle, George W. Childs Drexel and his wife Mary. Uncle George Drexel, a devoted Peabody & Stearns client, commissioned the architects to design a country house for each of the two boys upon their marriages—Laurento for Craig in 1901 and Westview for Livingston in 1917. Livingston was a graduate of Princeton University (Class of 1900), a quiet and contemplative man. When George Drexel retired in 1903 from the *Public Ledger*, Livingston accompanied him and his wife on most of their travels. Like his brother, Livingston was an avid sportsman, and indulged his love of big game hunting on the safaris that were part of the extensive cruises of the *Alcedo*; several dozen trophy heads adorned the library room of Westview.

The Westview property initially measured about ten acres of farmland—all within walking distance of Drexel's Wootton; at Drexel's death, an additional twenty-five acres was added to the Westview parcel. Reports suggest that Livingston Biddle was an avid horticulturist, and a description of the grounds in 1976 indicates the wide variety of ornamental trees and shrubs included in the original plantings.[32]

Unlike most of the country houses designed by Peabody & Stearns, Westview was intended as a year-round residence. The interior plan was reflective of the simpler American lifestyle of the time—however, this does not mean that it lacked design and decorative details. The paneled foyer leads the visitor under an arch topped by intricately carved wood panels, into the great room. Here the 16-foot-high coffered ceilings draw the eye up and around to take in the floor-to-ceiling arched windows, the massive corner fireplace, and the well-proportioned staircase that curves twenty-eight steps to the second floor. The delicate octagonal reception room

displayed the Biddles's collection of carved ivory. To the left the handsome library provided display space for Livingston's trophy heads; a small "Italian Room" was entered through the massive Yellin wood and iron door. The paneled dining room shared the view of the west lawn; a small porch was later enclosed as a breakfast room. On the second floor, a suite consisting of rooms for Mr. and Mrs. Biddle included a full bath for him as well as a bath and dressing room and an enclosed porch for her. A guest chamber and chambers for the Biddles's two sons completed the plan. On the third floor, the tower chamber is augmented by a series of small rooms with extensive built-in storage. Built-in cupboard and drawers line the hallway.

Westview remained in the Biddle family until Mrs. Biddle's death in 1974. The property was then sold and subdivided for a residential development. Happily, Westview and the adjoining carriage house and garage were retained on nearly two acres of the original grounds.

Westview is privately owned.

2.37. Westview, library/ trophy room. Courtesy of Thomas A. O'Callaghan, Jr.

Chapter 3

The South

Georgia and West Virginia

Peabody & Stearns's stronghold was in the Northeast and Middle Atlantic states, but there are examples of the firm's work in several areas of the South. The commissions that have been identified and researched are located in Georgia and West Virginia, but as-yet-unsubstantiated work has been identified in Eureka Springs and Hot Springs, Arkansas. One southern resort community in which Peabody & Stearns surprisingly did *not* participate was Jekyll Island, off of the coast of Georgia. The Jekyll Island Club was founded on April 4, 1886, initially as a hunting club, but it soon transitioned into a family-inclusive retreat for a select group of the Gilded Age's corporate, civic, and cultural leaders, their wives, children, and associates. Many of the members of the club were Peabody & Stearns clients in other locales—among them George Fisher Baker, John Sanford Barnes, James J. Hill, Charles Lanier, Pierre Lorillard, John Pierpont Morgan, Fairman Rogers, Dr. Henry F. Sears, John Sloane, William Warren Vaughan, and George Woodward. Although the firm never had a Jekyll Island commission, it was not for lack of interest. In a letter dated November 3, 1896, Peabody wrote in reply to a query from his Cumberland Island client Mrs. Lucy Carnegie: "We thank you for your suggestion about the houses near the Jekyll Island Club. Of course, we should be glad to do more work in that neighborhood, but we do not know precisely how to induce your neighbors to employ us."[1] The mystery behind Peabody's absence from Jekyll Island remains; for reasons as yet unknown, other architects dominated the limited field.

Peabody & Stearns was responsible for extensive additions and alterations to Lucy Carnegie's winter residence on Cumberland Island, Dungeness, in addition to creating Plum Orchard for her son. The correspondence between Peabody & Stearns and Mrs. Carnegie's superintendent of properties, William Page, is of great interest. In addition to the Jekyll Island Club inquiry referred to above, Peabody investigated other networking opportunities. In February of 1897, Peabody wrote to Page in care of Mrs. Carnegie:

We see that Mr. Andrew Carnegie is interesting himself in the matter of the new Pennsylvania State House Building. They will doubtless have some sort of a competition and if they are wise it will be a limited competition. We are most anxious to be counted in. We think that if we write to Mr. Carnegie he will scarcely recognize our letter in his large correspondence, but it occurs to us that he may be at Dungeness, or that in some way you or Mrs. Carnegie may have the opportunity to express to him our desires. If you find it possible to do this for us we should be greatly obliged.[2]

Peabody & Stearns was one of the six firms chosen to compete, but it did not secure the commission. The firm did become involved in other Carnegie family projects, including the renovations of the summer cottage in Magnolia, Massachusetts, which was purchased by Andrew Carnegie II.

In Elkins, West Virginia, records substantiate Peabody & Stearns's commission for Pinecrest, Richard C. Kerens's large summer cottage. While suggestions of the firm's involvement in several buildings in Eureka Springs, Arkansas, are intriguing—the town was founded by Kerens and his railroad connections, and he was central to the building of several of the town's public buildings—information to support the suggestions has not been located, and the commissions remain as tantalizing invitations for more research.

3.1. Pinecrest, front view. Postcard, collection of the author.

3.2. Pinecrest, garden view, 2007. Photograph by the author.

Pinecrest/
Kerens-Spears House

Elkins, West Virginia, 1891-95

Richard C. Kerens, 1842-1916

The village of Kerens was originally known as New Interest, but with the coming of the railroad to the area the name was changed in honor of R. C. Kerens, a member of the company's board of directors.

— *Randolph Country Profile,* 1976 [3]

A carved pinecone finial on the newel post in the main hall welcomed guests to the summer home of Richard C. Kerens. It was symbolic perhaps of the forested and mountainous terrain surrounding Pinecrest in Elkins, West Virginia, now the gateway to the Monongahela National Forest.

The coursed sandstone façade of Pinecrest is dominated by a picturesque landscape of steeply pitched roofs. The house is a wonderfully asymmetrical construction, with gables and twin rounded turret towers providing architectural detail to the elevation. Pinecrest is difficult to see all at one glance, as the

3.3. Pinecrest, front elevation, Peabody and Stearns Collection, courtesy of the Boston Public Library Fine Arts Department.

3.4. Pinecrest first story plan. Peabody and Stearns Collection, courtesy of the Boston Public Library Fine Arts Department.

3.5. Sketch, Kerens's Stable. Peabody and Stearns Collection, courtesy of the Boston Public Library Fine Arts Department.

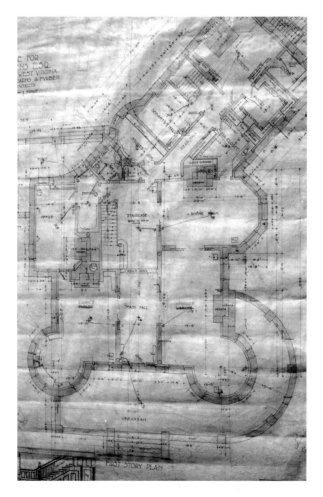

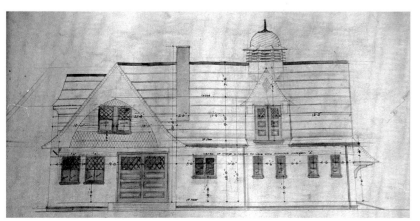

façade, porte-cochere and large covered porches snake around a basic blocky structure, providing as much variety of form and contrast as the once-panoramic view of Elkins and the landscaped grounds must have provided in the late 1890s.

Pinecrest's interiors are classically summer-cottage simple, unlike the two neighboring summer homes of Kerens's two business partners, Senators Henry G. Davis and Stephen B. Elkins, Hallihurst and Graceland, which boasted expansive formal rooms and great rooms intended for entertainments and public display. Warm-toned quartersawn white oak was a unifying theme throughout Pinecrest, extending even into the servants' wing. The first-floor plan consisted of three spacious rooms: a living room, a dining room, and a large office-library where meticulously crafted built-in oak bookcases lined the curve of one of the spacious turrets. Midway down the 15-by-50-foot main hall, a massive oak staircase led to the second floor, where several large chambers opened off of the gracious hall; additional bedchambers and storage were on the third floor. Elegant and spacious, but disarmingly simple and exceedingly livable, the plan is a reminder that Peabody & Stearns's designs most often succeeded on the human scale in even the largest cottages.

Richard C. Kerens's life was the classic story of a poor boy who succeeded in business beyond the wildest expectations. He was born in Kilberry, County Meath, Ireland, but came to America at an early age. During his lifetime he was counted among the ranks of the most influential men in the country, based on wealth and political connections. Kerens's prominence came through the transportation industries—like many others of his generation. He learned the communications and transportation business while serving in the Union Army in Missouri and Arkansas; his Army friendship with General Grant certainly aided him in later business contracts. Financial success resulted from his involvement in a number of railroad systems, among them the construction of the St. Louis Southwestern Railway, known as the Cotton Belt Route, and the West Virginia Central & Pittsburgh Railway, as well as the resultant land deals and business opportunities that railroad ventures threw off. His involvement with the Eureka Springs Railroad involved him personally and financially in that Arkansas resort community, where additional Peabody & Stearns commissions remain unsubstantiated. Kerens and his family resided at 36 Vandeventer Place in St. Louis, a private neighborhood which, as we saw earlier, included several homes designed by the Peabody & Stearns firm. He was appointed by President Harrison as commissioner-at-large to the World's Columbian Exposition, although he later resigned that commission to become one of the three U.S. representatives for the Intercontinental Railway Commission. Kerens was active in the Republican Party at the state and national levels and was appointed ambas-

3.6. Pinecrest, caretaker's cottage, c. 1957. Courtesy of Sidney and Barbara Tedford.

3.7. Pinecrest, detail of caretaker's cottage, c. 1957. Courtesy of Sidney and Barbara Tedford.

sador to Austria-Hungary (1909–13); more than one writer intimated that the position was awarded in appreciation of a $100,000 contribution made during President Taft's campaign.[4] Although Kerens had neither theoretical nor practical training in diplomacy, he evidently proved to be a popular representative in Vienna.

The original Pinecrest estate included twenty-seven acres on the hill overlooking Elkins. In 1957, years after Kerens's death and after several divisions of the property, the gatehouse was moved to a new site several hundred yards up the road. It is a charming cottage in its own right, landscaped with stones that came from the estate's dismantled icehouse. The main house was added to the National Register of Historic Places in 1979.

Pinecrest and the Pinecrest Gatehouse are private residences.

Plum Orchard

Cumberland Island, Georgia, 1898

George Lauder Carnegie, 1876-1921

> I was very much surprised and gratified to receive plans to-day. I had no idea they could be worked up so soon and so successfully. You have got my idea exactly, I think, in its perfection.
>
> — George L. Carnegie
> to Peabody & Stearns. July, 1898 [5]

3.8. Plum Orchard, front view after additions.
From The Collections of the Library of Congress (HABS GA 2362-2).

The Carnegie Estate archives in Georgia represent the only known instance where extensive correspondence between Peabody & Stearns and a client has been preserved, and this aspect alone makes the design of Plum Orchard of great value. The archives document that, in addition to Plum Orchard, Peabody & Stearns was commissioned to provide "every major architectural commission for the Carnegies' Cumberland Island homes from 1896 to 1907."[6] These included Dungeness, Greyfield, and numerous outbuildings.

Philadelphia steel entrepreneur Thomas Carnegie (1843-86), brother of Andrew, and his wife Lucy Coleman Carnegie (1847-1916) purchased 4,000 acres on the southern part of Cumberland Island in 1881. Much of the land had been deeded to Revolutionary War hero General Nathaniel Greene by the State of Georgia as a reward for his distinguished services; the Carnegies razed the remains of an historic mansion, Dungeness, built by Greene's widow, and replaced it with their new Dungeness mansion in 1884.[7] Lucy Carnegie planned a family compound on the island, and Plum Orchard was built as the winter residence for her son George Lauder Carnegie and his wife Margaret Thaw.[8]

Correspondence indicates that George and Margaret Carnegie were very involved in the design of Plum Orchard. It was initially conceived of as a square Classical Revival mansion raised on a ballustraded piazza. The enormous entry hall was finished in oak "with carved ornament" and richly embellished wall coverings and was dominated by a large fireplace alcove or inglenook located beneath the main staircase. To the left of the hall was the smaller living room, finished in sycamore, with an entrance to the gun room—an indication of the importance of the sporting activities on the island. To the right of the hall was the dining room, which was finished in oak, with a fireplace and built-in display shelves. Both the living room and the dining room had access to covered piazzas. The second floor was planned with six bedrooms and three baths, all finished in pine. The Boston firm of Irving & Casson provided much of the woodwork, flooring, mantels, and presumably the wallpapers, all of which were sent by steamer from their factory in East Cambridge to Cumberland Island. Other providers for the Carnegie projects included Davenport, Peters Company, lumber merchants from Boston, as well as Tiffany & Company for glass, McKenzie & Patterson of Quincy for stonework, and Cutting & Bardwell of Worcester for terra-cotta and brickwork.

A substantial addition to Plum Orchard completed in 1902-4 greatly expanded the public areas—and the footprint—of the house. An addition to the eastern end of the house included a swimming pool, locker room area, and squash court. The corresponding addition to the west reconfigured the living room area into a library and drawing room. At this time the exterior of the house was changed from clapboard to tabby, a local mix of shells and sand. A third building program in 1906-7 greatly enlarged and enhanced the service areas of the house. At the completion of these additions, Plum Orchard encompassed approximately 21,000 square feet with thirty principal rooms, eleven bathrooms and more than sixty service rooms and closets.

Landscaping at Plum Orchard included a formal ornamental garden along with sizable vegetable gardens. The front entrance was framed by two royal palms, which still flourish in the semitropical climate of the island. Tennis courts were added to the property for additional recreational opportunities, and a dedicated powerhouse provided Plum Orchard with electricity.

Plum Orchard was George and Margaret Carnegie's primary winter residence for nearly eighteen years. Recorded recollections by family members indicate that while much of the day was spent in outdoor activities—horseback riding, hunting, going to the beach, etc.—life in the house was of a more structured nature. "Dinners at Plum Orchard were formal affairs. . . . Two butlers dressed in green livery attended family dinners."[9] An injury confined George Carnegie to a wheelchair in 1915, and by 1917 he and Margaret were no longer spending time at Plum Orchard; they traveled extensively to spa resorts in the United States while maintaining a residence at the Plaza Hotel in

New York City. Lucy Carnegie had died in 1916, leaving all of the Cumberland Island properties in trust to her children—this included Plum Orchard. When George died in 1921, Margaret maintained her status as mistress of Plum Orchard, but in 1923 she remarried, and the property reverted to the family estate.

Plum Orchard was donated to the United States government by the Carnegie family in 1972, along with other family holdings on Cumberland Island. The house is owned and maintained by the National Park Service and is open to the public on a limited schedule.

Chapter 4
The West
Colorado and Iowa

We wanted the boys to see the West before it was too greatly changed. . . .

— Gertrude Houston Woodward, "Quita" [1]

In 1893, Frederick Jackson Turner announced the "closing of the frontier," and with his remarks, arguably, a new era in American history began. The end of the western frontier line coincided with new developments in transportation, with a "trickling down" of leisure time for a larger portion of the population, and with a new understanding of the American attitude toward the landscape as expressed by artists, writers, and landscape architects throughout the nation. Peabody & Stearns's practice straddled this exciting period of American history—it began twenty-three years before the "closing of the frontier" and extended for twenty-four years after. And, although the firm worked primarily on the East Coast of the United States, there were a number of opportunities in the development of the Midwest and the West, thanks in large part to the involvement in the railroad of many Peabody & Stearns clients.

The largest concentration of Peabody & Stearns resort-related designs in the western part of the United States is in Colorado Springs, Colorado. Like so many other western resort towns, Colorado Springs was created as an adjunct to a railroad line. General William Jackson Palmer first became aware of the landscape surrounding Pike's Peak in 1867 while surveying for the Kansas Pacific Railroad, an enterprise of the Pennsylvania Railroad. Tourists began visiting Colorado Springs almost as soon as it was established in 1871; they included hikers and adventurers, and women as well as men. Celebrities visited as well—a group as diverse as General Grant, John D. Rockefeller, Oscar Wilde, and retailer Marshall Field. The clear air of Colorado Springs made it a haven for the treatment of consumption (tuberculosis) and asthma—the Glockner Sanitarium was established in 1888. Peabody & Stearns's first commission in Colorado Springs was for Colorado College (fig. 4.1) (1878); the firm later designed the Antlers Hotel, major additions to Glen Eyrie, General Palmer's personal residence, and the United States Signal Service weather station on Pikes Peak—then the highest weather station in the world. [2]

(fig. 4.2) The Peabody & Stearns property record cards also indicate the firm's involvement in the design of permanent homes for several of Palmer's employees who were especially influential in the town's development. These men located their homes in a desirable area of town populated primarily by wealthy capitalists and professionals associated with the Colorado Springs Company and Colorado College, now known as the North Weber Street–Wahsatch Avenue Historic Residential District. Irving Howbert (1846-1934), a native of Columbus, Indiana, became the county clerk of El Paso County and later joined Palmer in the development of Colorado Springs. His fortune came out of the silver mines of Leadville, Colorado—we wonder if he knew Richard Kerens of St. Louis and Elkins, West Virginia, also an investor in Leadville. Other individuals associated with Palmer and with Peabody & Stearns were Edgar Ensign (1839-1918), a "founder and early builder" of the Colorado State Forestry Association; J. G. Warner, John Inglis, F. H. Sharpless, and A. E. Strettel, whom we assume to be Alma Strettel, an English friend of Palmer's wife, Queen.

Peabody & Stearns's commissions for the elusive B. F. Stevens in Spirit Lake, Iowa, are related to both railroad connections and the establishment of resort communities in the West. Although Iowa achieved statehood in 1846, the northwestern quarter of the state remained largely unpopulated until after the Civil War. When Congress made land grants to railroad companies interested in developing the so-called Great Lakes of Iowa, and connecting the major cities of this western region—Minneapolis and St. Paul, Chicago, and St. Louis—the path through Dickinson County, Iowa, was highly favored. Donovan Hofsommer's book *Prairie Oasis: The Railroads, Steamboats, and Resorts of Iowa's Spirit Lake Country* (1975) narrates the complicated negotiations that eventually resulted in a thriving recreational community. Attractions included guest accommodations of all sizes, fishing, boating, and swimming, in addition to croquet, relaxing in swings and hammocks, bowling, billiards, and musicales. Toboggan slides for swimmers

were available at several locations, and an amusement park was constructed in the early years of the twentieth century. It was in the midst of this actively promoted recreational area that Peabody, Stearns & Furber found their client, B. F. Stevens. The extensive plans for a boathouse, steamer dock, ice house, and water tower would have been natural additions to Mr. Stevens's other business holdings in the town of Spirit Lake.

Elsewhere in the western states, the James J. Hill mansion (1888), located in St. Paul, Minnesota, is one of Peabody & Stearns's best-known residences (see Preface, p.17). Other commissions were located in Cleveland, Kansas City, and St. Louis. In Wisconsin the firm produced sketches for several commissions in Madison, and designed the station for the Denver & Rio Grande Railroad in Manitou; in Duluth, Peabody & Stearns received the commission for the Union Depot and the station for the St. Paul & Duluth Railroad. The firm's connections stretched all the way to California, where it was reportedly involved in the design of the Oakland City Hall in 1910 as well as a hostelry in San Francisco.

FACING PAGE
4.1. Colorado College Building. *American Architect and Building News*, December 15, 1877. Collection of the author.

ABOVE
4.2. Signal Station, Summit of Pike's Peak. Postcard, collection of the author.

4.3. United States Signal Station, Pike's Peak, Colorado. *American Architect and Building News*, August 18, 1883, vol. XIV, p. 78. Courtesy of the Frances Loeb Library, Graduate School of Design, Harvard University.

Glen Eyrie

(alterations and additions, 1881)

Colorado Springs, Colorado

General William Jackson Palmer,

1836–1909

> ...till at length we reached Glen Eyie, an elegant modern residence, with balconies and porches and turrets and all the angles and eccentricities of an approved "Queen Anne" structure ...
>
> — OLIVE RAND,
> *A Vacation Excursion* [3]

The story of General Palmer and the lodge at Glen Eyrie parallels the development of Colorado Springs as a resort town and as an adjunct to the Denver & Rio Grande Railroad line. The first Glen Eyrie was built in 1871 by Palmer as a home for his bride, Mary Lincoln (Queen) Mellon; Peabody & Stearns's involvement with the house came ten years later. Named for the eagle's nest in the canyon leading in to his homesite, Glen Eyrie was originally a twenty-two-room frame house with separate carriage house.

The setting for the house was intended to be awe-inspiring, and it is just as remarkable today as it was 140 years ago. The property included 2,225 acres, surrounded by the massive red stone formations of the Garden of the Gods. When author Helen Hunt Jackson visited Glen Eyrie in the late 1890s, she described the locale as almost "overawing.... There are single shafts like obelisks or minarets, ... huge slabs laid tier upon tier like giant sarcophagi ..., massive like abbeys fallen into ruins; this is Glen Eyrie." [4]

The Peabody & Stearns additions and alterations to Glen Eyrie included a prominent tower and additional rooms, at a cost of approximately $50,000. An article in the *Denver Republican* suggests that the renovation project was not altogether successful. [5] "The architects have taken hold of the material at hand, an old frame house, and by adding something new here and taking away something incongruous there, aided by the free use of paint, stained glass and red brick have produced a tolerably harmonious appearance...." [6] The writer continued, finding fault with the heights of the chimneys and with the proportions of the tower, arguing that it had "rather a squatty appearance." His basic complaint was that General Palmer should have begun anew and should have built his house out of stone in order to be "in perfect harmony with its surroundings." He grudgingly concluded, however, that the parts the architects built anew, "especially the dormer windows, the gables, the porches and porticos, the entire kitchen and the conservatory, all of which are built in the Queen Anne or English cottage style," were "very creditable ... made under the guidance of good taste."

Peabody & Stearns's changes on the interior met with more approval. The windows were furnished new, in harmony with the Queen Anne style. Hardwood flooring was used on the main floor, and the "good taste" utilized in providing the new fireplaces, mantels, and hearths produced "beautiful effects." Wallpaper was made to order, and it appears that new wiring, plumbing, and fixtures were used throughout.

The hall of Glen Eyrie was furnished with a large fireplace with a "rustic cedar mantel" and opened into the library and the music room. The adjoining dining room was finished in oak, with a brick fireplace. Glass doors from the library and the dining room opened into the new 700-square-foot conservatory. The room that drew the most attention, though, was General Palmer's den, which was finished almost entirely in rustic stone (fig. 4.6). The den was dominated by the fireplace and mantel constructed of "native stones in the rough" and was so successful that it was preserved intact in subsequent renovations. A smoking room was located in the upper level of the tower—the *Republican* writer's praise of the view from this room was tempered by the thought that it was well located "barring the inconveniences of ascending to it after one of the General's hearty dinners."

A large carved and paneled staircase led from the hall to the second floor of the house, which was totally remodeled. The upstairs hall was designed in the shape of a square, with two pressed-brick fireplaces and ebony mantels reaching nearly to the ceiling. Chambers for the family members were located on the second floor, while the third floor included two chambers for guests.

In photographs made during the period, Glen Eyrie appears to be a uniquely charming and rustic country residence. The Denver writer's conclusion damned the house with faint praise: " . . . there are many faults, such as tortuous stairways and narrow halls, but when compelled at will, perhaps the best appointed home in the State of Colorado." The current reader hardly knows what to make of his descriptions.

Palmer's wife, Queen, suffered a mild heart attack in 1880 and moved to the East Coast and later to England—it is uncertain how much time she spent in the newly remodeled Glen Eyrie. General Palmer, however, remained in Colorado Springs to manage his railroad and other substantial business interests; indeed, he remained there until his death in 1909, having commissioned yet another even more ambitious renovation of the lodge in 1901 by Frederick J. Sterner, whose firm had won the commission for the second Antlers Hotel. Sterner encapsulated the Queen Anne house in 24-inch-thick stone walls quarried on the estate. The leaded-glass windows are trimmed with gray limestone; Flemish gable ends coexist with the remains of Tudoresque detailing on some of the gables and dormers. Sterner's plans called for twenty-four fireplaces, many of which were imported from Europe, and a total of sixty-five rooms and twenty-two bathrooms. It was this version of Glen Eyrie that was described in 1921:

> The house was a veritable château—the garden a wonderland of Colorado plants and flowers, skillfully disposed among the native ledges and scattered along the bases of the cliffs whose rugged sides enclosed

the mansion grounds. The towers (of gray stone) were English, . . . In a very real fashion "Glen Eyrie" bodied forth the singular and powerful character of its owner, who was at once an English squire, a Pennsylvania civil war veteran, and a western railway engineer.[7]

4.5. Glen Eyrie, Denver Public Library, Western History Collection, J. L. Clinton, photographer (X-1581).

4.6. Gen. William J. Palmer relaxing in his den at Glen Eyrie. Denver Public Library, Western History Collection, Jackson C. Thode (X-14703).

General Palmer incorporated all of the latest technological developments in Glen Eyrie. Over the years it had its own power plant, a water storage facility, a highly sophisticated interior ventilation system, as well as sewage and trash-disposal facilities, pollution control, a schoolhouse, greenhouses, and recreational swimming areas.

The Peabody & Stearns–designed Glen Eyrie was, of course, encased by the 1901 renovation. The new Glen Eyrie was added to the National Register of Historic Places in 1975. The Castle, as it is now deservedly called, is owned by the Navigators, an evangelical Christian nonprofit group that maintains the house and grounds for conferences and individual vacation stays.

The Antlers

Colorado Springs, Colorado, 1882-83

General William Jackson Palmer,

1836-1909

[Mrs. Forrester] and her husband always spent the winter in Denver and Colorado Springs ... he had been drinking with some old friends at the Antlers....
— Willa Cather, *A Lost Lady* [8]

There is still an Antlers Hotel located at the intersection of Cascade and Pikes Peak avenues in Colorado Springs, and it still provides its guests with breathtaking views of Pikes Peak. But the comparison between the current twelve-story hotel (completed in 1967) and the original Peabody & Stearns design ends with the view.

The Antlers designed by Peabody & Stearns of Boston and New York, was intended to be the ultimate in luxury and technology in the growing resort town of Colorado Springs, whose population numbered approximately 5,000 at the time of the hotel's completion. It boasted hydraulic elevators, a state-of-the-art ventilation system, central heat, gaslights, Turkish baths, and a staff imported from the hotels of the East Coast.

General William Jackson Palmer and the Colorado Springs Company donated four acres at the end of Pikes Peak Avenue in 1881 for a fine resort hotel and commissioned the design shortly thereafter. The *Daily Gazette* of August 3, 1881, reported that "Mr. P. P. Furber of New York, representing Messrs. Peabody & Stearns, the architects of the new hotel, has arrived in the city and will superintend the construction of the building." An article on October 8, 1882, reported that "a meeting of the board of directors of the Colorado Springs Hotel Company was held in Architect Furber's office" during which it was decided to prepare circulars containing a lithograph of the exterior and photographs of the interiors of the building to send to "all of the leading hotel men in the country" in hopes of attracting a manager with a "national hotel reputation." The first manager of the hotel was a woman, Miss A. A. Warren, who selected all of the furnishings for the headline-making hotel.[9] The hotel opened on June 1, 1883, with an eight-course celebratory dinner banquet that lasted two and a half hours.

An article in the September 11, 1881, *Daily Gazette* described the planned hotel in great detail:

It will be built on the side hill sloping toward the experimental garden and fronting the mountains. This frontage will have an elevation of two stories including basement and a length of one hundred and fifty-three feet with prominent bays, balconies, and other projections. The outer walls of the hotel will be of Douglas Lava stone with Manitou magnesia stone trimmings. It will to a great extent be surrounded by spacious

verandas and balconies. On the Cascade Avenue front the building will be four stories in height, the offices, dining rooms, etc., being on a level with that street. The basement properly speaking will be devoted to kitchen, laundry, billiard room, card room, barber shop, also nurses', childrens' and servants' halls. On the north end of the basement will be four large spaces with pressed brick walls and tile floors for Turkish baths....

The building was designed in the Queen Anne style with two towers that rose from the inner corners of the courtyard. The lower three floors were constructed of gray stone, while the top two floors were made of wood; the building reached 101 feet into the air.[10] Dr. Edwin Solly, author and tuberculosis specialist, consulted on the health aspects of the hotel design.

The large lobby greeted the many visitors to the hotel. The dining room was located directly across the main hall from the office, fronting to the north and west It featured "a large and well-lighted bay projecting westward." On the west side of the hall was the "ordinary," or supper, room, a music room, and a drawing room with a large bay in the westward as on the dining room. The ladies private entrance was on the north end of the hotel, with a private reception room as well as a separate suite of rooms that included a parlor, two chambers and a bathroom, with a private corridor. The interior finish of the main rooms was of oiled Colorado pine, with the exception of the main staircase, which was finished in brown ash. The public rooms were furnished with leather-upholstered walnut furniture. The newspaper reported that "all of the rooms are large and well lighted."

The second, third, and fourth stories were devoted almost exclusively to sleeping rooms. Each floor included three suites of rooms, many with fireplaces and all with bathrooms attached, in addition to almost two dozen other rooms—many of which were connected with doors and which could be used as suites. There were eight public and six private bathrooms on each floor, in addition to the Turkish baths in the basement. Many of the south rooms on the second and third stories had small private balconies provided "especially for the use of invalids" in response to the need for treatment of tuberculosis and related illnesses. Female servants had quarters on the fourth floor; male servants were housed elsewhere.

Although the economy was shaky at the time that the Antlers opened, the management persevered. With the return of national and local prosperity, the hotel flourished, with renovations and additions completed in the early 1890s doubling its size.

Politicians and wealthy businessmen, celebrities and foreign dignitaries, all stayed at the Antlers. A newspaper report in 1890 stated, "The many who stopped their [sic] went away with nothing but praises for the management, and the fame of the hotel rapidly spread over this continent and even across the Atlantic."[11] Perhaps the hotel's most memorable guest was Katherine Lee Bates, a professor of English

4.7. The Antlers, from Pike's Peak Avenue. Drawn by Charles Graham, *Harper's Weekly*, November 20, 1880. Collection of the author.

at Wellesley College, who in 1893 was so inspired by the view from atop Pikes Peak that she wrote the patriotic hymn "America the Beautiful" in her room at the Antlers.

On October 1, 1898, fire broke out at the Denver & Rio Grande freight depot located several blocks away. Airborne sparks ignited the hotel and despite the best efforts of the hotel employees and fire departments of Colorado Springs, Denver, and Pueblo, the Antlers was destroyed. General Palmer immediately arranged for a replacement hotel, which was designed by the firm of Varian & Sterner of Denver, Colorado, architects of the Greenbrier Hotel in White Sulphur Springs, West Virginia. The new Italian Renaissance-style Antlers

opened in July 1901, and was again purported to be one of the finest accommodations in the country, if not the world. This, the second Antlers was unrivaled in Colorado Springs for nearly twenty years. However, with the construction of the nearby Broadmoor Hotel in 1918, its superiority began to slip, and by the mid twentieth century the property was sold to the Fairmont Hotel Company of San Francisco. Refurbished and rejuvenated, the Antlers lived on for another ten years. But in 1964, it was torn down to make way for the third Antlers, the Antlers Plaza Hotel, constructed by the Western International Hotels chain; the Antlers Hilton Colorado Springs currently operates on the property.

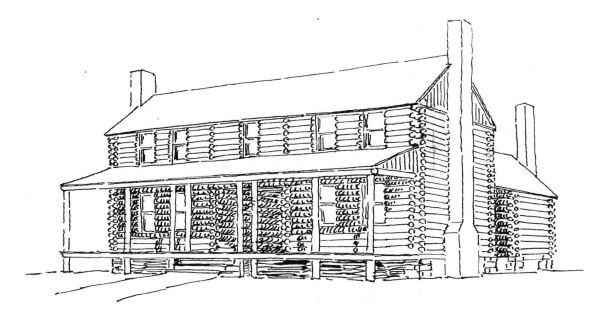

Log Cabin and Boat House

Spirit Lake, Iowa, 1908

B. F. Stevens, n.d.

Details on the projects for B. F. Stevens in Spirit Lake, Iowa, are maddeningly elusive. It is probable that the client was B. F. Stevens of St. Louis, Missouri, who was the owner of the Stevens Block on Lake Street, Spirit Lake, pictured in postcards of the early 1900s. The Lake Region Blue Book contains an entry regarding "the five hundred and thirty acre farm, formerly owned by Ben. Stevens, of St. Louis."[12] However, further identification and biographical material on Mr. Stevens has been unavailable.

The interest in B. F. Stevens comes from the diversity of projects that Peabody, Stearns & Furber designed for him in Spirit Lake. Drawings show a dock, boathouse, ice and milk house, and water tower—all of which would have been planned for the waterfront area of Spirit Lake. Further drawings are for dairy buildings, an oven, and a smokehouse—perhaps intended for the farm complex in the above-referenced *Blue Book* entry.

The most delightful design, however, is the "Cottage for B. F. Stevens" in the form of a log house carefully featured in a perspective sketch in the Peabody & Stearns drawings at the Boston Public Library. The plans indicate a main block measuring about 41 feet wide by 20 feet deep, with an 8-foot-deep farmer's porch stretching across the front of the cottage and a roomy kitchen extension and screened porch ("enclosed in wire nettings") to the rear. The first-floor plan included entry into a central hall with staircase. The living room measured 15 feet by 20, with arched entry from the

hall and built-in bookcases on either side and a large fireplace on the outside wall. On the opposite side of the hall was a chamber with en suite bath and fireplace. The kitchen to the rear was accessed from the rear of the hall and led out to a porch "enclosed in lattice." On the second floor were two chambers and a gun room, alluding to the popularity of the area for sportsmen interested in hunting as well as fishing.

The city of Spirit Lake is the largest municipality in Dickinson County, in the northwest portion of Iowa, long known for its year-round recreational opportunities. This is the Iowa Great Lakes region, and the city is located on the shore of East Okoboji Lake, to the south of Big Spirit Lake. Spirit Lake was first settled in the 1850s, but was not incorporated until 1879, when it was designated as the county seat. The abundance of natural resources and the recreational potentials of the area led to the building of two railroad lines to the area, one of which was the Chicago, Milwaukee & St. Paul. The first tourist accommodation, the Lake View House, was built in 1859; other inns and cottages followed, including one coincidentally named the Antlers Hotel, built on the same site in 1902.

There are suggestions that Peabody & Stearns was involved in the construction of the Stevens Block, the first brick block of the town, located at the corners of Hill Avenue and Lake Street. The building has been restored, although the early opera house that was located in the block was destroyed by fire in the late 1920s.

If indeed the boathouse and steam launch docks were constructed in Spirit Lake, they would represent the most western of all of Peabody & Stearn's known resort commissions. Photographs of the buildings have not been located, and further information is much desired about these public buildings as well as the log house designed for Mr. Stevens.

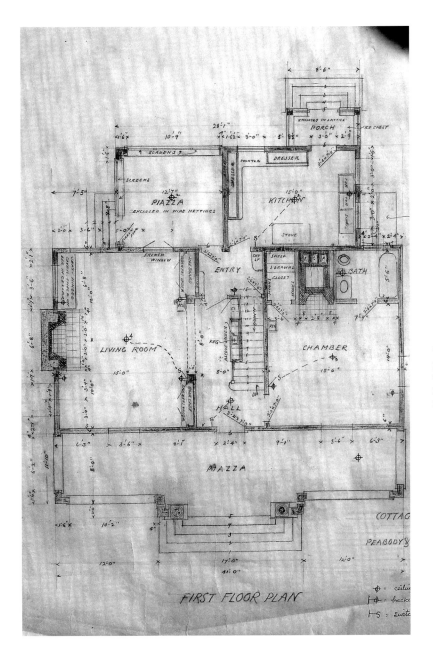

FIRST FLOOR PLAN

4.9. Log cabin, first floor plan. Peabody and Stearns Collection, courtesy of the Boston Public Library Fine Arts Department.

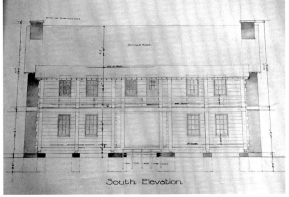

South Elevation.

4.10. Log cabin, south elevation. Peabody and Stearns Collection, courtesy of the Boston Public Library Fine Arts Department.

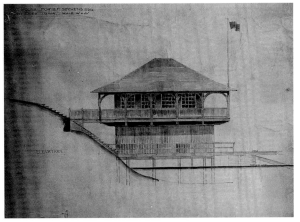

4.11. Boathouse for B. F. Stevens, Esq. Peabody and Stearns Collection, courtesy of the Boston Public Library Fine Arts Department.

Notes

RSP refers to Robert Swain Peabody;
JGS refers to John Goddard Stearns;
MJDP refers to Mary Jane Derby Peabody.

Preface

1. George Stanley Woodward, *Memoirs of a Mediocre Man* (Philadelphia: Harris & Partridge, 1935), p. 95.

Introduction: Narrative of a Practice

1. Julius Schweinfurth, "Robert Swain Peabody, Tower Builder, 1845-1917," *American Architect*, September 3, 1926, vol. 130, no. 2304, 181-91. Robert Day Andrews, *Architectural Review*, November 1917, p. x. Further information on office staff is based on interviews with Cornell Appleton conducted by Wheaton Holden in January and February 1968, and reported in his dissertation, pp. 19-21. Holden, Wheaton Arnold. *Robert Swain Peabody of Peabody and Stearns in Boston—The Early Years (1870-1886)*. Boston University of Graduate School, Ph.D., 1969, Fine Arts.
2. Francis G. Peabody, *A New England Romance: The Story of Ephraim and Mary Jane Peabody (1807-1892) Told by Their Sons* (Boston and New York: Houghton Mifflin Company, 1920), p. v.
3. Moorfield Storey, "Obituary," *Harvard University Class 1866 Class Report*, 1917 Report, pp. 10-11.
4. E. Digby Baltzell, *Philadelphia Gentlemen: The Making of a National Upper Class*. xxx
5. Ibid (Glencoe, IL: The Free Press, 1958), p. 21.
6. Robert Swain Peabody, "Early Reminiscences," an unpublished typescript in the Wheaton Holden collection at the Hay Library, Box 2, Brown University.
7. Edward D. Lindsey to RSP, December 6, 1866, Letter #5, Folder 1860-69. From the Collection of Historic New England.
8. RSP, "Architecture as a Profession for College Graduates," *Harvard Monthly*, October 1989-February 1890, vol. IX, no. 5, pp. 185, 192.
9. John Ruskin, introductory lines to "The Lamp of Sacrifice," *The Seven Lamps of Architecture* (New York: Dover Publications [reprint of the 1880 second edition of the book], 1989), p. 8.
10. JGS to RSP. Folder #2, from the Collection of Historic New England. The letter is undated, but a reference to the wedding of Van Brunt taking place the next week places it in the beginning of October 1869.
11. RSP to MJDP, September 12, 1867; RSP to MJDP, September 15, 1867. In 1867 almost 7,000,000 people visited Paris to view the architectural exhibition at the Champs-de-Mars. Peabody wrote to his mother on October 6 that "yesterday. . . . I spent all day at the Exposition."
12. RSP, *Early Reminiscences*, p. 2.
13. RSP, *Early Reminiscences*, p. 3.
14. RSP to MJDP, Letter #19, Historic New England (hereafter, HNE).
15. I am indebted to Richard Chafee for sharing information regarding Peabody's record at the École.
16. RSP to MJDP, Letter #98, May 23, 1869, HNE.
17. RSP to MJDP, Letter #103, June 20, 1869, HNE.
18. Roth, Leland, *McKim, Mead & White Architects*, (New York: Harper & Row, 1983).
19. RSP to MJDP, Letter #98, May 23, 1869, HNE.
20. RSP to MJDP, Letter #101, June 7, 1869, HNE.
21. RSP to MJDP, Letter #102, June 14, 1869, HNE.
22. I am indebted to Colin Cunningham of the Open University, Canterbury, for providing documents from Waterhouse office journals regarding the projects on which Peabody worked.
23. RSP to MJDP, Letter #103, June 20, 1869, HNE.
24. "Georgian" [RSP], "Georgian Houses of New England," *American Architect and Building News*, October 20, 1877, p. 339.
25. RSP, "On the Design of Houses," *An Architect's Sketch Book*, pp. 77-89.
26. Ibid., p 83.
27. RSP, "An Architect's Vacation," *Atlantic Monthly*, July 1895, pp. 23-28.
28. RSP, "On the Design of Houses," p. 86.
29. See Colin Cunningham and Prudence Waterhouse, *Alfred Waterhouse, 1830-1905: Biography of a Practice* (Oxford, England: Clarendon Press, 1992), for background on Waterhouse.
30. According to Brad Edgerly in "The Sketches of Robert Swain Peabody," *Dichotomy*, University of Detroit School of Architecture, vol. 6 (1983); pp. 46-53.
31. JGS to RSP, undated letter.
32. RSP to MJDP, Letter #115, August 11, 1869, HNE.
33. RSP to MJDP. September 12, 1869, HNE.
34. *North Shore Breeze, a weekly journal devoted to the best interests of the North Shore*, vol. 1, no. 1, Beverly, Mass., Saturday May 21, 1904.
35. Bruce Price, "The Suburban House," *Scribner's Magazine*, July 1890, pp. 3-19.

Chapter 1: New England

1. Robert Grant. "The North Shore of Massachusetts, *Scribner's Magazine* Vol. xvi, July 1894 New York: Charles Scribner's Sons, p. 10.
2. "Lenox in October," *Newport Mercury*, October 15, 1887.
3. "To Miss Arnold." *The Letters of Matthew Arnold 1848-1888*. Collected and arranged by George W. E.

Russell. Vol. III. London: MacMillan and Co., Limited. 1904, p. 294.

4. As related by Cleveland Amory in *Last Resorts A Portrait of American Society at Play*. New York: Harper & Brothers, 1952, p. 3.

5. Samuel Eliot Morison, *The Story of Mount Desert Island* (Boston: Little Brown & Co., 1960), p. 54.

6. *Encyclopaedia Britannica: A Dictionary of Arts, Sciences, Literature, and General Information*, Ed. Hugh Chisholm (Cambridge, England and New York: At the University Press, 1910), p. 553.

7. George Champlin Mason, *Newport and Its Cottages*, Boston: James R. Osgood & Co., 1975. p. 85.

8. *Boston Daily Globe* "Nathan Matthews Sr. Dead," Aug. 31, 1904, p. 3.

9. George Champlin Mason, *Newport and Its Cottages*, Boston: James R. Osgood & Co., 1875. p. 85.

10. Henry-Russell Hitchcock, *The Architecture of H. H. Richardson and His Times* (Cambridge, MA: MIT Press, 1966), p. 160. Hitchcock does praise Peabody for retaining the piazza feature of earlier Newport cottages.

11. I thank Dr. James Yarnall of Newport for information on the McPherson Stained Glass Company commissions.

12. RSP, *The Architectural Sketchbook, Edited by the Portfolio Club* (Boston: James R. Osgood & Co., 1873-74). A notebook of measurements in the collection of the Boston Public Library includes a sketch of "Nathan Matthews' China Closet."

13. *Newport Mercury*, April 20, 1878.

14. Ibid., May 26, 1882.

15. Mason, p. 60.

16 *Newport Mercury*. November 25, 1871.

17. *Sears Genealogical Catalogue*, Ed. L. Ray Sears III (Duncan, OK: Advanced Business Systems, 1992), 6.58.

18. Preservation Society of Newport County, *The Lost Houses of Newport, www.newportmansions.org*. See Education and Research/Lost Newport/The Lost Houses/1866-1875.

19. *Newport Journal,* April 29, 1876.

20. Ibid., January 24, 1877.

21. George William Sheldon, *Artistic Country Seats: Types of Recent American Villa and Cottage Architecture with Instances of Country Club Houses*, 2 vols. New York: D. Appleton & Co., 1886-1887.

22. *American Builder*, May 1878, p. 115.

23. Charles H. Dow, *Newport Past and Present*, Newport: J. P. Sanborn, 1880, p. 74.

24. *Newport Mercury*, September 29, 1877. R. E. Sales: "Hon. Wm. Beach Lawrence to Pierre Lorillard, about eleven acres of land on Ruggles Avenue, Ochre point Avenue and the sea, for $96,147.20."

25. From Robert Peabody's Diary, in the Hay Library Collection at Brown University. Wheaton Holden A94-125.

26. Maude Howe Elliott, *This Was My Newport* (Cambridge, Mass.: Mythology Company, 1944), p. 211.

27. Bernard Harper Friedman and Flora Miller Irving, *Gertrude Vanderbilt Whitney: A Biography* (Garden City, NY: Doubleday, 1978), p. 90.

28. Walter Nebiker, Robert Owen Jones, and Charlene K. Roice, *Historic and Architectural Resources of Naragansett, Rhoode Island* (Providence: Rhode Island HistoricalPreservation Commission, 1991), p. 65.

29. Richard Champlin. "Newport Estates and their Flora," *Newport History, Bulletin of the Newport Historical Society*, vol. 53, pt. 2, no. 178 (Spring 1980): 49-66.

30. Edith Wharton, *The Age of Innocence* (New York: D. Appleton and Company, 1921), p. 309

31. *Brickbuilder*, February 1910, vol. 19, p. 47.

32. Walter Crane, *An Artist's Reminiscences* (New York: Macmillan, 1907), p. 374.

33. Sheldon, p. 186.

34. *Newport Mercury*, December 25, 1886.

35. Russell Sturgis, "Peabody and Stearns," *Architectural Record, Great American Architects Series*, July 1896, pp. 84-85.

36. *Newport Mercury*, July 2, 1886.

37. George Champlin Mason, *Newport and Its Cottages*. Boston: James R. Osgood & Co., 1875, p. 27.

38. *Newport Mercury*, November 6, 1886.

39. Ibid., April 16, 1887.

40. Russell Sturgis, "A Critique of the Work of Peabody and Stearns," *Great American Architects Series*. New York: The Architectural Record Co., no. 3, July 1896. Reprint, New York: Da Capo, 1971, p. 84.

41. Mrs. John King Van Rensselaer, *Newport, Our Social Capitol*, Philadelphia and London: J. P. Lippincott Co., 1905, p. 63.

42. E.g., *New York Times,* June 10, 1889.

43. Van Rensselaer, p. 60.

44. Henry James, *The American Scene* (Bloomington & London: Indiana University Press, 1968), p. 153.

45. *Newport Mercury*, June 28, 1890.

46. Ibid., September 20, 1890.

47. *Boston Daily Globe*, August 16, 1896, p. 25.

48. Sturgis, p. 93.

49. Harriet Jackson Phelps. *Newport in Flower*. Newport: RI: The Preservation Society of Newport County, 1979, p. 45.

50. Wheaton A. Holden. "The Peabody Touch: Peabody and Stearns of Boston, 1870-1917." *Journal of the Society of Architectural Historians*, May 1973, p. 122.

51. *Newport Mercury*, December 31, 1887.

52. Ibid., September 15, 1894.

53. *New York Times*, June 9, 1882.

54. Ibid., November 22, 1897.

55. *Boston Daily Globe*, November 22, 1897.

56. *New York Times*, November 22, 1897.

57. E.g., *Boston Daily Globe*, June 28, 1905; ibid., September 15, 1912.

58. *Architectural Review*, March 1908, p. 56.

59. Barr Ferree. *American Estates and Gardens*. 1906. New York: Munn and Company, p. 97.

60. *Boston Sunday Globe*, August 18, 1906.

61. Frederick A. Ober. "Beverly" Chapter XLVII in *History of Essex County, Massachusetts: With Biographical Sketches of Many of its Pioneers and Prominent Men*. Ed. D. Hamilton Hurd. (Philadelphia: J. W. Lewis & Co., 1888, p. 750).

62. William Phillips, newsclipping in the Hightower-Phillips file at Beverly Public Library. Excerpted from *Ventures in Diplomacy* (Boston: Beacon Press, 1952).

63. "Moraine Farm Since 1880: A Frederick Law Olmsted Landscape, Forest, and Farm," in Charles E. Beveridge (Ed.), *The Frederick Law Olmsted Papers*, American University, Washington, DC, p. 1.

64. Robert Grant. *Fourscore, An Autobiography*. Boston and New York: Houghton Mifflin Company, 1934, p. 164.

65. *Boston Daily Globe*, March 15, 1895.

66. Longfellow, on August 28, 1850, in Henry Wadsworth Longfellow, *Life of Henry Wadsworth Longfellow with Extracts from His Journals*, ed. Samuel Longfellow (Boston: Ticknor & Co., 1886), p. 176.

67. Wheaton Holden, "Robert Swain Peabody of Peabody and Stearns in Boston—the Early Years (1870-1886)" (dissertation, Boston University, 1969), p. 136.

68. George William Sheldon. *Artistic Country Seats.* New York: D. Appleton & Co., 1886-87, p. 169.

69. *The Inland Architect and News Record,* April 1889, p. 53.

70. Charles Eliot, *Diary,* September 1884, as quoted by Charles Bevridge, in "Moraine Farm," p. 5.

71. Benjamin D. Hill and Winfield S. Nevins, *The North Shore of Massachusetts Bay, An Illustrated Guide . . .* (Salem, Mass., 1881), p. 55.

72. Joseph Garland, *Boston's North Shore and Boston's Gold Coast* Beverly, MA: Commonwealth Editions 1998, p. 127.

73. In collection of Boston Public Library's Peabody & Stearns Collection. PS/MA.258.

74. Robert E. Peabody, "Peach's Point, Marblehead," Essex Institute Historical Collections, vol. CII, no. 1 (January 1966), p. 13.

75. Now a private residence.

76. Robert E. Peabody, "Peach's Point, Marblehead," p. 10.

77. Ibid., p 11.

78. Dorothy B. Wexler, *Reared in a Greenhouse.* (New York: Taylor & Francis, 1998), p 195.

79. Letter, John W. Sears to the author, December 20, 2006.

80. Garland, p. 315.

81. References to the *Manchester Cricket* courtesy of letters from Miss Frances L. Burnett to Weston Milliken, dated August 8, 1983, and March 30, 1984.

82. From plans PS/MA.294 in the Peabody & Stearns collection of the Boston Public Library.

83. *New York Times,* November 25, 1891.

84. *The North Shore Breeze: A Weekly Journal Devoted to the Best Interests of the North Shore* (Beverly, Mass.) May 21, 1904.

85. *Boston Daily Globe,* May 4, 1911.

86. The first Bussey Institute building was completed in 1871, one of Peabody & Stearns's first full commissions, and it served as headquarters for an undergraduate school of agriculture. See fig. I.11.

87. "Visit to Lenox and Stockbridge Estates," *Transactions of the Massachusetts Horticultural Society for the year 1913* (Boston: MHS, 1913), p. 262.

88. *Book of Berkshire,* Springfield, MA: Clark W. Bryan & Co., Publishers. 1887, p. 43.

89. An article in the *New York Times* as well as a later article in the November 29, 1911, *Berkshire Gleaner* noted that the Barnes's den in their 10 East 79th Street residence in New York City was fitted out like a pilot house, in keeping with Barnes's interest in naval history and artifacts.

90. George Sheldon, *Artistic Country Seats* (New York: D. Appleton & Co., 1887), pp. 165-67.

91. Library of Congress, Manuscript Division, Frederick Law Olmsted Collection, as quoted by Carole Owens, *The Berkshire Cottages: A Vanishing Era* (Stockbridge, MA: Cottage Press, Inc., 1984), p. 113.

92. *New York Times,* May 27, 1894.

93. RSP, "On the Design of Houses," p. 77.

94. *American Architect and Building News,* April 5, 1902, p. 6.

95. C. S. Hayward, "Vespers in Formal Garden of Wheatleigh," *Springfield Republican,* July 18, 1943.

96. Obituary, *New York Times,* October 11, 1905.

97. Russell Sturgis. "A Critique", p. 84.

98. *New York Times,* September 29, 1895, p. 12.

99. *New York Times,* May 27, 1894, p. 21.

100. Robert Peabody's diary, as referenced by Ann Swallow in, "The Eclecticism of Peabody and Stearns in Lenox, MA, 1881-1905," Thesis, M. Arch History, University of Virginia, 1984.

101. *New York Times,* September 25, 1897, p. 7.

102. Stone House Guest Book (W. H. Forbes), p. 9. Permission granted to use materials in the possession of the family. Thank you to Beatrice Manz for bringing this material to my attention.

103. William Hathaway Forbes to John Murray Forbes, January 23, 1871, Box 17PRJ Correspondence, Collection of the Massachusetts Historical Society. John Glidden (the Larches, 1879) was employed as treasurer of the Pacific Guano Company in Woods Hole.

104. RSP to W. H. Forbes, February 25, 1871, WHF letter book 1865-1873, Carton 28, Edith Emerson Forbes and William Hathaway Forbes Papers, 1827-ca. 1964; bulk: 1827-1953, Massachusetts Historical Society.

105. RSP to W. H. Forbes, July 12, 1871, Box 20 (Financial), Edith Emerson Forbes and William Hathaway Forbes Papers, 1827-ca. 1964; bulk: 1827-1953, Massachusetts Historical Society.

106. *Naushon Data,* collected by Amelia Forbes Emerson. (Concord, Mass.: privately printed, 1963), p. 173.

107. *The Celebration of the Two Hundredth Anniversary of the Town of Falmouth, Massachusetts, June 15, 1886* (Falmouth, 1887), pp. 138-39.

108. Heiner Gillmeister, *Tennis: A Cultural History* (New York: New York University Press, 1998), p. 207.

109. Susan Fletcher Witzell, "Gardeners and Caretakers of Woods Hole," *Spritsail,* Summer 2005, p. 2.

110. *Boston Daily Globe,* March 11, 1889.

111. Witzell, p. 3.

112. From "For My Children," an unsigned typescript in the Fay Family Collection, Woods Hole Historical Museum.

113. George Moses, *Ring Around the Punchbowl* (Taunton, Mass.: Sullwold Publishing, 1976), p. 22.

114. Arnold W. Dyer, *Residential Falmouth. . . . Homes, New and Old.* " An 1897 Souvenir for the Sojourner Brought Up to Date." (Falmouth, Mass.: Falmouth Historical Society, 1995), p. 58.

115. See Joseph Fay, "The Track of the Norseman," *Magazine of American History,* 1882. A letter from Frederic A. Fernald in *Popular Science Monthly,* vol. 42 (1893), p. 123, however, points out that "the village of Woods Holl takes its name from the adjacent strait. Any one who remembers the 'swimming-hole' of his boyhood will see no need of explaining the word hole as applied to a body of water by means of the Norwegian word for the neighboring hill."

116. *From Pocasset to Cataumet: The Origins and Growth of a Massachusetts Seaside Community,* based on the files of Elmer Watson Landers, ed. Richard P. Sawyer. (Bourne, Mass.: Bourne Historic Commission, 1988), pp. 74-75.

117. Undated Obituary, *Boston Herald.* Alumnus file, William Ellery Channing Eustis, Class of 1871, Harvard University Archives (HUA), Pusey Library, Harvard University.

118. *From Pocasset to Cataumet,* pp. 74-75.

119. Charles W. Eliot, *Charles Eliot, Landscape Architect,* with an introduction by Keith N. Morgan (Amherst: University of Massachusetts Press, 1999), p. 207. Thank you to Janice Chadbourne for providing this reference.

120. Ibid., p. 207. Charles W. Eliot, the biographer, indicates that the planting was done in 1887, which predates the construction date listed on the photo-

graph at the Bourne Historical Society and the work documented by the Peabody & Stearns record card.

121. William F. Macy. *The Story of Old Nantucket: A Brief History of the Island and its People from its Discovery Down to the Present Day*. Nantucket, MA: The Inquirer and Mirror Press, 1915, p. 103.

122. Clay Lancaster, *Holiday Island: The Pageant of Nantucket's Hostelries and Summer Life From Its Beginnings to the Mid-Twentieth Century* (Nantucket, MA: Nantucket Historical Association, 1993), p. 203.

123. Cora Codman Wolcott, "Random Recollections of Much Ado About Nothing," (1934), chap. 7 in Mrs. John M. B. Churchill, *Codman Point, 1872-1972* (Wareham, MA, 1972), p. 18.

124. "Smart Set Like Golf," *Boston Globe*, July 21, 1895.

125. See Craig Lambert, "The Welds of Harvard Yard" included in *The Seven Weld Brothers, 1800 to 2000*, compiled by Nicholas Benton (New York: iUniverse, 2004).

126. Mrs. Bigelow, FOP New York: iUniverse, 2004, page v, *The Call of the Weld: A Contemporary Genealogy: Five Generations of Descendants of Stephen Minot Weld, Jr.*, compiled by Nicholas Benton.

127. Moses Foster Sweetser, *King's Handbook of Newton, Massachusetts* (Newton, MA, 1889), p. 325.

128. Susan Abele, *Newton's 19th Century Architecture: Newton Center, Oak Hill, Chestnut Hill, Commonwealth Avenue* (Newton, Mass.: Historic Newton, 1985), p. 21.

129. Francis H. Brown, M.D., "Edwin Shepard Barrett," *New England Historical and Genealogical Register, at the Annual Meeting 10 January 1900 with Memoirs of Deceased Members, 1898-1900*, p. cxi, supplementary number, 1900.

130. Leslie Perrin Wilson, "Battle Lawn: A House with a View of History," *Concord Journal*, April 26, 2001, p. 19.

131. *American Architect and Building News*, November 23, 1898, p. 172.

132. Wilson, p. 19.

133. John Shepard Keyes, "Houses, & Owners or Occupants in Concord, 1885," as referenced by Wilson, p. 19.

134. The New England Historical and Genealogical Register, Supplement to April Number, 1915, Proceedings of the New England Historic Genealogical Society at the Annual Meeting, 3 February 1915, with Memoirs of Deceased Members, 1914, p. lxvii.

135. *Official Guide to Harvard*, Ed. The Harvard Memorial Society. Cambridge, MA: Harvard University Press, 1907, p. 148.

136. Ibid, p. 148.

137. *Report of the President of Harvard College and Reports of Departments*. Harvard University Press, 1906, p. 119.

138. Wallace Nutting. *Maine Beautiful*. New York: Bonanza Books, 1924, p. 8.

139. Edith Wharton. *The Age of Innocence*. New York: D. Appleton and Company, 1921, p. 207.

140. Theodore Richards. "Charles William Eliot." *Later Years of the Saturday Club 1870-1920*, Ed. M. A. DeWolfe Howe. (Freeport, NY: Books for Libraries Press, 1968) p. 3.

141. Henry James, *Charles W. Eliot, President of Harvard University, 1869-1909* (Boston: Houghton Mifflin Co., 1930), p. 344.

142. Ibid., p. 341.

143. *Dictionary of American Biography*, vol. III (New York: C. Scribner's Sons, 1930), p. 71.

144. *The Unitarian*, vol. XII, ed. Frederick B. Mott (Boston: Geo. H. Ellis, 1897), p. 430.

145. T. Mark Cole, "Architecture of Mt. Desert," in *Mount Desert: An Informational History*, ed. Gunnar Hansen (Town of Mt. Desert, Maine, 1989), p. 159.

146. *Illustrated Boston: The Metropolis of New England Containing Also Reviews of its Principal Environs* (Boston: American Publishing & Engraving Co., 1889), p. 119.

147. Henry S. Howe. *Eleventh Report of the Class of 1869 of Harvard College Fiftieth Anniversary, June 1919*. Cambridge: The Riverside Press, 1919. p. 149.

148. Weston Milliken, "Peabody and Stearns," in *A Biographical Dictionary of Architects in Maine*, Vol. IV, no. 2 (Augusta: Maine Historic Preservation Commission, 1987), n.p.

149. Earle G. Shettleworth, Jr., *The Summer Cottages of Isleboro, 1890-1930* (Islesboro, Maine: Islesboro Historical Society, 1989), p. 68.

150. As quoted in Shettleworth, p. 69.

151. Leslie Day, "The City Naturalist—American Hornbeam Tree," http://www.nysite.com/nature/flora/muscle.htm

152. Conversation with Edward Lawrence, December 18, 2006.

153. Moses King, *Harvard Register*, Harvard University, 1880, p. 70.

154. "Harvard Divinity School at the Turn of the Last Century: Francis Greenwood Peabody (1847-1936)." online exhibit from Andover-Harvard Theological Library, http://www.hds.harvard.edu/library/exhibits/online/hdsturncentury/peabody.html.

155. C. H. Toy, "Ravenscleft," a poem framed and hanging in Ravenscleft, quoted here with permission of the owner.

156. M.A. De Wolfe Howe, *James Ford Rhodes, American Historian* (Boston: Houghton Mifflin Co., 1929), pp. 69-70.

157. Obituary, *New York Times*, November 6, 1875.

158. Weston Milliken, "Peabody and Stearns." *A Biographical Dictionary of Architects in Maine* (Augusta, ME: Maine Historic Preservation Commission, vol. IV, no. 2, 1987), n.p.

159. Per conversation with Mrs. Roger Milliken, July 1998.

160. *Camden Herald*, October 24, 1902.

161. *New York Times*, June 8, 1913, and August 30, 1913.

162. H. H. Piper, "A Sketch of Dublin." *The Granite Monthly: A New Hampshire Magazine*. Concord, NH, vol XXI, no. 2. August 1896, p. 80.

163. George Willis Cooke, "Old Times and New in Dublin, New Hampshire," *New England Magazine*, 1899; from Dublin Historical Society Archives.

164. Conversation with Robert A. M. Stern, September 8, 2006.

165. "[Isa]Bell Bridge is said to be engaged to (George E.) Leighton, the late Provost-Martial, a very suitable match as they are all Yankees together." Missouri Historical Society Archives Catalog.

166. Nahum J. Bachelder. *New Hampshire Agriculture: Report of the Board of Agriculture from January 1, 1907 to September 1, 1908* (Nashua, N.H.: Telegraph Publishing Co., 1908), p. 260.

167. Jim Bowditch, *Chocorua Lake Basin, a National Historic District* (Chocorua, N.H., 2005), p. 66.

168. Edmund Wheeler, *The History of Newport, New Hampshire: From 1766 to 1878.* (Newport, N.H., 1879), p. 266.

169. Letter, Peabody & Stearns, Architects, to Miss Mary Stevens, November 4, 1905, privately owned.

170. Hamilton Busbey, *Recollections of Men and Horses.* (New York: Dodd, Mead & Company, 1907), pp. 115–116.

171. Obituary, *Boston Daily Globe*, December 5, 1907, p. 1.

172. Frances Weitzenhoffer, *The Havemeyers: Impressionism Comes to America* (New York: Harry N. Abrams, 1986), p. 52.

173. Letter, Harry Havemeyer to the author, July 12, 2006.

174. *Greenwich Graphic*, 1907, as quoted in *The Great Estates, Greenwich, Connecticut, 1880-1930.* (Canaan, N.H.: Junior League of Greenwich/Phoenix Pub., c 1986), p. 140.

175. *The Connecticut Magazine: An Illustrated Monthly*, vol. 11 (1907), p. 621.

176. *New York Times*, January 10, 1911.

177. Ibid.

178. Christopher Gray, "Boathouse Built for the Bulldogs Is Soon to Bow Out," *New York Times*, February 19, 2006.

Chapter 2: The Middle Atlantic States

1. S. Edwin Solly, *A Handbook of Medical Climatology, Embodying Its Principles and Therapeutic Application with Scientific Data of the Chief Health Resorts of the World.* (Philadelphia and New York: Lea Brothers & Co., 1897), p. 199.

2. J. W. Townsend. "The Old Main Line," *Personal Reminiscences of the Main Line in the Sixties and Seventies.* Philadelphia: s.n., 1919, p. 103.

3. "Gossip of Long Branch," New York Times, April 12, 1903, p. 24.

4. Gustav Kobbé, *The New Jersey Coast and Pines* (Short Hills, N.J.: G. Kobbé, 1889), p. 32. The church is referred to in various sources as St. Peter's or as St. Peter.

5. *Inventory of the Church Archives of New Jersey, Protestant Episcopal Diocese of New Jersey.* Prepared by the New Jersey Historical Records Survey Project, Newark, N.J., 1940, p. 157.

6. *Long Branch Daily Record*, May 2, 1955.

7. Sheldon. *Artistic Country Seats*, pp. 101–4.

8. Franklin Ellis, *History of Monmouth County, New Jersey.* in 1885 by R. T. Peck Co., Philadelphia, p. 761.

9. Ibid.

10. Carl Hovey, *The Life Story of J. Pierpont Morgan: A Biography* (New York: Sturgis & Walton Co., 1911), p. 319.

11. George Wheeler, *Pierpont Morgan & Friends: The Anatomy of a Myth* (Englewood Cliffs, N.J.: Prentice-Hall, 1973), pp. 125–26.

12. Jean Strouse, *Morgan: American Financier* (New York: Random House, 1999), p. 235.

13. L. H. M. Soulsby, *The America I Saw in 1916-1918* (London: Longmans, Green & Co., 1920), p. 35.

14. Strouse, p. 236.

15. Ibid.

16. Moreland Avenue Block File, Chestnut Hill Historic District Inventory.

17. HABS PA-194. Data pages prepared by Radnor Historical Society, 1958, for Historic American Buildings Survey. HABS PA-194, p. 1.

18. Mary C. Clarke, "Memoir of J. M. DaCosta, M.D.," *American Journal of the Medical Sciences*, vol. 125 (1903), p. 318.

19. John W. Townsend, "The Old Main Line." *Personal Reminiscences of the Main Line in the Sixties and Seventies.* Philadelphia, s.n., 1922.

20. "Continuing Installment: Wootton Began as 'Simple Home,'" *Bryn Mawr Home News*, February 18, n.p. From the archives at Radnor Historical Society.

21. Cordelia Drexel Biddle, *My Philadelphia Father* (Garden City, N.Y.: Doubleday & Co., 1955), p. 15.

22. Ibid.

23. Barr Ferree. "'Laurento,' the Estate of Craig Biddle, Esq., Wayne, Pennsylvania," *American Homes and Gardens*, February 1907, pp. 45–51.

24. Obituary, *New York Times*, December 23, 1947

25. All of the following references to correspondence between Olmsted Brothers and the Biddles are contained in the Olmsted Associates Correspondence from the collection of the Library of Congress, Roll 8, File Folder #30, E. Craig Biddle (Radnor, PA), Wayne, PA 1900-1916.

26. "The Gardeners' Club," *Gardening*, Vol. XII (September 15, 1903-September 1, 1904), p. 649.

27. Obituary, *New York Times*, March 7, 1943.

28. The *"Benedicite,"* in George Stanley Woodward, *Memoirs of a Mediocre Man* (Philadelphia: Harris & Partridge, 1935), p. 216.

29. Phebe Westcott Humphreys, *The Practical Book of Garden Architecture* (Philadelphia: J. B. Lippincott), 1914, p. 48.

30. Gertrude Houston Woodward, *"Quita," Gertrude Houston Woodward, Jr.* (Privately published, 1934), p. 35.

31. Per Boston Public Library Architectural Collections Archive Report, PS/PA.011; Edward Teitelman and Richard W. Longstreth. *Architecture in Philadelphia: A Guide.* Cambridge: MIT Press, 1974, p. 242.

32. A typescript by Phyllis C. Maier, "Westview 1919-1976," prepared for the 1976 Philadelphia Vassar Club Designers' Show House. From a private collection.

Chapter 3: The South

1. Carnegie Estate Records of Cumberland Island, AC69-501M, Series III: Peabody & Stearns Architects, correspondence, Georgia Department of Archives and History, Morrow, Georgia.

2. Letter, RSP to William Page, February 27, 1897.

3. *Randolph County Profile—1976: A Handbook of the County*, comp. and ed. Anna Dale Kek for the Elkins Branch of the American Association of University Women (Parsons, W. Va.: McClain Printing Co., 1976), p. 88.

4. Obituaries from the Necrologies files, vol. C 5, 6, 12, 19, at the Missouri Historical Society, St. Louis, Missouri.

5. Copy of a letter from George L. Carnegie to Peabody & Stearns, July 1898, reproduced and attached to a letter, Peabody & Stearns to W. W. Page, July 30, 1898. Carnegie Estate Records of Cumberland Island, AC69-501M, Series III, George Department of Archives and History.

6. Sarah Olson, *Plum Orchard: Cumberland Island National Seashore, St. Marys, Georgia, Historic Furnishings Report* (Harpers Ferry Center, National Park Service, 1988), p. 14.

7. Dungeness was later destroyed by fire, June 24, 1959. Nancy Carnegie Rockefeller, *The Carnegies and Cumberland Island* (Greenwich, Conn.: NCR, 1993), p. 19.

8. Margaret was the sister of Harry Thaw, murderer of architect Stanford White of the firm McKim, Mead & White. Other buildings in the compound: Greyfield was built for oldest daughter Margaret, and the Cottage for son Thomas Morrison Carnegie, Jr. An existing plantation, Stafford Place, was given to son William Coleman Carnegie.

9. Olson, p. 6.

Chapter 4: The West

1. Gertrude Houston Woodward, *"Quita," Gertrude Houston Woodward, Jr.* (Privately published, 1934.)
2. *American Architect and Building News*, August 18, 1883, p. 78.
3. Olive Rand. *A Vacation Excursion: From Massachusetts to Puget Sound*. Press of John B. Clarke, 1884, p. 30.
4. Helen Hunt Jackson, *Bits of Travel at Home* (Boston: Roberts Brothers, 1898), referenced in the ca. 1918 pamphlet *Beautiful Glen Eyrie and the Castle Adjoining the Garden of the Gods*, published by the Glen Eyrie Companies.
5. *Denver Republican*, October 24, 1881. As reproduced in the *Colorado Prospector*, April 1990, p. 8.
6. Ibid.
7. Hamlin Garland, *A Daughter of the Middle Border* (New York: Macmillan Co., 1921), p. 229.
8. Willa Cather, *A Lost Lady* (Thorndike, Maine: Thorndike Press, 1923), pp. 33–35.
9. Leland Feitz, *The Antlers: A Quick History of Colorado Springs' Historic Hotel* (Denver: Golden Bell Press, 1972. Also see Emily Faithfull, *Three Visits to America* (New York, Fowler & Wells Co., 1884).
10. Marshall Sprague, *Newport in the Rockies: The Life and Good Times of Colorado Springs*. Denver: Sage Books, 1961, p. 101.
11. *Colorado Springs Gazette*, March 23, 1880.
12. Henrietta Comstock Wright, *The Lake Region Blue Book and Club Directory of Spirit Lake and Vicinity* (Spirit Lake, IA, 1906), p. 71.

Bibliography

Abele, Susan. Newton's 19th Century Architecture: Newton Centre, Oak Hill, Chestnut Hill, Commonwealth Avenue. Newton, MA: Historic Newton, 1985.

Amory, Cleveland. *The Last Resorts: A Portrait of American Society at Play*. New York: Harper & Brothers, 1948.

The Architectural Sketchbook, Edited by the Portfolio Club. Boston: James R. Osgood & Co., 1873-74.

Bachelder, Nahum J. *New Hampshire Agriculture: Report of the Board of Agriculture from January 1, 1907 to September 1, 1908*. Nashua, NH: Telegraph Publishing Co., 1908.

Baltzell, E. Digby. *Philadelphia Gentlemen: The Making of a National Upper Class*. Philadelphia: University of Pennsylvania Press, 1958.

Beautiful Glen Eyrie and the Castle Adjoining the Garden of the Gods, pamphlet, published by The Glen Eyrie Companies, ca. 1918. In the collection of the Pikes Peak Library District, Colorado Springs, Colorado.

Benton, Nicholas. *The Call of the Weld: A Contemporary Genealogy: Five Generations of Descendants of Stephen Minot Weld, Jr.* New York: iUniverse, 2004.

——, comp. *The Seven Weld Brothers, 1800 to 2000: A Contemporary Genealogy*. Including "The Welds of Harvard Yard," by Craig Lambert. New York: iUniverse, 2004.

Beveridge, Charles E., series ed. "Moraine Farm Since 1880. A Frederick Law Olmsted landscape, Forest, and Farm, N. Beverly, Massachusetts." Frederick Law Olmsted Papers, The American University, Washington DC, 1984.

Biddle, Cordelia Drexel. *My Philadelphia Father*. Garden City, NY: Doubleday & Co., Inc., 1955.

Bowditch, Jim. *Chocorua Lake Basin: A National Historic District*. Chocorua, NH, 2005.

The Brooks Estate Preservation Association. *Historic Massachusetts Endangered Resource Program: 1998 Massachusetts Ten Most Endangered Historic Resources Nomination*. May 1998.

Brown, Francis H., MD, "Edwin Shepard Barrett." *New England Historical and Genealogical Register, at the Annual Meeting 10 January 1900 with Memoirs of Deceased Members 1898-1900*, Supplementary Number, 1900. Boston, MA: New England Historical and Genealogical Society, p. cxi.

Carnegie Estate Records of Cumberland Island, AC69-501M, Series III: Peabody & Stearns. Georgia Department of Archives and History, Morrow, Georgia.

Cather, Willa. *A Lost Lady*. Thorndike, ME: Thorndike Press, 1923.

The Celebration of the Two Hundredth Anniversary of the Town of Falmouth, Massachusetts, June 15, 1886. Falmouth, MA, 1887.

Chafee, Richard. "The Teaching of Architecture at the École des Beaux-Arts." In *The Architecture of the École des Beaux-Arts*, Edited by Arthur Drexler. New York: Museum of Modern Art; Cambridge, MA: MIT Press, 1977.

Champlin, Richard. "Newport Estates and their Flora." *Newport History, Bulletin of the Newport Historical Society*, 53, pt. 2, no. 178 (spring 1980), 49-66.

Clarke, Mary C. "Memoir of J. M. DaCosta, MD." *American Journal of the Medical Sciences* 125 (1903): 318-329. In the Jacob M. DaCosta Collection (MS 055) of the Scott Memorial Library at Thomas Jefferson University, Philadelphia.

"Col. Hugh Cochrane House," an unsigned typescript in the collection of the Manchester Historical Society, Manchester, Massachusetts.

Cole, T. Mark. "Architecture of Mt. Desert." In *Mount Desert: An Informational History*. Edited by Gunnar Hansen. Town of Mt. Desert, Maine, 1989.

Cooke, George Willis. "Old Times and New in Dublin, New Hampshire." *New England Magazine*, 1899.

Cunningham, Colin, and Prudence Waterhouse. *Alfred Waterhouse, 1830-1905: Biography of a Practice*. Oxford, UK: Clarendon Press, 1992.

Day, Leslie. "The City Naturalist—American Hornbeam Tree." Retrieved April 28, 2009 from http://www.nysite.com/nature/flora/muscle.htm.

Dow, Charles H. *Newport Past and Present*. Newport, RI: J. P. Sanborn, 1880.

Dyer, Arnold W. *Residential Falmouth . . . Homes, New and Old*. "An 1897 Souvenir for the Sojourner Brought Up to Date." Falmouth, MA: Falmouth Historical Society, 1995.

Edgerly, Brad. "Drawings of Robert Swain Peabody." *Dichotomy* (University of Detroit School of Architecture) 6 (1983): 46-53.

Eliot, Charles W. *Charles Eliot, Landscape Architect*. With an introduction by Keith N. Morgan. Amherst, MA: University of Massachusetts Press, 1999.

Elliott, Maud Howe. *This Was My Newport*. Cambridge, MA: Mythology Company, 1944.

Ellis, Franklin. *History of Monmouth County, New Jersey*. Philadelphia: R. T. Peck, Co., 1885.

Emerson, Amelia Forbes, comp. *Naushon Data*. Concord, MA: privately printed, 1963.

Encyclopedia Britannica: A Dictionary of Arts, Sciences, Literature, and General Information. Edited by Hugh Chisholm. Cambridge, UK and New York: At the University Press, 1910.

Faithfull, Emily. *Three Visits to America*. New York: Fowler & Wells Co., 1884.

Fay Collection, Woods Hole Historical Collection and Museum, Woods Hole, Massachusetts

Feitz, Leland. *The Antlers: A Quick History of Colorado Springs' Historic Hotel.* Denver: Golden Bell Press, 1972, 2000.

Ferree, Barr. *American Estates and Gardens.* New York: Munn & Co., 1906.

____. "Notable American Homes: 'Laurento,' the Estate of Craig Biddle, Esq., Wayne, Pennsylvania." *American Homes and Gardens*, February 1907, pp. 45–49.

Forbes, Edith Emerson, and William Hathaway Forbes. Papers, 1827–ca. 1964; bulk: 1827–1953, Massachusetts Historical Society.

From Pocasset to Cataumet: The Origins and Growth of a Massachusetts Seaside Community, based on the files of Elmer Watson Landers. Edited by Richard P. Sawyer. Bourne, MA: Bourne Historic Commission, 1988.

"The Gardeners Club." *Gardening* XII (September 15, 1903–September 1, 1904), p. 649.

Garland, Hamlin. *A Daughter of the Middle Border.* New York: Macmillan Co., 1921.

Garland, Joseph E. *Boston's North Shore and Boston's Gold Coast.* Beverly, MA: Commonwealth Editions, 1998.

Georgia Department of Archives, Georgia Archives and Manuscripts Automated Access Project: A Special collections Gateway Program of the University Center in Georgia. Collection no. AC 69-501-M.

Gillmeister, Heiner. *Tennis: A Cultural History.* New York: New York University Press, 1998.

Glennon, Beverly Morrison, and Judith Navas Lund. *Greetings from Dartmouth, Massachusetts. A Postcard History.* Dartmouth, MA: Garrison Wall Publishers, 2003.

Grant, Robert. *Fourscore: An Autobiography.* Boston and New York: Houghton Mifflin Co., 1934.

Gray, Christopher. "Boathouse Built for the Bulldogs Is Soon to Bow Out." In "Streetscapes," *New York Times,* February 19, 2006.

Gray, John Lynne. "Krisheim, A Magnificent Private Estate." *American Suburbs,* December 1910.

The Great Estates: Greenwich, Connecticut, 1880–1930. Canaan, NH: Phoenix Publishing for the Junior League of Greenwich, Connecticut, 1986.

"Harvard Divinity School at the Turn of the Last Century: Francis Greenwood Peabody (1847–1936)." Online exhibit from Andover-Harvard Theological Library: http://www.hds.harvard.edu/library/exhibits/online/hdsturncentury/peabody.html

Hill, Benjamin D., and Winfield S. Nevins. *The North Shore of Massachusetts Bay: An Illustrated Guide.* Salem, MA, 1881.

Hitchcock, Henry Russell. *The Architecture of H. H. Richardson and His Times.* Cambridge, MA: MIT Press, 1981 [1936].

Holden, Wheaton Arnold. "The Peabody Touch: Peabody and Stearns of Boston, 1870–1917." *Journal of the Society of Architectural Historians,* May 1973, pp. 114–131. [L. M. Roth, "Correction" *JSAH,* December 1973, pp. 348–349.]

____. "Robert Swain Peabody of Peabody and Stearns in Boston—the Early Years (1870–1866)." PhD diss., Boston University Graduate School of Fine Arts, 1969.

____. Papers. A-94-125. Hay Library Collection, Brown University, Providence, Rhode Island.

Hovey, Carol. *The Life Story of J. Pierpont Morgan: A Biography.* New York: Sturgis & Walton Co., 1911.

Howe, Mark A. Dewolfe. *James Ford Rhodes, American Historian.* Boston: Houghton Mifflin Co., 1929.

____. *Later Years of the Saturday Club: 1870–1920.* Boston: Houghton Mifflin Co., 1927.

Humphreys, Phebe Westcott. *The Practical Book of Garden Architecture.* Philadelphia: J. B. Lippincott, 1914.

Illustrated Boston, The Metropolis of New England. Boston: American Publishing & Engraving Co., 1889.

"Interesting Improvements at Glen Eyrie." *Denver Republican,* October 24, 1881. As reproduced in *The Prospector,* April 1990.

Inventory of the Church Archives of New Jersey, Protestant Episcopal Diocese of New Jersey. Prepared by the New Jersey Historical Records Survey Project, Newark, NJ, 1940.

Jackson, Helen Hunt. *Bits of Travel at Home.* Boston: Roberts Brothers, 1898. Referenced in *Beautiful Glen Eyrie and the Castle Adjoining the Garden of the Gods,* pamphlet, published by The Glen Eyrie Companies, ca. 1918.

James, Henry. *The American Scene.* Bloomington and London: Indiana University Press, 1968.

James, Henry. *Charles W. Eliot, President of Harvard University, 1869–1909.* Boston: Houghton Mifflin Co., 1930.

Jetties Beach Pavilion and Bath House: Historic Structures Report. Preservation Institute: Nantucket. Class of 2007.

Kobbe, Gustav. *The New Jersey Coast and Pines.* Short Hills, NJ: G. Kobbe, 1889.

Lambert, Craig. "The Welds of Harvard Yard." In Nicholas Benton, *The Call of the Weld. A Contemporary Genealogy: Five Generations of Descendants of Stephen Minot Weld, Jr.* New York: iUniverse, 2004.

Lancaster, Clay. *Holiday Island: The Pageant of Nantucket's Hostelries and Summer Life from Its Beginnings to the Mid-Twentieth Century.* Nantucket, MA: Nantucket Historical Association, 1993

Later Years of the Saturday Club, 1870–1920. Edited by M. A. DeWolfe Howe. Boston: Houghton Mifflin Co., 1927; reprinted 1968 by Books for Libraries Press.

Lewis, Arnold. *American Country Houses of the Gilded Age (Sheldon's Artistic Country-Seats).* New York: Dover Publications, 1982.

Lippincott, Bertram, III. "The Hutton Family of 'Shamrock Cliff.'" *Newport History,* 64, pt. 4, no. 221 (fall 1991).

Longfellow, Henry Wadsworth. *Life of Henry Wadsworth Longfellow with Extracts from his Journals.* Edited by Samuel Longfellow. Boston: Ticknor & Co., 1886.

Mason, George Champlin. *Newport and Its Cottages.* Boston: James B. Osgood & Co., 1875.

Milliken, Weston. "Peabody and Stearns." In *A Biographical Dictionary of Architects in Maine.* Augusta, ME: Maine Historic Preservation Commission, IV, no. 2, 1987.

Missouri Historical Society Archives Catalog, St. Louis, Missouri. George E. Leighton, Lane Collection.

Moses, George L. *Ring Around the Punch Bowl: The Story of the Beebe Woods in Falmouth on Cape Cod.* Taunton, MA: William S. Sullwold Publishing, 1976.

Nebiker, Walter, Robert Owen Jones, and Charlene K. Roice. *Historic and Architectural Resources of Narragansett, Rhode Island.* Providence: Rhode Island Historical Preservation Commission, 1991.

The New England Historical and Genealogical Register. Supplement to April Number, 1915. Proceedings of the New England Historic Genealogical Society at the Annual Meeting, 3 February 1915, with Memoirs of Deceased Members, 1914.

Olmsted Associates Letterbooks, 1884–1899, Olmsted Associates Correspondence from the Collection of the Library of Congress.

Olson, Sarah. *Plum Orchard, Cumberland Island National Seashore: Historic Furnishings Report.* Harpers Ferry Center, VW: National Park Service, 1988.

Peabody, Francis. *A New England Romance: The Story of Ephraim and Mary Jane Peabody (1807-1892) Told by Their Sons.* Boston and New York: Houghton Mifflin Co., 1920.

Peabody, Robert E. "Peach's Point, Marblehead." Essex Institute Historical Collections, CII, no. 1, January 1966.

Peabody, Robert Swain. *An Architect's Sketch Book.* Boston: Houghton Mifflin Co., 1912.

____. "An Architect's Vacation." *Atlantic Monthly* 76 (July 1895). Also:

"Rural England," July, pp. 23-28; "French and English Churches," August, pp. 174-181; "The Venetian Day," October, pp. 477-481; "The Italian Renaissance," November, pp. 634-640.

____. "Architecture as a Profession for College Students." *Harvard Monthly* 9, no. 5,

(February 1890): 185-194.

____. "Georgian Houses of New England." *American Architect and Building News* II, no. 95, (October 20, 1877): 338-9.

____. "The Georgian Houses of New England, II." *American Architect and Building News* III, no. 112 (February 16, 1878): 54-55.

____. *Hospital Sketches.* Boston: Houghton Mifflin Co., 1916.

____. *Note Book Sketches.* Boston: J. R. Osgood, 1873.

____. "A Talk About Queen Anne." *American Architect and Building News* II, no. 70 (April 28, 1877).

Peabody & Stearns Collection, Boston Public Library, Fine Arts Department, Boston Massachusetts.

Peabody & Stearns Collection, Historic New England, Boston, Massachusetts.

Peabody & Stearns Collection, Memorial Library, Boston Architectural College, Boston, Massachusetts.

Perry, E. G. *A Trip Around Buzzards Bay Shores.* Bourne, MA: Bourne Historic Commission, 1976.

Phelps, Harriet Jackson. *Newport in Flower: A History of Newport's Horticultural Heritage.* Newport, RI: Preservation Society of Newport County, 1979.

Phillips, William. *Ventures in Diplomacy.* Boston: Beacon Press, 1952.

Preservation Society of Newport County. *The Lost Houses of Newport County.* www.newportmansions.org. See Education and Research/History Highlights/Lost Newport/The Lost Houses/1866-1875.

Price, Bruce. "The Suburban House." *Scribner's Magazine*, VIII, no. 1 (July 1890): 3-19.

Randolph County Profil—1976: A Handbook of the County. Compiled and edited by Anna Dale Kek for the Elkins Branch of the American Association of University Women. Parsons, WV: McClain Printing Co., 1976.

Residential Falmouth: Homes, New and Old. Falmouth-by-the-Sea, MA: Board of Industry, 1897.

Rockefeller, Nancy Carnegie. *The Carnegies and Cumberland Island.* Greenwich, CT: NCR, 1993.

Roth, Leland. *McKim, Mead & White.* New York: Harper & Row, 1983.

Ruskin, John. *The Seven Lamps of Architecture.* New York: Dover Publishing, 1989.

Schuyler, Montgomery. "The Romanesque Revival in America." *Architectural Record* 1, no. 2 (October-December 1891).

Schweinfurth, Julius. "Robert Swain Peabody, Tower Builder, 1845-1917." *American Architect* CXXX, no. 2504 (September 5, 1926): 181-191.

Sears Genealogical Catalogue. Edited by L. Ray Sears, III. Boston: New England Historical Genealogical Society, 1992.

Sheldon, George W. *Artistic Country Seats—Types of Recent American Villas and Cottage Architecture with Instances of Country Club-Houses.* New York: Appleton and Company, 1886.

Shettleworth, Jr., Earle G. *The Summer Cottages of Isleboro, 1890-1930.* Islesboro, ME: Islesboro Historical Society, 1989.

Solly, S. Edwin. *A Handbook of Medical Climatology, Embodying Its Principles and Therapeutic Application with Scientific Data of the Chief Health Resorts of the World.* Philadelphia and New York: Lea Brothers & Co., 1897.

Soulsby, L. H. M. *The America I Saw in 1916-1918.* London: Longmans, Green & Co., 1920.

Sprague, Marshall. *Newport in the Rockies: The Life and Good Times of Colorado Springs.* Denver: Sage Books, 1961.

Storey, Moorfield. "Obituary," *Harvard University Class 1866 Class Report*, 1917 Report, pp. 10-11.

———. "Robert Swain Peabody." In *Later Years of the Saturday Club, 1870-1920.* Edited by M. A. DeWolfe Howe. Boston & New York, 1927.

Strouse, Jean. *Morgan, American Financier.* New York: Random House, 1999.

Sturgis, Russell. "A Critique of the Work of Peabody & Stearns." *Architectural Record Great Architects Series*, no. 3 (July 1896).

Sweetser, Charles H. *Book of Summer Resorts.* New York: Evening Mail, 1868.

Sweetser, Moses Foster. *King's Handbook of Newton, Massachusetts.* Newton, MA, 1899.

Teitelman, Edward, and Richard W. Longstreth. *Architecture in Philadelphia: A Guide.* Cambridge, MA: MIT Press, 1974.

Twain, Mark. *The Gilded Age.* In *The Family Mark Twain.* New York: Harper & Row, 1972.

Van Rensselaer, Mrs. John King. *Newport: Our Social Capital.* Philadelphia and London: J. B. Lippincott Co., 1905.

"Visit to Lenox and Stockbridge Estates." *Transactions of the Massachusetts Horticultural Society for the Year 1913.* Boston: Massachusetts Horticultural Society, 1913.

Weitzenhoffer, Frances. *The Havemeyers: Impressionism Comes to America.* New York: Harry N. Abrams, 1986.

Wexler, Dorothy B. *Reared in a Greenhouse.* New York: Taylor & Francis, 1998.

Wheeler, Edmund. *History of Newport, New Hampshire: From 1766 to 1878.* Concord, NH: Republican Press Association, 1879; reprinted 1994.

Wheeler, George. *Pierpont Morgan & Friends: The Anatomy of a Myth.* Englewood Cliffs, NJ: Prentice-Hall, 1973.

Who's Who Along the North Shore, Being a Register of the Noteworthy, Fashionable, and Wealthy Residents on the North Shore of Massachusetts Bay for Summer 1912. Salem, MA: Salem Press Co., 1912.

Wilson, Leslie Perrin. "Battle Lawn: A House with a View of History," *Concord Journal*, April 26, 2001: 19.

Witzell, Susan Fletcher. "Gardeners and Caretakers of Woods Hole." *Spritsail*, Summer 2005.

Wolcott, Cora Codman. "Random Recollections of Much Ado about Nothing," chap. 7 in Mrs. John M. B. Churchill. *Codman Point 1872-1972.* Wareham, MA: 1972.

Woodward, George Stanley. *Memoirs of a Mediocre Man.* Philadelphia: Harris & Partridge, 1935.

Woodward, Gertrude Houston. *Quita.* Gertrude Houston Woodward, Jr., privately published, 1934.

Wright, Henrietta Comstock. *The Lake Region Blue Book and Club Directory of Spirit Lake and Vicinity.* Spirit Lake, Iowa, 1906.

Additional Readings & Resources

Abbott, Elizabeth. "Northeast Notebook." *New York Times,* June 7, 1992.

Aimone, Barbara. "America's First Vacationland and the Rise and Fall of the West Point and Cozzens' Hotel." *Orange County Historical Society Magazine*, vol. 31, November 1, 2002.

Allen, Armin Brand. *The Cornelius Vanderbilts of the Breakers: A Family Retrospective* [exhibition]. Preservation Society of Newport County, Newport Art Museum, May 27-October 1, 1995.

Alonzo, Lewis. *The History of Lynn, Including Nahant.* Lynn, MA: S. N. Dickinson, 1844.

Appleton's Illustrated Handbook of American Summer Resorts. New York, NY: D. Appleton & Company, 1893.

Aslet, Clive. *The American Country House.* New Haven, CT: Yale University Press, 1990.

Bacon, Edwin Munroe. *Walks and Rides in the Country Round About Boston: Covering Thirty-six Cities and Towns.* Boston and New York: Houghton Mifflin & Co., 1898.

Benjamin, Samuel Greene Wheeler. "An Account of Cumberland Island Deeded to General Nathaniel Greene by the State of Georgia and the Greene Mansion "Dungeness." *Sea Island, Harper's New Monthly Magazine,* vol. 57, pp. 848-850, 1878.

Black, Celeste. *Queen of Glen Eyrie: The Story of Mary Lincoln Mellen Palmer, Wife of General William Palmer.* Colorado Springs, CO: Black Bear Publishing, 1999.

The Book of Berkshire Describing and Illustrating its Hills and Homes and Telling Where They Are, What They Are and Why They Are Destined to Become the Most Charming and Desirable Summer Homes in America: For the Season of 1887. Great Barrington and Springfield, MA: Clark W. Bryan & Company, 1887.

Bryan, John Morrill & Fred L. Savage. *Maine Cottages: Fred L. Savage and the Architecture of Mount Desert.* New York, NY: Princeton Architectural Press, 2005.

Bullard, Mary R. *Cumberland Island: A History.* Athens, GA and London: The University of Georgia Press, 2003.

Bunting, Bainbridge. *Houses of Boston's Back Bay.* Cambridge, MA and London: The Belknap Press of Harvard University, 1967.

Busbey, Hamilton. *Recollections of Men and Horses.* New York, NY: Dodd, Mead & Company, 1907.

Buttrick, James C., with the Jamestown Historical Society. *Jamestown—Images of America Series.* Charleston, SC: Arcadia Publishing, 2003.

Canfield, Cass. *The Incredible Pierpont Morgan: Financier and Art Collector.* New York: Harper & Row, 1974.

Carley, Rachel. *Building Greenwich: Architecture and Design, 1640 to the Present.* The Historical Society of the Town of Greenwich, 2005.

Catlin, Daniel Jr. *Good Work Well Done: The Sugar Business Career of Horace Havemeyer, 1903-1956.* Published by the author, 1988.

Childs, James Rives. *Reliques of the Rives.* Lynchburg, VA: J. P. Bell Company, 1929.

Contosta, David R. *A Philadelphia Family: The Houstons and Woodwards of Chestnut Hill.* Philadelphia, PA: University of Pennsylvania Press, 1988.

____. *Suburb in the City: Chestnut Hill, Philadelphia, 1850-1990.* Columbus, OH: Ohio State University Press, 1992.

Conway, James. "Nurture versus Nature." *Preservation,* vol. 49, no. 2, pp. 40-51, March/April, 1997.

Crane, Walter. *An Artist's Reminiscences, 1890-92.* New York, NY: Macmillan & Co., 1907.

Crowley, Michael S. "Opulence at Breakneck Speed." *Boats and Harbors Magazine,* August, 1987.

Downing, Antoinette F. & Vincent J. Scully Jr. *The Architectural Heritage of Newport, Rhode Island (1640-1915).* New York, NY: Bramhall House, 1967.

Dunkak, Harry M. *The Lorillard Family of Westchester County.* Westchester County Historical Society, 1995. From *Westchester Historian,* vol. 71, no. 3, summer 1995.

Faught, Millard Clark. *Falmouth, Massachusetts: Problems of a Resort Community.* New York, NY: Columbia University Press, 1945.

Foreman, John & Robbie Pierce Stimson. *The Vanderbilts and the Gilded Age: Architectural Aspirations, 1879-1901.* New York, NY: St. Martin's Press, 1991.

Fox, Pamela W. *North Shore Boston: Houses of Essex County, 1865-1930.* New York, NY: Acanthus Press, 2005.

Gabrielan, Randall. *Monmouth Beach and Sea Bright.* Dover, NH: Arcadia Publishing, 1998.

____. *Long Branch People and Places.* Charleston, SC: Arcadia Publishing, 1998.

Garland, Joseph E. *The North Shore: A Social History of Summers Among the Noteworthy, Fashionable, Rich, Eccentric, and Ordinary on Boston's Gold Coast, 1823-1929.* Beverly, MA: Commonwealth Editions, 2003.

Gebhard, David, & Deborah Nevins. *200 Years of American Architectural Drawing.* New York, NY: Watson Guptill Publications, 1977.

Girouard, Mark. "Blackmoor House, Hampshire." *Country Life,* August 29, 1974, pp. 554-557 and September 5, 1974, pp. 614-617.

Goodrich, Jane. "Curious George: Woodlawn's Enigmatic Benefactor." Woodlawn Museum Newsletter, summer 2006.

Harrison, Mitchell C. *Prominent and Progressive Americans: An Encyclopaedia of Contemporaneous Biography*, vol. 1. New York, NY: New York Tribune, 1902.

The Harvard Graduates' Magazine, vol. XX, 1911-1912.

Herbst, Jurgen. "Francis Greenwood Peabody: Harvard's Theologian of the Social Gospel." *The Harvard Theological Review*, vol. 54, no. 1, pp. 45-69, January 1961.

Heslin, James J. "John Sanford Barnes, Naval Officer, Financier, Collector." *New York Historical Society Quarterly*, vol. 47, pp. 41-65, 1963.

Higgins, Charles A. *To California and Back*. Chicago Passenger Department, Santa Fe Route, 1899.

Hoyt, Edwin P. *The Peabody Influence: How a Great New England Family Helped to Build America*. New York, NY: Dodd, Mead & Company, 1968.

Hyde, William & Howard L. Conrad (Eds.). *Encyclopedia of the History of St. Louis, A Compendium of History and Biography for Ready Reference*. New York and St. Louis: The Southern History Company, 1899.

Jackson, Richard S. Jr., & Cornelia Brooke Gilder. *Houses of the Berkshires 1870-1930*. New York, NY: Acanthus Press, 2006.

Jarvis, Elizabeth Farmer. *Chestnut Hill Revisited*. Charleston, SC: Arcadia Publishing, 2004.

Jordy, William H. & Christopher P. Monkhouse. *Buildings on Paper: Rhode Island Architectural Drawings 1825-1945*. Providence, RI: Brown University, Rhode Island Historic Society, Rhode Island School of Design, 1982.

Keels, Thomas H. & Elizabeth Farmer Jarvis. *Chestnut Hill*. Charleston, SC: Arcadia Publishing, 2002.

King, Moses. *Harvard Register*. Cambridge, MA: Harvard University, 1880.

____. *Philadelphia and Notable Philadelphians*. New York, NY: Blanchard Press, Isaac H. Blanchard Co., 1901.

King, Robert B. *The Vanderbilt Homes*. New York: Rizzoli, 1989.

Lewis, Arnold, James Turner & Steven McQuillin. *The Opulent Interiors of the Gilded Age*. New York: Dover Publications, Inc., 1987.

Limerick, Jeffrey, Nancy Ferguson & Richard Oliver. *America's Grand Resort Hotels*. New York, NY: Random House, 1979.

Marshall, Perry. *Vinland, or the Norse Discovery of America*. Chicago, IL: Charles H. Kerr & Company, ca. 1920.

Mathias, Christopher R. & Kenneth C. Turino. *Nahant*. Charleston, SC: Arcadia Publishing, 1999.

Miller, Paul. "Newport in the Gilded Age." *Magazine Antiques*, pp. 598-605, April 1995.

Morison, Samuel Eliot. *The Story of Mount Desert Island*. Boston, MA: Little, Brown & Co., 1960.

Morrison, William. *The Main Line: Country Houses of Philadelphia's Storied Suburb, 1870-1930*. New York, NY: Acanthus Press, 2002.

Moss, George H. Jr. *Another Look at Nauvoo to the Hook*. Sea Bright, NJ: Ploughshare Press, 1990.

Nightingale, B. N. "Dungeness." *Georgia Historic Quarterly*, vol. 22, no. 4, pp. 369-383, 1938.

Owens, Carole. *The Berkshire Cottages: A Vanishing Era*. Stockbridge, MA: Cottage Press, Inc., 1984.

____. *The Berkshires: Coach Inns to Cottages*. Charleston SC: Arcadia Publishing, 2004.

Philadelphia Architecture and Buildings. Accessed April 21, 2009 at www.philadelphiabuildings.org.

Porter, David L. *Biographical Dictionary of American Sports*. Santa Barbara, CA: Greenwood Press, 1988.

Rabinow, Rebecca A. "Catharine Lorillard Wolfe, The First Woman Benefactor of The Metropolitan Museum of Art." *Apollo Magazine*, pp. 48-55, March 1998.

Rand, Olive. *A Vacation Excursion: From Massachusetts Bay to Puget Sound*. Manchester, NH: Press of John B. Clarke, 1884.

Reed, Roger G. *A Delight to All Who Know It*. Augusta, ME: Maine Historic Preservation Commission, 1990.

Rhode Island Historical Preservation and Heritage Commission. *Historical and Architectural Resources of Jamestown, Rhode Island*. Accessed online April 21, 2009 at http://www.jamestownri.com/library/history.htm.

Robinson, Ann E. "The Resort Architecture of Peabody and Stearns in Newport, Rhode Island and Northeast Harbor, Maine." Master's Thesis, Tufts University, May, 1999.

Roth, Leland. *McKim, Mead & White*. New York: Harper & Row, 1983.

Roths, Jaylene. "Charles W. Eliot and John Gilley: Good Hope for Our Island." *History Journal of the Mount Desert Historical Society*, pp. 3-23, June 1998.

Sawyer, Richard P. (Ed.). *From Pocasset to Cataumet: The Origins and Growth of a Massachusetts Seaside Community* Based on the files of Elmer Watson Landers. Bourne, MA: Bourne Historic Commission, 1988.

Scott, Henry Edwards. "Fanny Foster." *The New England Historical and Genealogical Register*, vol. XC, pp. 306-314, October 1936.

Scully, Vincent. *The Shingle Style and the Stick Style*. New Haven, CT: Yale University Press, 1971.

Sloane, Florence Adele, with commentary by Louis Auchincloss. *Maverick in Mauve: The Diary of a Romantic Age*. Garden City, NY: Doubleday & Co., 1983.

Smith, George Washington. *History of Illinois and Her People*. Chicago and New York: American Historical Society, 1927.

Susan Alyson Stein (Ed.). *Sixteen to Sixty: Memoirs of a Collector* by Louisine Waldron Elder Havemeyer. New York: Metropolitan Museum of Art, 1961, 1993.

Story, Kenneth Byrd. "The Ecclesiastical Architecture of Peabody & Stearns: An Evaluation and Catalog." Masters Thesis, Tufts University, 1986.

Sloane, W. & J. *The Story of Sloanes*. New York: W. & J. Sloane, 1950.

Sutton, Horace. "The Berkshire Story." *Town & Country*, August 1949.

Swallow, Ann Virginia. "The Eclecticism of Peabody and Stearns in Lenox, MA, 1881-1905." Thesis, M. Arch History, University of Virginia, 1984.

Symmes, Richard W. *North Beverly—Remembered*. Beverly, MA: Beverly Historic Society, 1987.

Torres, Louis. *Historic Resource Study, Cumberland Island National Seashore, Georgia and Historic Structure Report, Historical Data Section of the Dungeness Area*. Denver, CO: National Park Service, October 1977.

Tschirch, John R. "The Evolution of a Beaux Arts Landscape." *Journal of the New England Garden History Society*, vol. 7, pp. 1-14, fall 1999.

Waterman, Arba Nelson. *Historical Review of Chicago and Cook County and Selected Biography*, vol. III. Chicago and New York: The Lewis Publishing Company, 1908.

Wilcox, Rhoda David. *The Man on the Iron Horse*. Manitou Springs, CO: Martin Associates, 1959.

Willard, Frances Elizabeth & Mary Ashton Rice Livermore. *American Women: Fifteen Hundred Biographies with Over 1400 Portraits*. New York, NY: Mast, Crowell & Kirkpatrick, 1897.

Wurman, Richard Saul. *The Newport Guide*. Newport, RI: The Initial Press Syndicate, 1995.

Yarnall, James L. *Newport Through Its Architecture: A History of Styles from Postmedieval to Postmodern*. Lebanon, NH: University of New England Press and Salve Regina University, 2005.

Youngman, Elsie P. *Summer Echoes from the 19th Century: Manchester-by-the-Sea.* Rockport, MA: Don Russell, 1981.

Periodicals Consulted

American Architect and Building News
American Architect
Architectural Record
Boston Globe
Brickbuilder
Builder
Camden Herald
Colorado Prospector

Colorado Springs Gazette
Connecticut Magazine: An Illustrated Monthly
Country Life in America
Daily Gazette, Colorado Springs
Indoors and Out, New York and London
Inland Architect and News Record
Newport Journal
Newport Mercury
Newport Social Index
New York Times
North Shore Breeze: A Weekly Journal Devoted to the Best Interests of the North Shore
Sanitary Engineer
Village Gleaner
Woods Hole Oceanographic Institution Newsletter

Index